Database Systems Using Oracle

A Simplified Guide to SQL and PL/SQL

Nilesh Shah

DeVry College of Technology, North Brunswick, New Jersey
Monroe College, New Rochelle, New York

Prentice Hall
Upper Saddle River, NJ 07458

Library of Congress Cataloging-in-Publication Data

Shah, Nilesh.
  Database systems using Oracle: a simplified guide to SQL & PL/SQL/Nilesh Shah.
    p. cm.
  Includes bibliographical references and index.
  ISBN 0-13-090933-5
    1. Oracle (Computer file) 2. Relational databases. I. Title.

QA76.9.D3 S487 2001
005.75'85–dc21   2001034596

Vice President and Editorial Director, ECS: *Marcia J. Horton*
Acquisitions Editor: *Petra J. Recter*
Editorial Assistant: *Karen Schultz*
Vice President and Director of Production and Manufacturing, ESM: *David W. Riccardi*
Executive Managing Editor: *Vince O'Brien*
Managing Editor: *David A. George*
Production Editor: *Kevin Bradley*
Director of Creative Services: *Paul Belfanti*
Creative Director: *Carole Anson*
Art Director: *Jayne Conte*
Art Editor: *Adam Velthaus*
Cover Designer: *Bruce Kenselaar*
Manufacturing Manager: *Trudy Pisciotti*
Manufacturing Buyer: *Lisa McDowell*
Senior Marketing Manager: *Jennie Burger*

©2002 by Prentice-Hall, Inc.
Upper Saddle River, New Jersey 07458

Printed in the United States of America
10 9 8 7 6 5 4 3

ISBN 0-13-090933-5

PRENTICE-HALL INTERNATIONAL (UK) LIMITED, *LONDON*
PRENTICE-HALL OF AUSTRALIA PTY. LIMITED, *SYDNEY*
PRENTICE-HALL CANADA INC., *TORONTO*
PRENTICE-HALL HISPANOAMERICANA, S.A., *MEXICO CITY*
PRENTICE-HALL OF INDIA PRIVATE LIMITED, *NEW DELHI*
PRENTICE-HALL OF JAPAN, INC., *TOKYO*
PEARSON EDUCATION ASIA PTE. LTD., *SINGAPORE*
EDITORA PRENTICE-HALL DO BRASIL, LTDA., *RIO DE JANEIRO*

To my two children,
Naman, 8
(For constantly worrying about the progress of this book)
and
Navan (Jinku), 3
(For frequently clicking the Save button for me)

To my wife,
Prena
(For her support)

To my parents,
Dhiraj and Hansa
(For their sacrifice)

Contents

Foreword

Computer science educators and IT administrators are, and have traditionally been, faced with a common problem. In an industry that is characterized by rapid and dramatic changes the manager must determine how can he or she maintain state-of-the-art skills among IT staff. The educator, in a similar vein, must be able to judge how students can be best prepared to work as professionals in a field that may have gone through revolutionary transitions between the time that student first entered college and the time he or she graduates.

Certainly a technical education must incorporate a strong foundation in the core concepts of operating systems, file or database structure, computer architecture, and general programming theory. The difficulty arises when the educator seeks to select an application or development platform to use as introducing these concepts and providing students with practical, functional, and marketable hands-on skills. As the ones responsible for such preparation, we often look for a package that not only will give the student the most vivid demonstration of the theoretical concepts the professor or trainer is attempting to portray, but also will offer the student an opportunity to use knowledge almost immediately in any of a variety of environments. In addition, we seek packages that are in heavy and common demand, with a "track record" of success, reliability, and longevity.

The area of relational database management systems (DBMS) is one crowded with a vast number of quality DBMS products. There is only one, however, that addresses the many concerns the educator has for students. That product, of course, is Oracle. It has been on the market for more than twenty years and holds a major portion of market share, which accounts for Larry Ellison's position as one of the world's wealthiest men and Oracle's position among the largest global corporations. There are versions of the product for nearly every hardware platform from personal computers through minicomputers and supercomputers, and operating systems from DOS, Windows, and Linux through MVS, OS/400, PICK, and the multitudinous flavors of Unix. Of all the DBMS systems available, Oracle is the one the student is most likely to encounter on the job and the one in which employers most eagerly seek expert applicants and employees.

From an educator's perspective, Oracle, as a truly relational database, incorporates virtually all the relational operations that any database theory course must encompass. This allows the student to actually see the result of such operations.

Similarly, the instructor retains flexibility to design customized exercises that combine a single, multiple, or all of the standardized operations discussed in lectures on relational theory. In addition, Oracle's ease of use allows the professor to concentrate on the purpose of the course rather than how to utilize the DBMS software.

Computer science has never been one of the "pure" sciences concerned solely with theoretical constructs. Like engineering, its concern and preparation is directly and fully aimed at practical application of knowledge. In today's economy, a comprehensive grasp of database design, use, and implementation is a basic skill required of IT professionals, and, as an educator and CIO, it is my opinion that any university course or professional training seminar focusing on database concepts that does not also provide the student with at least an introduction to Oracle is deficient.

Nilesh Shah's *Database Systems Using Oracle* includes everything both the educator seeking to present essential database concepts and the student wishing to learn Oracle in either a guided classroom or independent study approach would be looking for. It is organized in such a manner that the beginner is presented with enough background to quickly progress to a functional mastery of the more complex material, and the progression of topics and degree of coverage is comprehensive enough to meet the needs of the demanding professional. In recognition of the need to go beyond theory, numerous hands-on exercises are included and examples are given of features, such as Web interfaces to Oracle tables, from Oracle's most recent versions.

For those of you who are first entering the world of DBMS, the Shah text is a reliable vehicle that will assist you in meeting your objectives and assure that you finish with confidence in your ability.

To the database professional, Shah will give you a reference and guide that you will use frequently.

To the university professor or professional trainer, Shah has given you a uniquely flexible educational tool. With it you can develop, plan, and implement your course in a manner that will give your students the necessary academic understanding of core database concepts while simultaneously giving them a skill that is hugely sellable within the computer industry.

As a professor of computer science at Monroe College, as well as the college's Senior Database Programmer, Nilesh Shah has demonstrated the dual abilities of fully comprehending the broad range of complexities involved in database management as well as the gift of presenting complex subject matter in an easily understandable format. To the reader's benefit, these abilities come across clearly in the text before you.

ALEX EPHREM, Ph.D.
Vice-President and Chief Information Officer
Monroe College

Preface

THE READER

The Relational Database Management System (RDBMS) is the most important database model today. The Oracle Corporation has established the Oracle database product as the prime database package in the world. Structured Query Language (SQL) is the universal query language for relational databases. Programming Language/Structured Query Language (PL/SQL), an Oracle extension to SQL, brings all the benefits and capabilities of a high-level programming language to the database environment.

This text is designed for use as a primary textbook in a database course at the college level or as a self-study guide for the information systems or business professional. With its in-depth coverage of relational database concepts, SQL, and PL/SQL, the textbook serves as an introductory guide as well as a future reference resource. The textbook can be used in a course that concentrates on database design and uses SQL to complement it. It also makes a perfect textbook to teach SQL only. Another use of this book is in an advanced database management system course, where more advanced features of SQL, along with PL/SQL and database administration, are emphasized. In a classroom environment, it is not possible to cover all 14 chapters in one semester. The book serves as a great resource to expand on the topics learned in the classroom.

THE TEXTBOOK

The first part of the book provides adequate knowledge of relational concepts and database designing techniques to allow students to design and implement accurate and effective database systems. The second part concentrates on the primary nonprocedural relational database language SQL. SQL is supported by most relational database software packages installed on various platforms. The book primarily concentrates on Oracle 8 and points out the features available in Oracle8i. In reality, the SQL part of the book can be utilized in Oracle release 7.x, 8, or 8i. The third part of the textbook is devoted to the procedural language PL/SQL, which is Oracle's proprietary language extension to SQL. PL/SQL features data encapsulation, error handling, and information hiding, which are the capabilities of a typical high-level programming language. The fourth part of the textbook introduces the architecture and administration of Oracle 8, as well as new features of Oracle8i and the concept of object orientation.

Throughout the text, the general syntax of SQL and PL/SQL are supplemented by simple examples and illustrations. Each chapter in the textbook includes a brief summary, exercise questions, and lab activities. The textbook is supported by sample databases—one a typical college's student database with demographic, schedule, and registration information, and the other a corporation's employee database with employees' demographic and job-related data. In most cases, the examples are based on one of the sample databases and the lab activity is based on the other to test a student's ability to apply queries in a different scenario. A separate section on supplementary examples is included at the end of the SQL part of the textbook.

As the book is primarily designed as a college textbook, it also includes (exclusively for instructors) answers to the exercise questions and SQL queries and PL/SQL blocks for the lab activities. The script to create both sample databases is also included for the instructors.

THE SOFTWARE

Oracle comes in many flavors. At your business or in college laboratory, Oracle might be implemented in a Windows NT, Unix, Linux, Solaris, or Novell Netware environment. The version of Oracle might vary from Oracle 7.x to Oracle 8 to Oracle8i. The beauty of this textbook is its versatility. The SQL and PL/SQL features covered in this text work with all versions, and the exceptions are pointed out in the individual topics, wherever necessary.

The reader is advised to join the Oracle Technology Network (OTN) by using the URL *www.technet.oracle.com*. One of the benefits of being a registered OTN user is access to a free download of Enterprise, Personal, or Lite version of Oracle 8i software. A user can also order a free Oracle software CD from the OTN site.

USING THE TEXTBOOK

The book is designed for sequential reading from Chapter 1 through Chapter 14. If you are familiar with relational database concepts, you may skip the first two chapters. From my personal experience with students, Chapter 2 on data modeling and normalization helps students tremendously in designing effective databases. You will need access to the computer system to practice SQL statements and PL/SQL programs from Chapters 3 through 12. The fourth part of the text contains reading material on the architecture and administration of Oracle, and the object and Internet features of Oracle8i. Many popular SQL*Plus commands are also covered in Chapter 13. The reader must perform exercise questions and labs at the end of each chapter before moving over to the next chapter. Whether it is procedural or nonprocedural, you cannot learn programming by just reading about it. You need to practice to master the material.

NILESH SHAH

Acknowledgments

I would like to thank Petra Recter and her staff for all her understanding and support, and for prompt responses to my questions throughout this project. It is my pleasure to work with a prestigious publishing company such as Prentice Hall. I also thank Scott Montgomery at Prentice Hall for his help in the early stages of the project.

I am also grateful to my employers—DeVry College of Technology, North Brunswick, New Jersey, and Monroe College, New Rochelle, New York. I would like to mention two individuals in particular: Dean Bhupinder Sran at DeVry first asked me to write a book when we could not find a suitable text for our Database Systems course, and Dr. Alex Ephrem at Monroe supported and encouraged me throughout the text's development process.

I would like to thank all my students, past and present, for being themselves. Without my students, I would not be in a position to write a book. Their enthusiasm in the classroom, respect toward me, and desire to learn has inspired me to take up this project.

Finally, I would like to thank my family for their understanding and patience during the whole process: my 8-year old son Naman, who always wanted to know if the book is finished so he could play basketball with me; my 3-year-old son Navan, who helped me login to my notebook and came back every few minutes to click on the disk-icon to save my work; my wife Prena for her support and for entertaining both children so I could work on this project; and last, my parents Dhiraj and Hansa for the sacrifice they have made in their life by sending their only son to the United States for a better future.

1

Database Concepts:

A Relational Approach

IN THIS CHAPTER . . .

- You will learn about basic database terminology and relational database concepts.
- The Database Management System (DBMS) and its functions are covered.
- Integrity rules and types of relationships are outlined.
- Two theoretical relational languages, relational algebra and relational calculus, are introduced for data retrieval.

DATABASE: AN INTRODUCTION

A database is an electronic storage of data. It is a depository that stores information about different "things" and also contains relationships among those different "things." Let us examine some of the basic terms to examine structure of a database:

- A person, place, event, or item is called an **entity.**
- The facts describing an entity are known as **data.** For example, if you were a registrar in a college, you would like to have all the information about students. Each student is an entity in such a scenario.

1

- Each entity can be described by its characteristics, which are known as **attributes.** For example, some of the likely attributes for a student in a college are student identification number, last name, first name, phone number, social security number, and so on.

- All the related entities are collected together to form an **entity set.** An entity set is given a name. For example, the STUDENT entity set contains data about students only. All related entities in the STUDENT entity set are students. Similarly, a company keeps track of all its employees in an entity set called EMPLOYEE. The EMPLOYEE entity set does not contain information about company's customers, because that wouldn't make any sense.

- A **database** is a collection of entity sets. For example, a college's database may include information about entities such as student, faculty, course, term, course section, building, registration information, and so on.

- The entities in a database are likely to interact with other entities. The interactions between the entity sets are called **relationships.** The interactions are described using active verbs. For example, a student *takes* a course section (CRSSECTION), so the relationship between STUDENT and CRSSECTION is *takes*. A faculty *teaches* in a building, so the relationship between FACULTY and BUILDING is *teaches*.

RELATIONSHIPS

The database design requires you to create entity sets, each describing a set of related entities. The design also requires you to establish all the relationships between entity sets within the database. The different database management software packages handle the creation and the use of relationships in different manners. Depending upon the type of interaction, the relationships are classified into three categories:

- **One-to-one relationship:** A one-to-one relationship is written as **1:1** in short form. It exists between two entity sets, X and Y, if an entity in entity set X has only one matching entity in entity set Y and vice versa. For example, a department in a college has one chairperson and a chairperson chairs one department in a college. An employee manages one department in a company, and only one employee manages a department.

- **One-to-many relationship:** A one-to-many relationship is written as **1:M.** It exists between two entity sets, X and Y, if an entity in entity set X has only one matching entity in entity set Y, but an entity in entity set Y has many matching entities in entity set X.

    For example, a faculty teaches for one department in a college but a department has many faculty members. An employee works in a department, but a department has many employees.

- **Many-to-many relationship:** A many-to-many relationship is written as **M:N.** It exists between two entity set, X and Y, if an entity in entity set X has many matching entities in entity set Y and an entity in entity set Y has many matching entities in entity set X. For example, a student takes many courses and many students take a course. An employee works on many projects, and a project has many employees.

Many times, students find it difficult to determine the type of relationship. You need to ask the following two questions to make the determination:

1. Does an entity in entity set X have more than one matching entity in entity set Y?
2. Does an entity in entity set Y have more than one matching entity in entity set X?

If your answers to both questions are No, the relationship is 1:1. If one of the answers is Yes and the other answer is No, it is a 1:M relationship. If both answers are Yes, you have an M:N relationship.

DATABASE MANAGEMENT SYSTEM (DBMS)

The database system consists of the following components (see Fig. 1-1):

- A database management System (DBMS) software package such as MS-Access, Visual Fox Pro, or Oracle.

User		
Applications	**DBMS**	**Database**
Software		
Hardware		

Figure 1-1 Database system.

- A user developed and implemented database or databases that includes tables, a data dictionary, and other database objects.
- Custom applications such as data-entry forms, reports, queries, blocks, and programs.
- Computer hardware—personal computers, minicomputers, and mainframes in a network environment.
- Software—an operating system and a network operating system.
- Personnel—a database administrator, a database designer/analyst, a programmer, and end users.

Data is the raw material. Information is processed, manipulated, collected, or organized data. The information is produced when a user uses the applications to transform data managed by the DBMS. The database system is utilized as a decision-making system and is also referred to as an information system (IS).

A DBMS based on a relational model is also known as a Relational Database Management System (RDBMS). An RDBMS not only manages data, but it is also responsible for other important functions:

- It manages data and relationships stored in the database. It creates a Data Dictionary as a user creates a database. The Data Dictionary is a system structure, which stores **Metadata** (data about data). The Metadata include table names, attribute names, data types, physical space, relationships, and so on.
- It manages all day-to-day transactions.
- It performs bookkeeping duties, so the user has data independence at application level. The applications do not have information about data characteristics.
- It transforms logical data requests to match physical data structures. When a user requests data, the RDBMS searches through the data dictionary, filters out unnecessary data, and displays the results in user readable and understandable form.
- It allows users to specify validation rules. For example, if only M and F are possible values for the attribute GENDER, users can set validation rules to keep incorrect values from being accepted.
- It secures access through passwords, encryption, and restricted user rights.
- It provides backup and recovery procedures for physical security of data.
- It allows users to share data with data locking capabilities.
- It provides import and export utilities to use data created in other database or spreadsheet software or to use data in other software.

- It reduces data redundancy by enabling users to join tables within a database. Less redundancy means fewer data entry errors, fewer data corrections, and better data integrity, and a more efficient database.

THE RELATIONAL DATABASE MODEL

The need for data is always present. In the computer age, the need to represent data in easy to understand logical form has led to many different models, such as the relational model, the hierarchical model, and the network model. Due to its simplicity in design and ease in retrieval of data, the relational database model has been very popular, especially in the personal computer environment.

E. F. Codd developed the relational database model in 1970. The model is based on mathematical set theory, and it uses a **relation** as the building block of the database. The relation is represented by a two-dimensional flat structure known as a **table.** The user does not have to know the mathematical details or the physical aspects of the data, but the user views data in a logical two-dimensional structure. The database system that manages a relational database environment is known as Relational Database Management System (RDBMS). Some of the popular relational database systems are Oracle 8 by Oracle Corporation, Microsoft Access 2000, and Microsoft Visual Fox Pro 6.0.

A table is a matrix of rows and columns in which each row represents an entity and each column represents an attribute. In other words, a table represents an entity set as per the database theory and it represents a relation as per the relational database theory. In daily practice, the terms *table, relation,* and *entity set* are used interchangeably.

Figure 1-2 shows six relational tables, PROJ1999, PROJ2000, PARTS, PRJPARTS, DEPARTMENT, and EMPLOYEE. PROJ1999 has three attributes and four entities. PROJ2000 contains three attributes and five entities. PROJ1999 consists of three attributes and four entities. PRJPARTS has three attributes and five entities. In relational terminology, a row is also referred to as a **tuple.** In a relational database, it is easy to establish relationships between tables. For example, it is possible to find the name of the vendor who supplies parts for a project.

Each column in a relation or a table corresponds to an attribute of the relation, and each row corresponds to an entity. The number of attributes in a table is called the **degree** of the relation. For example, if a table has four attributes, then the table is of degree 4.

It is assumed that there is no predefined order to rows of a table and that no two rows have exact same set of values. The order of columns is also immaterial, but correct order is used in the illustrations.

The set of all possible values that an attribute may have is called the **domain** of that attribute. Two domains are same only if they have the same meaning and

Domain — set of all possible values that an attribute may have.

PROJ1999

ProjNo	Loc	Customer
1	Miami	Stocks
2	Orlando	Allen
3	Trenton	Smith
4	Charlotte	Jones

PROJ2000

ProjNo	Loc	Customer
1	Miami	Stocks
3	Trenton	Smith
5	Phoenix	Robins
6	Edison	Shaw
7	Seattle	Douglas

PRJPARTS

ProjNo	PartNo	Qty
1	11	20
2	33	5
3	11	7
1	22	10
2	11	3

PARTS

PartNo	PartDesc	Vendor	Cost
11	Nut	Richards	19.95
22	Bolt	Black	5.00
33	Washer	Mobley	55.99

EMPLOYEE

Empno	Ename	DeptNo	ProjNo	Salary
101	Carter	10	1	25000
102	Albert	20	3	37000
103	Breen	30	6	50500
104	Gould	20	5	23700
105	Barker	10	7	75000

DEPARTMENT

DeptNo	DeptName
10	Production
20	Supplies
30	Marketing

Figure 1-2 Relational database tables.

use. ProjNo, PartNo, EmpId, DeptNo, and StudentId are attributes with numeric values, but their domains are different.

Figure 1-3 shows a simple comparison between terminology used in relational databases and file systems. Many times terms are borrowed from file system for the relational field and vice versa.

A **key** is a minimal set of attributes used to uniquely define any row in a table. If a single attribute can be used to describe each row, there is no need to use two attributes as a key. For example, in PROJ1999, ProjNo uniquely defines each row, and in PARTS, PartNo uniquely defines each row. In PRJPARTS, none of the

Relational Terminology	File System Terminology
Entity Set or Table or Relation	File
Entity or Row or Tuple	Record
Attribute or Column	Field

Figure 1-3 Terminology comparison.

attributes defines each row uniquely by itself. The attribute ProjNo is not unique, and PartNo is not unique either. In such a table, a combination of attributes can be used as a key. For example, ProjNo and PartNo together make a key for PRJPARTS table. When a single attribute is used as a unique identifier, it is known as a **primary key.** When a combination of attributes is used as a unique identifier, it is known as a **composite primary key.**

Sometimes, a more human approach is used to identify or retrieve a row from a table, because it is not possible to remember primary key values for the employee number, part number, department number, and so on. For example, a vendor's name, an employee's last name, a book's title, or an author's name can be used for the data retrieval. Such a key is known as a **secondary key.** If none of the attributes is a candidate for the primary key in a table, sometimes database designers use an extra attribute as a primary key instead of using a composite key. Such a key is known as a **surrogate key.** For example, attributes such as customer's identification number, term identification number, or vendor number can be added in a table to describe a customer, term, or vendor respectively.

In a relational database, tables are related to each other through a common attribute. An attribute in a table that references an attribute in another table is known as a **foreign key.** For example, the PartNo attribute in PRJPARTS is a foreign key attribute that references the PartNo attribute in PARTS.

Figure 1-4 shows typical illustrations showing the notation used for tables in a relational database. The table name is followed by a list of attributes within parentheses. The primary key or composite primary key attributes are shown underlined. In Oracle, the primary key, composite key, or surrogate key is defined as a primary key only, and a foreign key in a table can reference a primary key attribute only.

PROJ1999 (ProjNo**, Loc, Customer)**
PROJ2000 (ProjNo**, Loc, Customer)**
PARTS (PartNo**, Vendor, Cost)**
PRJPARTS (ProjNo**, **PartNo**, Qty)**
DEPARTMENT (DeptNo**, DeptName)**
EMPLOYEE (EmpNo**, Ename, DeptNo, ProjNo, Salary)**

Figure 1-4 Notation used for tables.

INTEGRITY RULES

In a large database managed by an RDBMS, it is very important that the data in the underlying tables be consistent. If consistency is compromised, the data is not usable. This need has led the peers to formulate two integrity rules:

Row entity

1. *Entity Integrity*. No attribute in a primary key may be null.
   The primary key provides the means of uniquely identifying a row or an entity. A null value means a value that is not known, not entered, not defined, or not applicable. A zero or a space is not considered a null value. If the primary key value is a null value in a row, we do not have enough information about the row to uniquely identify it. The RDBMS software strictly follows the entity integrity rule and does not allow users to enter a row without a unique value in the primary key attribute.

2. *Referential Integrity*. A foreign key value may be a null value, or it must exist as a value of a primary key in another table.

Referential integrity is not fully supported by all commercially available systems, but Oracle supports it religiously! Oracle does not allow you to declare a foreign key if it does not exist as a primary key in another table. It allows you to leave the foreign key attribute value as a null. If a user enters a value in the foreign key attribute, Oracle cross-references the referenced primary key attribute in the other table to confirm the existence of such a value.

It is not a good practice to use null values in any non-primary-key attributes, because this results in extra overhead on system's part in search operations. The programmers or query users have to add extra measures to include or exclude rows with null values. In certain cases, it is not possible to avoid null values. For example, an employee does not have middle initial, an employee is hired but does not have an assigned department, or a student's major is undefined. In Oracle, a default value can be assigned to an attribute and a user does not have to enter a value for that attribute.

THEORETICAL RELATIONAL LANGUAGES

E. F. Codd suggested two theoretical relational languages to use with the relational model:

1. *Relational algebra,* a procedural language.
2. *Relational calculus,* a nonprocedural language.

The third-generation high-level compiler languages can be used to manipulate data in a table, but they can only work with one row at a time. In contrast, the relational languages can work on the entire table or a group of rows. The multiple-row manipulation does not even need a looping structure! The relational languages provide more power with a very little coding. Codd proposed these languages to embed them in other host languages for more processing capability and more sophisticated application development. In the database systems available today, nonprocedural Structured Query Language (SQL) is used as a data manipulation sublanguage. The theoretical languages have provided the basis for SQL.

Relational Algebra

Relational algebra is a procedural language because the user accomplishes desired results by using a set of operations in a sequence. It uses set operations on tables to produce new resulting tables. These resulting tables are used for subsequent sequential operations.

The nine operations used by relational algebra are

1. Union
2. Intersection
3. Difference
4. Selection
5. Projection
6. Product
7. Join
8. Assignment
9. Division

Union. The union of two tables consists of all rows that are in one or both tables. The duplicate rows are eliminated from the resulting table. The resulting table does not contain two rows with identical data values. There is a basic requirement to perform a union operation on two tables:

- Both tables must have the same degree.
- The domains of the corresponding attributes in two tables must be same.

Such tables are said to be *union compatible.* In mathematical set theory, a union can be performed on any two sets, but in relational algebra, a union can be performed only on union-compatible tables.

Suppose we want to see all the projects from years 1999 and 2000. We obtain it by performing a union (∪) on PROJ1999 and PROJ2000 tables as given in Fig. 1-1.

If we call the resulting table TABLE_A, the operation can be denoted by:

TABLE_A = PROJ1999 ∪ PROJ2000

TABLE_A

ProjNo	Loc	Customer
1	Miami	Stocks
2	Orlando	Allen
3	Trenton	Smith
4	Charlotte	Jones
5	Phoenix	Robins
6	Edison	Shaw
7	Seattle	Douglas

Intersection.   The intersection of two tables produces a table with rows, that are in both tables. The two tables must be union compatible to perform intersection on them.

If we use the same two tables that were used in the union operation, the intersection will give us the projects that appear in the year 1999 and in the year 2000. Let us call the resulting table, which is produced by the intersection (∪) operation, TABLE_B.

TABLE_B = PROJ1999 ∪ PROJ2000

TABLE_B

ProjNo	Loc	Customer
1	Miami	Stocks
3	Trenton	Smith

Difference.   The difference of two tables produces a table with rows that are present in the first table and are not present in the second table. The difference can be performed on union-compatible tables only.

If we find the difference (−) of the same two tables used in the previous operations and create TABLE_C, it will have projects for the year 1999, that are not projects for the year 2000:

TABLE_C = PROJ1999 − PROJ2000

TABLE_C

ProjNo	Loc	Customer
2	Orlando	Allen
4	Charlotte	Jones

Now just as in mathematics, $A - B$ is not equal to $B - A$. If we perform the same operation to find projects from year 2000 that did not exist in year 1999,

TABLE D = PROJ2000 – PROJ1999

the resulting TABLE_D will look like this:

TABLE_D

ProjNo	Loc	Customer
5	Phoenix	Robins
6	Edison	Shaw
7	Seattle	Douglas

Projection.   The projection operation allows us to create a table based on desirable attributes from all existing attributes in a table. The undesired attributes are ignored. The projection operation returns the "vertical slices" of a table. The projection is indicated by including the table name and a list of desired attributes.

TABLE_E = PARTS (PartDesc, Cost)

TABLE_E

PartDesc	Cost
Nut	19.95
Bolt	5.00
Washer	55.99

Selection.   The selection operation selects rows from a table based on a condition or conditions. The conditional operators ($=, <>, >, >=, <, <=$) and the logical operators (AND, OR, NOT) are used along with attributes and values to create conditions. The selection operation returns "horizontal slices" from a table.

Let us apply the selection (**Sel**) operation to the PARTS table:

TABLE_F = Sel (PARTS: Cost>10.00)

TABLE_F

PartNo	PartDesc	Vendor	Cost
11	Nut	Richards	19.95
33	Washer	Mobley	55.99

The resulting table has the same number of attributes as the original table but fewer rows. The rows that satisfy the given condition are returned.

Product.   A product of two tables is a matching of every row in the first table with each and every row in the second table. It is also known as a Cartesian product. If the first table has x rows and the second table has y rows, the resulting product has $x \cdot y$ rows. If the first table has m attributes and the second table has n attributes, the resulting product has $m + n$ attributes.

For simplicity, let us take two tables with one attribute each and perform the product (*) operation on them.

DEPARTMENT

DeptName
Production
Supplies
Marketing

EMPLOYEE

Ename
Carter
Albert

TABLE_G = EMPLOYEE * DEPARTMENT

TABLE_G

Ename	DeptName
Carter	Production
Carter	Supplies
Carter	Marketing
Albert	Production
Albert	Supplies
Albert	Marketing

In this example, EMPLOYEE has 2 rows and DEPARTMENT has 3 rows, so TABLE_G has $2 \cdot 3 = 6$ rows. EMPLOYEE has 1 attribute and DEPARTMENT has 1 attribute, so TABLE_G has $1 + 1 = 2$ attributes.

Assignment.   This operation creates a new table from existing tables. We have been doing it throughout all the other operations. Assignment ($=$) gives us an ability to name new tables that are based on other tables.

For example,

TABLE_A = PROJ1999 ∪ PROJ2000
TABLE_C = PROJ1999 − PROJ2000

Join.   The join is one of the most important operations due to its ability to get related data from a number of tables. The join is based on a common attribute, which does not have to have the same name in both tables but has the same domain in both tables. When a join is based on equality of value, it is known as a natural join. In Oracle, you will learn about the natural join, or equijoin, and also about other types of joins, such as outer join, nonequijoin, and self-join, that are based on the operators other than just the equality operator.

For example, if we are interested in employee information along with department information, a join can be carried out using the EMPLOYEE and DEPARTMENT tables. The DeptNo column is the common attribute in both tables and will be used for the join condition.

TABLE_H = join (EMPLOYEE, DEPARTMENT: DeptNo = DeptNo)

TABLE_H

EmpNo	Ename	DeptNo	ProjNo	Salary	DeptName
101	Carter	10	1	25000	Production
102	Albert	20	3	37000	Supplies
103	Breen	30	6	50500	Marketing
104	Gould	20	5	23700	Supplies
105	Barker	10	7	75000	Production

The expression is read as "join a row in the EMPLOYEE table with a row in the DEPARTMENT table, where the DeptNo value in the EMPLOYEE table is equal to the DeptNo value in the DEPARTMENT table."

Join operation is an overhead on the system because it is accomplished using a series of operations. A product is performed first, which results in $5 \cdot 3 = 15$ rows. A selection is performed next to select rows where the DeptNo values are equal. Finally, a projection is performed to eliminate duplicate DeptNo attributes.

Division.   The division operation is the most difficult operation to comprehend. It is not as simple as division in mathematics. In relational algebra, it identifies rows in one table that have a certain relationship to all rows in another table. Let us consider the following two tables:

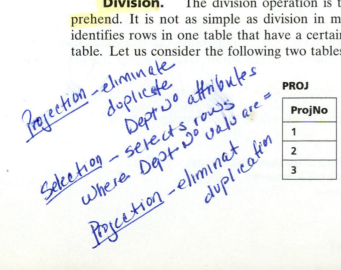

Projection - eliminate duplicate DeptNo attributes

Selection - selects rows where DeptNo value are =

Projection - eliminat duplication

PROJ

ProjNo
1
2
3

PRJPARTS

ProjNo	PartNo
1	11
2	33
3	11
1	22
2	11

Suppose we want to find out which parts are used in every project. We have to divide (/) PRJPARTS by PROJ:

TABLE_I = PRJPARTS / PROJ

TABLE_I

PartNo
11

The attributes of TABLE_I are those from the dividend PRJPARTS, that are not in the divisor PROJ. The rows of TABLE_I are a subset of the projection PRJPARTS (PartNo). The row (PartNo) is in TABLE_I if and only if (ProjNo, PartNo) is in the dividend PRJPARTS for every value of (ProjNo) in the divisor PROJ.

The nine operations provide users with a sufficient set of operations to work with the relational databases. Some of the operations are combinations of other operations, as we saw in the case of the join operation, but such operations are very useful in actual practice. In later chapters on Oracle, you will find the actual query statements used to accomplish the different operations outlined here. You will learn to perform these operations using Oracle's Structured Query Language (SQL).

Applications of Relational Algebra

Relational algebra is a procedural language in the sense that a user is required to use a series of operations to obtain a certain result. This language has its capabilities and limitations.

Problem 1

Which employee is working on a project in Miami during year 2000?
Solution

```
A = join (PROJ2000, EMPLOYEE : ProjNo = ProjNo)
B = Sel (A : Loc = 'Miami')
C = B (Ename)
```

Alternative solution

A = Sel (PROJ2000 : Loc = 'Miami')
B = join (EMPLOYEE, A : ProjNo = ProjNo)
C = B (Ename)

In these solutions, Table C will have one entry, *Carter,* an employee who works on project 1 in Miami. Relational algebra is called a procedural language because a user has to perform a series of operations in order to achieve the desired result.

Problem 2

Who has supplied parts for the project in Trenton?
Solution

D = PROJ1999 ∪ PROJ2000
E = Sel (D : Loc = 'Trenton')
F = join (E, PRJPARTS : ProjNo = ProjNo)
G = join (F, PARTS : PartNo = PartNo)
H = G (Vendor)

The solution uses four tables from the database. First the union operation is performed to put all projects together. Then the selection operation is performed to find all rows for projects in Trenton. Then the result is joined with the PRJPARTS table to merge part number with project information. Then the PARTS table is merged with the resulting table to get part–vendor information. At last, name of the vendor is retrieved using projection, which returns *Richards*.

The solutions illustrated here show a fundamental weakness in relational algebra as a programming language. The solutions are difficult to develop and comprehend for users who have not come across problems like these before. Relational algebra cannot group related information together. Neither can it perform calculations on numeric values or sort rows in any particular order. Printing information with formatting is out of question! The actual implementation of relational languages is an integral part of fourth-generation query languages. These languages are supported by many other tools, which provide users with full application development capabilities.

RELATIONAL CALCULUS

Relational calculus is a nonprocedural language. The programmer specifies the data requirement, and the system generates operations needed to produce a table with the required data. In this section, we will try to understand relational calculus briefly with sample examples, using the general syntax

Result = (attribute list) : Expression

The list of attributes is on the left of the colon and the conditions are on the right.

Problem

Find projects where part number 11 is used.
Solution

(r.ProjNo) : r in PRJPARTS and r.PartNo = 11

In this expression, *r* is known as a **row variable.** The expression is read as "ProjNo in row *r*, where *r* is a row in the PRJPARTS table and PartNo in row *r* is 11." Each row in PRJPARTS is examined using the condition to the right of the colon. The resulting table will contain project numbers 1, 3, and 2:

ProjNo
1
3
2

The solution for the same problem in relational algebra would look like this:

M = Sel (PRJPARTS : PartNo = 11)
N = M (ProjNo)

Problem

Find employee names and salary for employees who work in Production.
Solution

(r.Ename, r.Salary) : r in EMPLOYEE and
s in DEPARTMENT and
s.DeptName = 'Production' and
r.DeptNo = s.DeptNo

RESULT

Ename	Salary
Carter	25000
Barker	75000

Problem

Find employee names, department names, and locations for projects in the year 2000 for all employees who are working on project 1.

Solution

(r.Ename, s.DeptName, t.Loc) : r in EMPLOYEE and
                                   s in DEPARTMENT and
                                   t in PROJ2000 and
                                   r.ProjNo = 1 and
                                   r.ProjNo = t.ProjNo and
                                   r.DeptNo = s.DeptNo

RESULT

Ename	DeptName	Loc
Carter	Production	Miami

The theoretical relational languages discussed in this chapter are the basis for the commercially available relational languages. Structured Query Language (SQL) is a nonprocedural query language based on relational calculus that is supported by many relational database systems.

Final Note

A database is an electronic data depository that is supposed to answer users' data requests correctly, quickly, and efficiently. Most end users execute applications that work on databases. The most important task for the database designer is to create a properly designed database. If the database is not designed well, it will not be implemented well. The result is a nightmare for application developers. Even if the application is well written, a defective database may result in incorrect and sometimes meaningless results.

In Chapter 2, we will study the fundamentals of database design and modeling techniques in the first half. In the latter half, we will learn the normalization process to control data redundancies. If you have learned a programming language before, you are familiar with the tools used in the program development cycle. If you use a short cut and create a wrong algorithm for a problem, you have to start the cycle all over again to rectify your logic. Database design is also like programming. The designing tools are aids for creating a "good" database. Remember that the database is a collection of tables. Do not build individual tables, but design a database as a whole.

IN A NUTSHELL . . .

- A database is an electronic storage of data.
- An entity is a person, place, event, or item.
- Data are the facts describing an entity.

- An entity's characteristics are known as attributes.
- An entity set is a collection of related entities.
- A database is a collection of entity sets.
- Relationships are interactions between entity sets.
- Three types of relationships are one-to-one (1:1), one-to-many (1:M), and many-to-many (M:N).
- In a relational model, a row is known as a tuple.
- The degree is the number of attributes in a table, and the domain is a set of all possible values for an attribute.
- A key is a minimal set of attributes used to uniquely define a row. When a single attribute is used as a key, it is known as a primary key. When a combination of attributes is used as a key, it is known as a composite key.
- The foreign key is an attribute in a table that references a primary key in another table.
- Two integrity rules of relational model are entity integrity (the primary key may not be null) and referential integrity (the foreign key value may be null or it must exist as a primary key value in another table).
- The relational algebra is a theoretical procedural language for data retrieval. It provides users with a set of operations such as union, intersection, difference, selection, projection, product, join, assignment, and division.
- Relational calculus is a nonprocedural relational language, which is the basis for today's popular relational database language Structured Query Language (SQL).

EXERCISE QUESTIONS

1. Define the following terms.
   (a) Entity
   (b) Entity set
   (c) Attribute
   (d) Tuple
   (e) Domain
   (f) Key
   (g) Null
2. What are the two integrity rules of relational database?
3. What are the different types of keys?
4. Identify the primary key and foreign key for the following tables. Also, specify the table referenced by the foreign key. If a table does not have a foreign key, leave the entry blank. (*Note:* Some tables have a composite primary key. Identify all composite key attributes for such tables.)

STUDENT (StudentId, Last, First, StartTerm, Birthdate, FacultyId, MajorId, Phone)
FACULTY (FacultyId, Name, RoomId, Phone, DeptId)
COURSE (CourseId, Title, Credits)
CRSSECTION (CsId, CourseId, Section, TermId, FacultyId, Day, RoomId)
REGISTRATION (StudentId, CsId, Midterm, Final)
ROOM (RoomType, RoomDesc)
TERM (TermId, TermDesc, StartDate, EndDate)
LOCATION (RoomId, Building, RoomNo, Capacity, RoomType)
MAJOR (MajorId, MajorDesc)
DEPARTMENT (DeptId, DeptName, FacultyId)

Table	Primary Key	Foreign Keys	Tables Referenced
STUDENT			
FACULTY			
COURSE			
CRSSECTION			
REGISTRATION			
ROOM			
TERM			
LOCATION			
MAJOR			
DEPARTMENT			

5. Discuss different types of relationships with examples.

6. What do we mean by "union compatible"? Which operations require tables to be union compatible?

7. State the difference between the following:
   (a) Union and intersection
   (b) Product and join
   (c) Selection and projection

8. Use the tables given in Fig. 3-1. The relational database notation of tables is

> PROJ1999 (ProjNo, Loc, Customer)
> PROJ2000 (ProjNo, Loc, Customer)
> PARTS (PartNo, Vendor, Cost)
> PRJPARTS (ProjNo, PartNo, Qty)
> DEPARTMENT (DeptNo, DeptName)
> EMPLOYEE (EmpNo, Ename, DeptNo, ProjNo, Salary)

Retrieve the following information by using a series of relational algebraic operations and also by using a relational calculus statement.
   (a) All employee names.
   (b) All employees working in department number 20.
   (c) All employees who are making $50,000 or more.
   (d) All employees who are working in department 20 and also making more than $25,000.
   (e) Vendors who supplied parts for the project in Miami during the year 2000.

2

Database Design:
Data Modeling and
Normalization

IN THIS CHAPTER . . .

- You will learn about database modeling techniques
- You will work with symbols and E-R diagrams for representation of entity and relationship.
- Types of dependencies within a table are examined and illustrated by using dependency diagrams.
- Reduction of data redundancy and the process of normalization are covered.

In Chapter 1 you learned about relational database concepts. You also learned about theoretical languages and operations on tables. The relational model is very popular due to its simplicity. It shows data to the user in a very simple logical view as a two-dimensional table. Anyone can create tables, but the strongest characteristic of the relational model is its ability to establish relationships among tables, which helps reduce redundancy. Your queries are as good as the database you create. The first and the foremost step in database creation is database design. Database design involves a certain degree of common sense. If the given list of attributes describes different entities, you would create a separate table for each entity type. You would use foreign keys to establish relationships. To join two tables, you need at least one common or redundant attribute in both tables. All situations are not the same. There are complex cases where common sense does not do the job.

Many proven modeling and designing tools are available for a better database design. In this chapter, you will learn about different pictorial methods, techniques, and concepts to create a "near-perfect" database.

DATA MODELING

A model is a simplified version of real-life complex objects. Databases are complex, and data modeling is a tool to represent the various components and their relationships. The Entity Relationship (E-R) model is a very popular modeling tool among many such tools available today. The E-R model provides

- An excellent communication tool.
- A simple graphical representation of a database.

The E-R model uses **E-R diagrams** for graphical representation of the database components. An **Entity** (or an entity set) is represented by a rectangle. The name of the entity (set) is written within the rectangle. The name of an entity set is a singular noun in uppercase letters. For example, EMPLOYEE, CUSTOMER, and DEPARTMENT are singular entity set names (see Fig. 2-1).

EMPLOYEE

Figure 2-1   Entity representation in an E-R diagram.

A diamond-shaped box represents the relationship between the two entity sets. The name of the relationship is an active verb in lowercase letters. For example, *works, manages,* and *employs* are examples of active verbs. Passive verbs can be used, but active verbs are preferable (see Fig. 2-2).

Figure 2-2   Representation of relationship in an E-R diagram.

The types of relationships (1:1, 1:M, and M:N) between entities are called **connectivity.** The connectivity is written with a label next to each entity. For example, an EMPLOYEE supervises a DEPARTMENT and a DEPARTMENT has one EMPLOYEE supervisor, a DIVISION contains many FACULTY members but a FACULTY works for one DIVISION, and an INVOICE contains many ITEMs and an ITEM can be in more than one INVOICE.

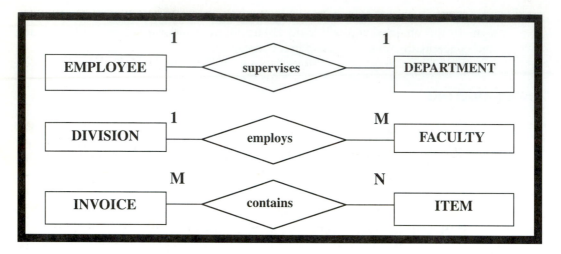

Figure 2-3   Entity, relationship, and connectivity.

Let us put everything together and represent these scenarios with the E-R diagram. Figure 2-3 shows entities, relationships, and connectivity.

The relationship between two entities can be given using the lower and upper limits. This information is called the cardinality. The cardinality is written next to each entity in the form (n,m), where n is the minimum number and m is the maximum number. For example, (1,1) next to EMPLOYEE means that an employee can supervise a minimum of 1 and a maximum of 1 department. Similarly, (1,1) next to DEPARTMENT says that one and only one employee supervises the department. The value (1,N) means a minimum of 1 and a maximum equal to any number (see Fig. 2-4). In reality, corporations set rules for the minimum and maximum values for cardinality. A corporation may decide that a department must have a minimum of 10 employees and a maximum of 25 employees, which results in cardinality of (10,25). A college decides that a computer science course section must have at minimum 5 students in order to recover the cost incurred and at maximum 35 students because the computer lab contains only 35 terminals. An employee can be part of zero or more than one department, and an item may not be in any invoice! These types of decisions are known as business rules.

Figure 2-4 shows the E-R diagram with added cardinality. In real life it is possible to have an entity that is not related to another entity at all times. The relationship becomes optional in such a case. In the example of a video rental store, a customer can rent video movies. There are times when the customer has not rented any movie, and there are times when the customer has rented 1 or more movies. Similarly, there can be a movie in the database that is or is not rented at a particular time. These are called optional relationships and are shown with a small circle next to the optional entity (see Fig. 2-5). The optional relationship

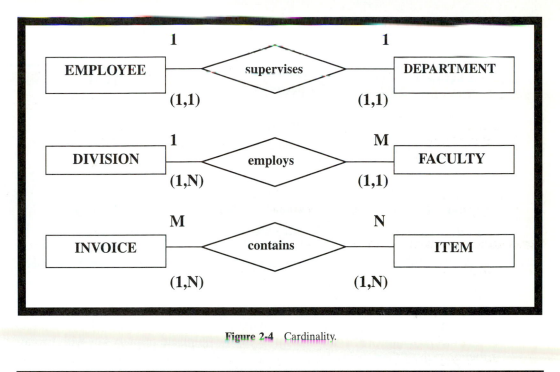

Figure 2-4 Cardinality.

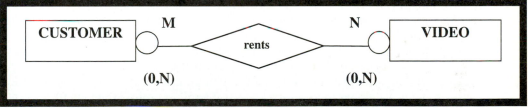

Figure 2-5 Optional relationships.

can occur in 1:1, 1:M, or M:N relationships, and it can occur on one or both sides of the relationship.

In relational databases, many to many (M:N) relationships are allowed, but they are not easy to implement. For example, an invoice has many items and an item can be in many invoices. Refer to the INVOICE and ITEM relationship in Fig. 2-4. At this point, you will be introduced to the relational schema, a graphical representation of tables, their attribute names, key components, and relations between the primary key in one table and the foreign key in another. You will also see the decomposition of a M:N relationship into two 1:M relationships. The decomposition from M:N to 1:M involves a third entity known as a **composite entity.** The composite entity is created with the primary key from both tables with M:N relationships. The new entity has a composite key, which is a combination of primary keys from the original two

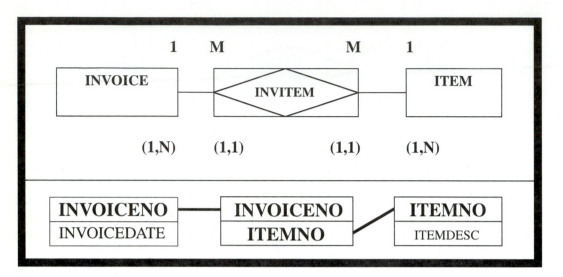

Figure 2-6   Composite entity and relational schema.

entities. In the E-R diagram, a composite entity is drawn as a diamond within a rectangle (see Fig. 2-6). The composite entity has a composite primary key with two attributes, each of them being foreign keys referencing other two entities in the database. For example, the foreign key INVOICENO in the INVITEM table references the INVOICENO attribute in the INVOICE table and the foreign key ITEMNO in the INVITEM table references the ITEMNO attribute in the ITEM table.

In a database there are entities that cannot exist by themselves. Such entities are known as **weak entities.** In Chapter 3, you will be introduced to two different sample databases. In the employee database there is an entity called EMPLOYEE with employees' demographic information and another entity called DEPENDENT with information about each employee's dependents. The DEPENDENT entity cannot exist by itself. There are no dependents for an employee who does not exist. In other words, you need the existence of an employee for his/her dependent to exist in the database. The weak entities are shown by double-lined rectangles. The weak entity is shown in Fig 2-7.

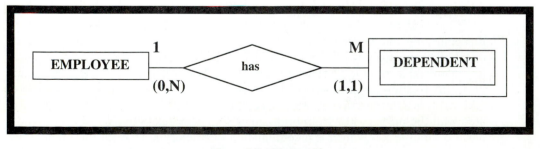

Figure 2-7   Weak entity.

Some of the other elements considered in the database design are

- **Simple attributes**—attributes that cannot be subdivided, for example, last name, city, or gender.
- **Composite attributes**—attributes that can be subdivided, into atomic form, for example, a full name can be subdivided into the last name, first name, and middle initial.
- **Single-valued attributes**—attributes with a single value, for example, Employee ID, social security number, or date of birth.
- **Multivalued attributes**—attributes with multiple values, for example, degree codes or course registration. The multivalued attributes have to be given special consideration. They can be entered into one attribute with a value separator mark, or they can be entered in separate attributes with names like Course 1, Course 2, Course 3, and so on, or a separate composite entity can be created.

DEPENDENCY

In Chapter 1, you learned that the primary key in a table describes an entity. Every table in the database has a primary key, which uniquely identifies an entity. For example, PartNo is a primary key in the PARTS table and DeptNo is a primary key in the DEPARTMENT table. Each table has other attributes that do not make up the primary key for the table. Such attributes are called the nonkey attributes. The nonkey attributes are functionally dependent on the primary key attribute. For example, PartDesc and Cost in the PARTS table are dependent on the primary key PartNo, and DeptName is dependent on the primary key attribute DeptNo in the DEPARTMENT table.

Now, let us take a scenario as shown in Figure 2-8. The INVOICE table in Fig. 2-8 does not have any single attribute that can uniquely identify an entity.

INVOICE

InvNo	InvDate	CustNo	ItemNo	CustName	ItemName	ItemPrice	Qty
1001	04/14/00	212	1	Starks	Screw	$2.25	5
1001	04/14/00	212	3	Starks	Bolt	$3.99	5
1001	04/14/00	212	5	Starks	Washer	$1.99	9
1002	04/17/00	225	1	Connors	Screw	$2.25	2
1002	04/17/00	225	2	Connors	Nut	$5.00	3
1003	04/17/00	239	1	Kapur	Screw	$2.25	7
1003	04/17/00	239	2	Kapur	Nut	$5.00	1
1004	04/18/00	211	4	Garcia	Hammer	$9.99	5

Figure 2-8 INVOICE table and its attributes.

The first choice would be InvNo, but it is not a unique value in the table because an invoice may contain more than one item and there may be more than one entry for an invoice. CustNo cannot be the primary key because there can be many invoices for a customer and CustNo does not identify an invoice. ItemNo cannot be the primary key because an item may appear in more than one invoice and ItemNo does not describe an invoice. The table has a composite key or a composite primary key, which consists of InvNo and ItemNo. InvNo and ItemNo together make up unique values for each row. All other attributes that do not constitute the primary key are nonkey attributes, and they are dependent on the primary key.

There are three types of dependencies in a table:

- *Total Dependency.* A nonkey attribute dependent on all primary key attributes shows total dependency.
- *Partial Dependency.* In partial dependency, a nonkey attribute is dependent on part of the primary key.
- *Transitive Dependency.* In transitive dependency, a nonkey attribute is dependent on another nonkey attribute.

For example, in the INVOICE table, ItemName and ItemPrice are nonkey attributes that are dependent only on a part of the primary key attribute ItemNo. They are not dependent on the InvNo attribute. Similarly, the nonkey attribute InvDate is dependent only on InvNo. They are *partially dependent* on the primary key attributes. The nonkey attribute CustName is not dependent on any primary key attribute but is dependent on another nonkey attribute, CustNo. It is said to have *transitive dependency*. The nonkey attribute Qty is dependent on both InvNo and ItemNo, so it is said to have *total dependency*.

DATABASE DESIGN

Relational database design involves an attempt to *synthesize* the database structure to get the "first draft." The initial draft goes through an *analysis* phase to improve the structure. More formal techniques are available for the analysis and improvement of the structure. In the synthesis phase, entities and their relationships are identified. The characteristics or the attributes of all entities are also identified. The designer also defines the domains for each attribute. The candidate keys are picked, and primary keys are selected from them. The minimal set of attributes is used as a primary key. If one attribute is sufficient to uniquely identify an entity, there is no need to select two attributes to create a composite key. You should avoid using names as primary keys and should also break down composite attributes into separate columns. For example, a name should be split into last name and first name. Once entities, attributes, domains, and keys are defined, each entity is synthesized by creating a table for it. A process called **normalization** analyzes tables created by the synthesis process.

NORMAL FORMS

In Fig. 2-8, data is repeated from row to row. For example, InvDate, CustNo, and CustName are repeated for same InvNo. The ItemName is entered repeatedly from invoice to invoice. There is a large amount of redundant data in a table with just eight rows! The **redundant data** can pose a huge problem in databases. First of all, someone has to enter same data repeatedly. Second, if there is a change in one piece of data, the change has to be made in many places. For example, if customer Starks changes his/her name to Starks-Johnson, you would go to the individual row in INVOICE and make that change. The redundancy may also lead to **anomalies.**

Anomalies

A deletion anomaly results when the deletion of information about one entity leads to the deletion of information about another entity. For example, in Fig. 2-8, if an invoice for customer Garcia is removed, information about item number 4 is also deleted. An insertion anomaly occurs when the information about an entity cannot be inserted unless the information about another entity is known. For example, if the company buys a new item, it cannot be entered unless an invoice is created for a customer with that new item.

The unnecessary and unwanted redundancy is not appropriate in databases. Such tables are in lower normal form. The normalization is a technique to reduce redundancy. It is a decomposition process to split tables up. The splitting is performed carefully so that no information is lost. The higher the normal form is, the lower the redundancy. The table in Fig. 2-8 is in first normal form.

First Normal Form (1NF)

A table is said to be in first normal form, or can be labeled 1NF, if the following conditions exist:

- The primary key is defined. That includes a composite key if a single attribute cannot be used as a primary key. In our INVOICE table, InvNo and ItemId are defined as the composite primary key components.
- All nonkey attributes show functional dependency on the primary key components. If you know the invoice number and the item number, you can find out the invoice date, customer number and name, item name and price, and quantity ordered. For example, if the InvNo = 1001 and ItemNo = 5 are known, then InvDate = 04/14/00, ItemName = Washer, ItemPrice = $1.99, CustNo = 212, and CustName = Starks.

• The table contains no multivalued attributes. In a single-valued attribute, the intersection of a row and a column returns only one value. In a normalized table, the intersection of a row and a column is a single value. Some database packages allow multiple values in an attribute in a row. Unidata and Prime Information are two examples of such software. Figure 2-9 shows the INVOICE table of Fig. 2-8 in nonnormalized form. In Fig. 2-9, the ItemNo, ItemName, ItemPrice, and Qty attributes are multivalued.

INVOICE

Multivalued attributes — *attributes with multiple values.*

InvNo	InvDate	CustNo	ItemNo	CustName	ItemName	ItemPrice	Qty
1001	04/14/00	212	1	Starks	Screw	$2.25	5
			3		Bolt	$3.99	5
			5		Washer	$1.99	9
1002	04/17/00	225	1	Connors	Screw	$2.25	2
			2		Nut	$5.00	3
1003	04/17/00	239	1	Kapur	Screw	$2.25	7
			2		Nut	$5.00	1
1004	04/18/00	211	4	Garcia	Hammer	$9.99	5

Figure 2-9 Nonnormalized table with multivalued attributes.

A table that is in 1NF has redundant data. A table in 1NF does not show data consistency and integrity in the long run. The normalization technique is used to control and reduce redundancy and bring the table to a higher normal form.

Second Normal Form (2NF)

A table is said to be in 2NF if the following requirements are satisfied:

Partial dependency — a nonkey attribute is dependent on part of the primary key.

• All 1NF requirements are fulfilled.
• There is no partial dependency.

As you already know, partial dependency exists in a table in which nonkey attributes are partially dependent on part of a composite key.

• **Question:** A table is in 1NF and it does not have a composite key. Is it in the second normal form also?
• **Answer:** Yes, it is in 2NF because there is no partial dependency. Partial dependency only exists in a table with the composite key.

Third Normal Form (3NF)

A table is said to be in 3NF if the following requirements are satisfied:

- All 2NF requirements are fulfilled.
- There is no transitive dependency.

[handwritten: Transitive dependency — a nonkey attribute is dependent on another nonkey attribute.]

A table in 2NF with no transitive dependency is automatically in 3NF.

Other, higher, normal forms are defined in some database texts. Boyce–Codd normal form (BCNF), fourth normal form (4NF), fifth normal form (5NF), and domain key normal form (DKNF) are not covered in this text. In the following section, you will learn the normalization process by using dependency diagrams.

DEPENDENCY DIAGRAMS

A dependency diagram is used to show total, partial, and transitive dependencies in a table.

- The primary key components are highlighted. They are in bold letters and in boxes with a darker border. The primary key components are connected to each other using a bracket.
- The total dependencies are shown with arrows drawn above the diagram.
- The partial and transitive dependencies are shown with arrows at the bottom of the diagram.

Conversion from 1NF to 2NF

We see in Fig. 2-10 that there is a composite key in the table and 1NF to 2NF conversion is required. In this conversion, you remove all partial dependencies.

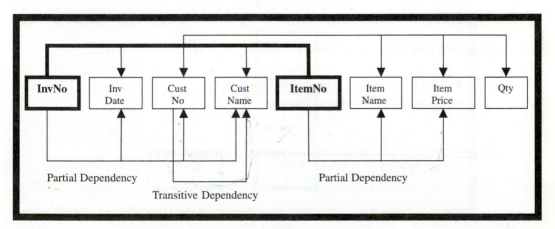

Figure 2-10 Dependency diagram.

- First write each primary key component on a separate line because they will become primary keys in two new tables.
- Write the composite key on the third line. It will be the composite key in the third table.

Figure 2-11 shows the decomposition of one table in 1NF into three tables in 2NF. The reason behind the decomposition is moving attributes with partial dependency to the new table along with the primary key. If only one of the two primary key attributes has nonkey attributes dependent on it, you will create only one new table to remove the partial dependency. The InvNo, CustNo, and CustName attributes will move to the INVOICE table because they are partially dependent on InvNo. ItemNo and ItemPrice will move to the ITEM table because they are partially dependent on ItemNo in Fig. 2-10. The Qty attribute moves to INVITEM because it is totally dependent on the composite key. The database will look like the one shown in Fig. 2-12.

Conversion from 2NF to 3NF

The database tables in 2NF (see Fig. 2-12) have no partial dependency, but the INVOICE table still has transitive dependency.

- Move attributes with the transitive dependency to a new table.
- Keep the primary key of the new table as a foreign key in the existing table.

In Fig. 2-13, you see the decomposition from 2NF to 3NF to remove transitive dependency. A new CUSTOMER table is created with CustNo as its primary key. The CustNo attribute is kept in the INVOICE table as a foreign key to establish a relationship between INVOICE and CUSTOMER tables. The final database in 3NF looks like the one in Fig. 2-14.

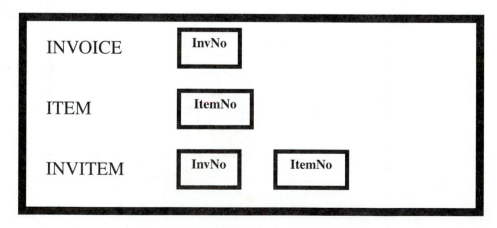

Figure 2-11   1NF to 2NF decomposition.

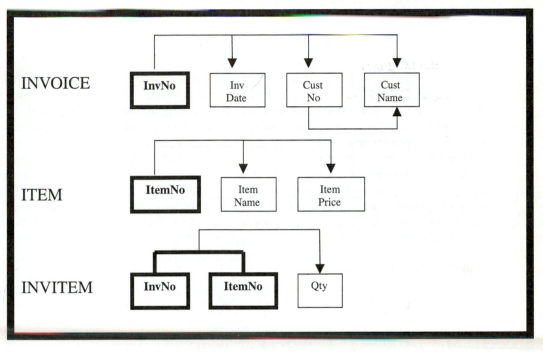

Figure 2-12 Tables in 2NF.

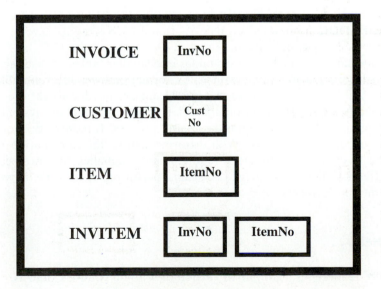

Figure 2-13 2NF to 3NF decomposition.

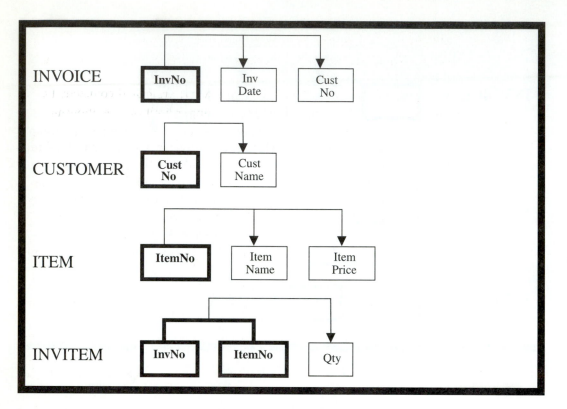

Figure 2-14   Tables in 3NF.

DENORMALIZATION

The normalization process splits tables into smaller tables. These tables are joined through common attributes to retrieve information from different tables. The more tables you have in a database, the more joins are needed to get the desired information. In a multiuser environment it is a costly overhead and system performance is affected. Denormalization is the reverse process. It reduces the normal form and increases data redundancy. With denormalization, the information is stored with duplicate data, more storage is required, and anomalies and inconsistent data exist. The designer has to weigh this against performance to come up with a good design and performance.

IN A NUTSHELL . . .

- A model is a simplified version of real-life complex objects.
- The Entity Relationship (E-R) diagram is an excellent communication tool that represents a database graphically.

- In an E-R diagram an entity (set) is represented by a rectangle with name of the entity set written as an uppercase singular noun.
- An E-R diagram represents a relationship as an active verb inside a diamond-shaped box.
- The types of relationships (1:1, 1:M, and M:N) are called connectivity.
- The cardinality shows the lower and the upper limit of a relationship.
- All entities are not related to each other at all times. Such a relationship is known as an optional relationship. It can occur in 1:1, 1:M, and M:N relationships, and it can occur on one or both sides of the relationship.
- M:N relationships are complex to implement. Each M:N relationship is decomposed into two 1:M relationships using a third entity, known as a composite entity. A composite entity has a composite primary key, which is combination of primary keys from the other two entities.
- Simple attributes cannot be divided, but composite attributes can be subdivided.
- Attributes can be single valued or multivalued.
- Nonkey attributes are functionally dependent on the primary key attributes in a table.
- In partial dependency, a nonkey attribute is dependent on part of the composite primary key.
- In transitive dependency, a nonkey attribute is dependent on another nonkey attribute.
- A database design involves synthesis and analysis. Normalization is a process of analyzing a database created with synthesis.
- Normalization is a decomposition process to reduce data redundancy and data anomalies.
- A database in 1NF does not have any multivalued attributes.
- A database in 2NF does not have any partial dependencies.
- A database in 3NF does not have any transitive dependencies.
- Higher normal forms are also possible, and the process of denormalization is also performed on a database to weigh performance against redundancy.

EXERCISE QUESTIONS

True/False:
1. *Connectivity* is a term used for relationships in the E-R diagram.
2. Partial dependency can exist in a table with a simple primary key.
3. In transitive dependency, an attribute is dependent on the primary key in another table.
4. The higher the normal form is, the lower the redundancy.
5. Normalization is a process of converting database from lower to higher normal form.

Define the following terms:
1. Partial dependency
2. Transitive dependency
3. Normalization
4. Data anomalies
5. Cardinality

E-R diagram exercise:
A student takes many courses, and many students take a course. Create an E-R diagram to represent the entities, connectivity, and cardinality. Decompose the E-R diagram with a composite entity to reduce each M:N relationship to two 1:M relationships. Also draw the relational schema for the database.

Dependency diagram exercise:

EMP

EMP_ID	LAST	FIRST	DEPT_ID	DEPT_NAME	DEPENDENT_NO	DEPENDENT_SSN	DEPENDENT_DOB

Create a dependency diagram for the set of given attributes for the EMP table:

EMP_ID	Employee's ID
LAST	Employee's last name
FIRST	Employee's first name
DEPT_ID	Employee's department number
DEPT_NAME	Employee's department name
DEPENDENT_NO	Employee's number of dependents
DEPENDENT_SSN	Dependent's social security number
DEPENDENT_DOB	Dependent's date of birth

The primary key attributes are EMP_ID and DEPENDENT_NO.

Normalization exercise:
Using the dependency diagram of the EMP table from the previous exercise, normalize the table to third normal form (3NF). Use 1NF to 2NF and then 2NF to 3NF conversion.

3

Oracle 8: An Overview

IN THIS CHAPTER . . .

- You will learn the differences between a client/server database, such as Oracle, and PC-based database software.
- The Oracle client/server Database Management System (DBMS) and its utilities are introduced.
- The Oracle development environment SQL*Plus and its various types of commands are covered.
- The primary language SQL (Structured Query Language) to communicate with the Oracle Server is also introduced.
- Designs of a college's student registration system database and a company's employee database system are discussed.

PERSONAL DATABASES

Personal database management systems, such as Microsoft's MS-Access and Visual Fox Pro, are usually stored on a user's desktop computer system or a **client computer.** These database packages are developed primarily for single-user applications. When such a package is used for a multiuser or a shared access environment, the database applications are stored on a file server, or a **server** and files are transmitted

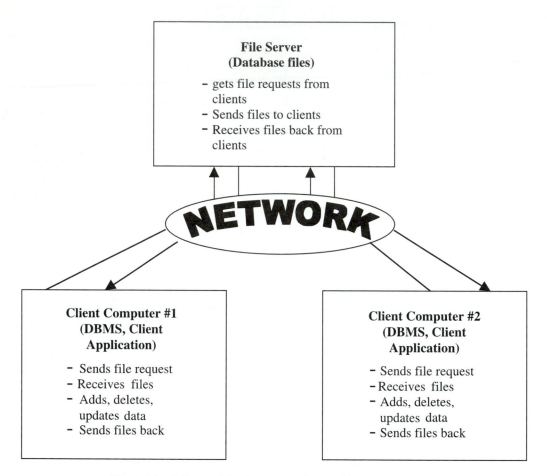

Figure 3-1 A Personal database system in a multiuser environment.

to the client computers over the network (see Fig. 3-1). A server is a computer that accepts and services requests from other computers, such as client computers. A server also enables other computers to share its resources. A server's **resources** could include the server's hard disk drive space, application programs on a server's hard drive, data stored on the server's drive, or printers. A network is an infrastructure of hardware and software that enables computers to communicate with each other.

Demand on Client and Network. In a network environment with a personal DBMS, the client computer must load the entire database application along with the client database application in its memory. If the client requires a small piece of data from the server's large database, the server has to transmit the entire database to the client over the network. In some database packages, only part of the database is transmitted. In any case, the client computer hardware has to handle heavy demand and the network must sustain heavy traffic in both directions. In the network environment, the system response to various client requests depends on the speed of the network and the amount of traffic over it.

Table Locking. The personal database system assumes that no two transactions will happen at the same time on one table, which is known as optimistic locking. In optimistic locking, the tables are not locked by the database system. If one agent sells a seat for a basketball game and another agent tries to sell the same seat at the same time, the database system will notify the second agent about the update on the table after his/her read, but it will go ahead and let the second agent sell the seat anyway. Application programmers can write code to avoid such a situation, but that requires an added effort on programmer's part. Personal database software does not lock tables automatically.

Client Failure. When a client is performing record insertions, deletions, or updates, those records are locked by that client and are not available to the other clients. Now, if the client with all the record locks fails due to software or hardware malfunction, or due to power outage, the locked records stay locked. The transactions in progress at the time of failure are lost. The database can get corrupted and needs to be repaired. In order to repair the database, all users have to log off during the repair, which can take a few minutes to a few hours! If the database is not repairable, data can be restored from the last backup, but the transactions since the last backup are lost and have to be reentered.

Transaction Processing. Personal databases, such as MS-Access, do not have file-based transaction logging. Transactions are logged in the client's memory. If the client fails in the middle of a batch of transactions, some transactions are written to the database and some are not. The transaction log is lost because it is not stored in a file. If a client writes a check to transfer money from a savings account to a checking account, the first transaction debits money from the savings account. Suppose the client fails right after that. The checking account never gets credited with the amount because the second transaction is lost!

CLIENT/SERVER DATABASES

Client/server databases, such as Oracle, run the DBMS as a process on the server and run client database application on each client. The client application sends a request for data over the network to the server. When the server receives the client request, the DBMS retrieves data from the database, performs required processing on the data, and sends only the requested data (or query result) back to the client over the network (see Fig. 3-2).

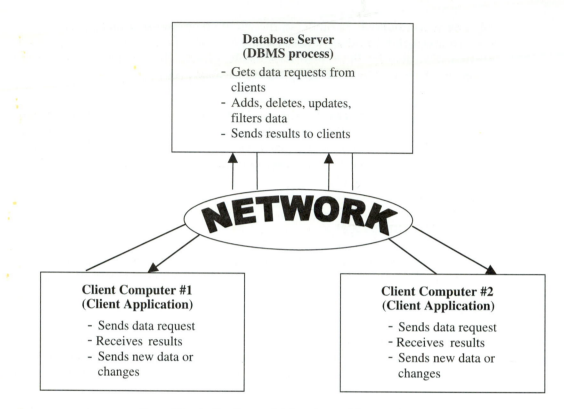

Figure 3-2   A client/server database in a multiuser environment.

Demand on Client and Network. The client computer does not run the entire DBMS, only the client application that requests data from the server. The client does not store the entire database on its local drive but receives only the requested data from the server. Data processing is performed on the server's side. The demand at the client's end is minimal. The clients request data from the server, and only requested data is sent back via the network, which results in less network traffic.

Table Locking. In a client/server system, such as Oracle, when an agent reads a table to sell a seat for a basketball game, it is locked totally or partly by the DBMS. The second agent cannot read the part of the table with available seats. Once the first agent sells the seat and it is marked as *sold,* the lock is released for the next agent. The DBMS takes care of the locking automatically, and it involves no extra effort on application programmer's part.

Client Failure. In case of a client failure, the client/server database is not affected. The other clients are not affected either. The failed client's transactions in progress are lost. If the server fails, a **central transaction log,** which keeps a log of all current database changes, allows the Database Administrator (DBA) to complete or roll back unfinished transactions. The rolled-back transactions are not implemented in the database. The DBA can notify clients to resubmit rolled-back transactions again. Most client/server database packages have fast and powerful recovery utilities.

Transaction Processing. If a grouped transaction or batch transaction fails in the middle, all transactions are rolled back. The DBMS will enable the bank to make sure that both accounts' balances are changed if the batch transaction goes through. If the batch transaction fails, the balance in none of the accounts is changed.

ORACLE 8: AN INTRODUCTION

Oracle 8 is a client/server DBMS that is based on the relational database model discussed in Chapter 1. Oracle 8 is one of the most popular database management software packages available today. The Oracle Corporation is the second largest software company in the world today, with revenue of $10.13 billion in the fiscal year ending May 2000 and net income of $6.30 billion. Oracle 8 is capable of supporting over 10,000 simultaneous users and a database size of up to 100 terabytes! It is preferred to the other PC-based DBMS packages due to its client/server database qualities, failure handling, recovery management, administrative tools to manage users and the database, object-oriented capabilities, Graphical User Interface (GUI) developer tools, and web interface capabilities. It is widely used by corporations of all sizes to develop mission-critical applications. It is used as a teaching tool by educational institutions to teach object-relational database technology, **Structured Query Language (SQL), PL/SQL** (Oracle's procedural language extension to SQL), developer tools, and interfacing web and Oracle databases. Oracle has an educational initiative program to form partnerships with educational institutions that enables institutions to obtain Oracle database software at a nominal membership fee.

The Oracle 8 environment consists of the following tools:

- *SQL*Plus.* The SQL*Plus environment is for writing command-line SQL queries to work with database objects such as tables, views, and sequences.
- *PL/SQL.* PL/SQL is Oracle's extension to SQL for creating procedural code to manipulate data.
- *Query Builder.* The query builder is for creating SQL query using graphical environment.
- *Developer.* This tool is used for developing database applications
  - Form Builder—to create graphical forms and menus
  - Report Builder—to create reports to view and print data
  - Graphic Builder—to create charts based on data

- *Enterprise Manager.* A tool for managing users and databases. Enterprise Manager uses the following tools:
  - Storage Manager—to create and manage "table spaces"
  - Instance Manager—to start, stop, or tune databases
  - Security Manager—to create and manage users and roles
- *Oracle Web Application Server.* A tool for creating a web site that allows users to access Oracle databases through web pages.

THE SQL*PLUS ENVIRONMENT

When a user logs in to connect to the Oracle server, SQL*Plus provides the user with the **SQL>** prompt, where the user writes queries or commands.

FEATURES OF SQL*PLUS:

- Accepts ad hoc entry of statements at the prompt
- Accepts SQL statements from files
- Provides a line editor for modifying SQL queries
- Provides environment, editor, format, execution, interaction, and file commands
- Formats query results and displays reports on the screen
- Controls environmental settings
- Accesses local and remote databases

STRUCTURED QUERY LANGUAGE

The standard query language for relational databases is SQL (Structured Query Language). It is standardized and accepted by ANSI (American National Standards Institute) and the ISO (International Standards Organization). Structured Query Language is a fourth-generation high-level nonprocedural language, unlike third-generation compiler languages such as C, COBOL, or Visual Basic, which are procedural. Using a nonprocedural language query, a user requests data from the DBMS. The SQL language uses English-like commands such as CREATE, INSERT, DELETE, UPDATE, and DROP. The SQL language is standardized, and its syntax is same across most DBMS packages. The different packages have minor variations, and they do support some additional commands.

Oracle 8 uses the following types of SQL statements for command-line queries to communicate with the Oracle server from any tool or application:

- *Data retrieval* retrieves data from the database, for example, SELECT.
- *Data Manipulation Language (DML)* inserts new rows, changes existing rows, and removes unwanted rows, for example, INSERT, UPDATE, and DELETE.

- *Data Definition Language (DDL)* creates, changes, and removes a table's structure, for example, CREATE, ALTER, DROP, RENAME, and TRUNCATE.
- *Transaction control* manages and changes logical transactions. Transactions are changes made to the data by DML statements grouped together, for example, COMMIT, SAVEPOINT, and ROLLBACK.
- *Data Control Language (DCL)* gives and removes rights to Oracle objects, for example, GRANT and REVOKE.

The SQL queries are typed at the SQL> prompt. If a query exceeds one line, SQL*plus displays the next line number on the line editor. A SQL query is sent to the server by ending a query with a semicolon (;). A query can also be sent to the server by using a forward slash (/) on a new line instead of ending the query with a semicolon.

LOGGING IN TO SQL*PLUS

In the Windows environment, Click **Start** → **Programs** → **Oracle for Windows xx** → **SQL*Plus 8.0.** In Windows Explorer, change to folder **ORAWINxx\BIN** and then double click on **plus80w.exe** (where **xx** stands for 95 or NT depending on your Windows operating system). A Log On window will pop up. Enter your **Username, Password,** and **Host String** as provided by your Database Administrator (see Fig 3-3).

In a command-line environment such as DOS, type **sqlplus [username [/password [@host/database]]]**

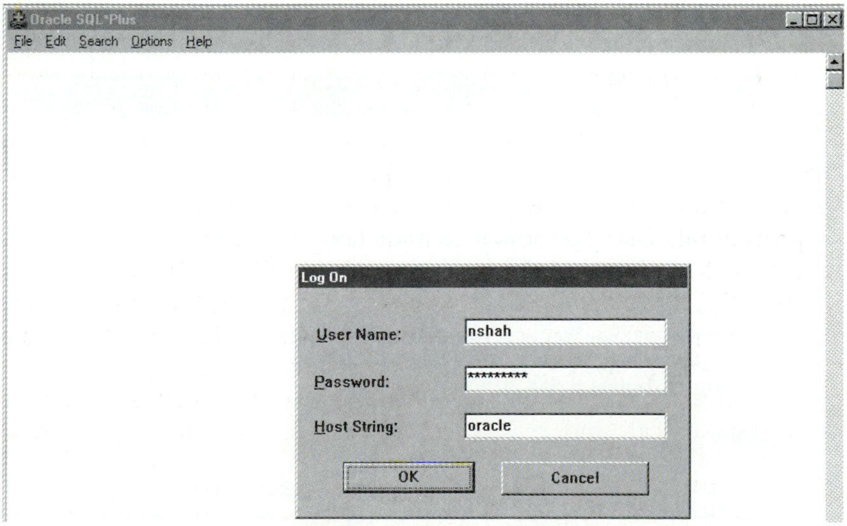

Figure 3-3   SQL*Plus login window.

If the entire command is typed, the password will be visible on screen. If you enter your username only, a prompt will be displayed for your password. The password typed at this prompt will be masked to maintain its integrity.

Once a user logs in and SQL> prompt is displayed, the user can start a new Oracle session. The SQL queries and SQL*Plus commands are typed at the SQL> prompt. The SQL*Plus commands do not have a terminator, but SQL queries are terminated using a semicolon (;) at the end or by typing a forward slash (/) on a new line. Figure 3-4 shows the differences between SQL statements and SQL*Plus commands.

SQL	SQL*Plus
1. A nonprocedural language to communicate with Oracle server	1. An environment for executing SQL statements
2. ANSI standard	2. Oracle proprietary
3. Keywords cannot be abbreviated	3. Keywords can be abbreviated
4. Last statement is stored in the buffer	4. Commands are not stored in the buffer
5. Statements manipulate data and table structures in the database	5. Commands do not allow manipulation of data in the database
6. Uses a termination character to execute command immediately	6. Commands do not need a termination character

Figure 3-4   SQL queries versus SQL*Plus commands.

SQL*PLUS COMMANDS

A user can enter only one SQL*Plus command per SQL>prompt (see Fig. 3-5). As you already know, SQL*Plus commands are not stored in the buffer. If a command

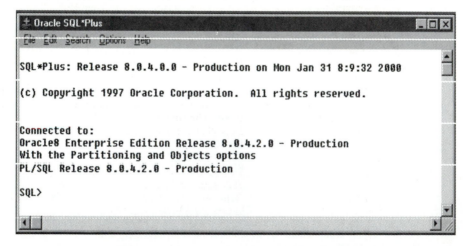

Figure 3-5   SQL*Plus environment—SQL prompt.

is very long, you can continue the command on the next line by using a hyphen at the end of the current line.

In the following tables, file-related (see Fig. 3-6) and editor-related (see Fig. 3-7) commands are described. The command words are in bold letters, and user-supplied filenames and extensions are in lowercase. The abbreviations allowed for the SQL*Plus commands are underlined. The optional parameters are enclosed within a pair of brackets [   ].

A query typed at the prompt is loaded in to the SQL*Plus buffer. When the query is sent to the server, the server processes data and sends back the result to

COMMAND	DESCRIPTION
GET filename [.ext]	Writes previously saved file to the buffer. The default extension is .SQL
START filename [.ext]	Runs a previously saved command from file
@filename	Same as START
EDIT	Invokes the default editor (such as Notepad) and saves buffer contents in a file called *afiedt.buf*
EDIT [filename [.ext]]	Invokes editor with the command from a saved file
SAVE filename [.ext] REPLACE I APPEND	Saves current buffer contents to a file with option to replace or append
SPOOL [filename [.ext] I OFF I OUT]	Stores query results in a file. OFF closes the file, and OUT sends the file to the system printer.
EXIT	Leaves SQL*Plus environment

Figure 3-6   SQL*Plus file-related commands.

COMMAND	DESCRIPTION
APPEND text	Adds text to the end of the current line
CHANGE / old / new	Changes old text to new text in the current line
CHANGE / text /	Deletes text from the current line
CLEAR BUFFER	Deletes all lines from the SQL buffer
DEL	Deletes current line
DEL n	Deletes line number *n*
DEL m n	Deletes lines *m* through *n*
INPUT	Inserts an indefinite number of lines
INPUT text	Inserts a line of text
LIST	Lists all lines from the SQL buffer
LIST n	Lists line number *n*
LIST m n	Lists lines from *m* through *n*
RUN	Displays and runs an SQL statement in the buffer
N	Makes line *N* current
n text	Replaces line *n* with text
0 text	Inserts a line before line 1
CLEAR SCREEN	Clears screen

Figure 3-7   SQL*Plus editing commands.

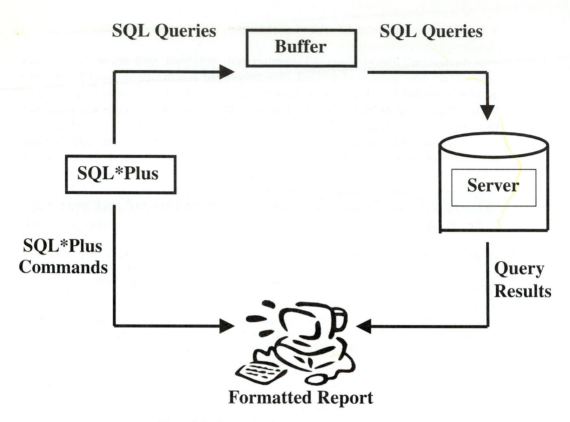

Figure 3-8   Interaction between SQL and SQL*Plus.

the client computer, which can be formatted using SQL*Plus formatting commands (see Fig. 3-8).

SAMPLE DATABASES

In this textbook, each chapter uses examples and lab activities to teach various Oracle query statements and utilities, using two fictitious databases. One database is developed for the Indo–US College, which keeps track of students, faculty, courses offered, and enrollment by semester. The other database is designed for the NamanNavan Corporation, which has employee, department, dependent, and salary-level information. These databases are created using the normalization techniques covered in Chapter 2. Each database table contains appropriate data to explain the results obtained from different query statements in the later chapters.

The Indo–US College Student Database

The Indo–US College has a computerized database system in place. They have spent a large sum of money in establishing a network infrastructure. The database management system that resides on their minicomputer system is a nonnormalized database. Nonnormalized databases are rare in the relational database software family. Their main feature is multivalued fields, which is a custom programmer's nightmare. This database does support its own version of query language, but it is not common in the business world. It is not easy to find Information Systems personnel with experience using such a database system. The administration is fed up with the "holes" in the system due to redundant data, bad data, and lack of data integrity. Students do not have the ability to retrieve course information, register on-line, or retrieve their unofficial transcript records using computers in the laboratory or the library. Faculty members do not have on-line access to their own course information, rosters, or student information.

The college has decided to use a standard relational database management system to overcome deficiencies of the existing system. The tables for the Indo–US College are illustrated in Fig. 3-9.

The Indo–US student database consists of 10 tables to store student master records, faculty master records, course master records, term-by-term course offerings, and student registration by each term. It also uses other supporting tables for lookup and additional information for basic entities in the database. The faculty and students are given on-line access to the system to view demographic information,

STUDENT (StudentId, Last, First, Street, City, State, Zip, StartTerm, BirthDate, FacultyId, MajorId, Phone)

StudentId	Last	First	Street	City	State	Zip	StartTerm	BirthDate	FacultyId	MajorId	Phone
00100	Diaz	Jose	1 Ford Avenue #7	Hill	NJ	08863	WN00	02/12/80	123	100	9735551111
00101	Tyler	Mickey	12 Morris Avenue	Bronx	NY	10468	SP00	03/18/79	555	500	7185552222
00102	Patel	Rajesh	25 River Road #3	Edison	NJ	08837	WN00	12/12/82	111	400	7325553333
00103	Rickles	Deborah	100 Main Street	Iselin	NJ	08838	FL00	10/20/70	555	500	7325554444
00104	Lee	Brian	2845 First Lane	Hope	NY	11373	WN00	11/28/75	345	600	2125555555
00105	Khan	Amir	213 Broadway	Clifton	NJ	07222	WN00	07/07/81	222	200	2017585555

Figure 3-9   Sample tables for the Indo–US College database.

FACULTY (FacultyId, Name, RoomId, Phone, DeptId)

FacultyId	Name	RoomId	Phone	DeptId
111	Jones	11	525	1
222	Williams	20	533	2
123	Mobley	11	529	1
235	Vajpayee	12	577	2
345	Sen	12	579	3
444	Rivera	21	544	4
555	Chang	17	587	5
333	Collins	17	599	3

COURSE (CourseId, Title, Credits)

CourseId	Title	Credits
EN100	Basic English	0
LA123	English Literature	3
CIS253	Database Systems	3
CIS265	Systems Analysis	3
MA150	College Algebra	3
AC101	Accounting	3

CRESSECTION (CsId, CourseId, Section, TermId, FacultyId, Day, StartTime, EndTime, RoomId, MaxCount, ActualCount)

CsId	CourseId	Section	TermId	FacultyId	Day	StartTime	EndTime	RoomId	MaxCount	ActualCount
1101	CIS265	01	WN01	111	MW	09:00	10:30	13	30	21
1102	CIS253	01	WN01	123	TR	09:00	10:30	18	40	39
1103	MA150	02	WN01	444	F	09:00	12:00	15	25	25
1104	AC101	10	WN01	345	MW	10:30	12:00	16	35	35
1205	CIS265	01	SP01		MW	09:00	10:30	14	35	12
1206	CIS265	02	SP01	111	TR	09:00	10:30	18	30	27
1207	LA123	05	SP01		MW	09:00	10:30	15	30	29
1208	CIS253	21	SP01	123	TR	09:00	10:30	14	40	40
1209	CIS253	11	SP01	111	MW	09:00	10:30	18	40	5
1210	CIS253	31	SP01	123	F	TBA	TBA	11	1	1

TERM (TermId, TermDesc, StartDate, EndDate)

TermId	TermDesc	StartDate	EndDate
SP00	Spring 2000	05/01/2000	08/11/2000
FL00	Fall 2000	09/04/2000	12/15/2000
WN01	Winter 2001	01/02/2001	04/13/2001
SP01	Spring 2001	04/30/2001	08/10/2001
FL01	Fall 2001	09/03/2001	12/14/2001

ROOM (Room Type, RoomDesc)

RoomType	RoomDesc
L	Lab
C	Classroom
O	Office

Figure 3-9 Sample tables for the Indo–US College database (*continued*).

REGISTRATION (StudentId, CsId, Midterm, Final)

StudentId	CsId	Midterm	Final
00100	1101	C	F
00100	1102	B	B
00100	1104	B	A
00101	1102	F	D
00101	1103	A	A
00103	1101	F	W
00103	1104	D	D
00100	1207		
00103	1206		
00104	1206		
00104	1207		
00104	1210		
00105	1208		
00105	1209		
00101	1205		
00102	1210		
00102	1207		
00102	1206		

DEPARTMENT (DeptId, DeptName, FacultyId)

DeptId	DeptName	FacultyId
1	Computer Science	111
2	Telecommunications	222
3	Accounting	333
4	Math & Science	444
5	Liberal Arts	555

MAJOR (MajorId, MajorDesc)

MajorId	MajorDesc
100	AAS-Accounting
200	AAS-Computer Science
300	AAS-Telecommunications
400	BS-Accounting
500	BS-Computer Science
600	BS-Telecommunications

LOCATION (RoomId, Building, RoomNo, Capacity, RoomType)

RoomId	Building	RoomNo	Capacity	RoomType
11	Gandhi	101	2	O
12	Gandhi	103	2	O
13	Kennedy	202	35	L
14	Kennedy	204	50	L
15	Nehru	301	50	C
16	Nehru	309	45	C
17	Gandhi	105	2	O
18	Kennedy	206	40	L
19	Kennedy	210	30	L
20	Gandhi	107	2	O
21	Gandhi	109	2	O

Figure 3-9   Sample tables for the Indo–US College database (*continued*).

course information, unofficial transcript records, availability of course sections by term, and so on. The faculty and student logins are created by the Information Systems department. Each student or faculty login name consists of the first letter of the first name, three letters of the last name, and the last four digits of the social security number. The social security number data is intentionally omitted from the STUDENT and FACULTY tables. Student and faculty members use their social security numbers as passwords to access the system.

The STUDENT table contains demographic information. StudentId is used as a primary key field. Social security numbers could have been used as the primary key, but system-generated StudentId is used instead. The table contains FacultyId as a foreign key, which references the FACULTY table to keep track of student advisors' information throughout the curriculum. Another foreign key, MajorId, uses the MAJOR table for a description of students' majors.

The FACULTY table contains location, phone extension, and department information for faculty members identified by a FacultyId, the table's primary key. To get further information, the DeptId foreign key field is used for department or chairperson's data from the DEPARTMENT table. Similarly, RoomId field is used to get the location of the faculty offices.

The COURSE table (primary key CourseId) is the course master with course title and credit information. The prerequisite information, which is ignored in this sample table can be added.

Each term and its dates are entered in the TERM table. An abbreviated term and year are used together to create four-character-long primary key, for example WN00 for the Winter 2000 term. The LOCATION table with a unique RoomId serves multiple purposes by keeping all types of rooms: It helps academic departments in locating a room available for a new course section; and the room capacity helps academic administration in scheduling classes with maximum allowable enrollment less than or equal to the room capacity.

Two of the most important tables are CRSSECTION and REGISTRATION. These tables are related to many other tables in the database, and they grow with each term. The CRSSECTION table contains courses offered during each term. It uses CsId as its primary key. The table references COURSE, TERM, FACULTY, and LOCATION tables with foreign keys CourseId, TermId, FacultyId, and RoomId respectively. The table helps college administration in flagging each section as *Open* or *Closed* based on maximum enrollment and actual current enrollment.

The REGISTRATION table contains each student's schedule for every registration term. It can be used for printing class rosters, for obtaining mid-term and final grades, and for grade point averages. The database contains three lookup tables, which are MAJOR, DEPARTMENT, and ROOM.

The NamanNavan Corporation Employee Database

The NamanNavan Corporation is an up-and-coming name in the Information Systems field. They are distributors of computer hardware and software, and providers of computer-related services. Recently, they have joined the web marketing community with a broad product line. The management feels that it is the right time for a changeover from an existing hard copy, paper-only system to a more sophisticated system to keep track of their employees' basic information and the company's organizational structure, payroll, raises, and promotion-related issues. The tables shown in Fig. 3-10 are created for the corporation's database.

EMPLOYEE (Employeeld, Lname, Fname, PositionId, Supervisor, HireDate, Salary, Commission, DeptId, Qualld)

EmployeeId	Lname	Fname	PositionId	Supervisor	HireDate	Salary	Commission	DeptId	Qualld
111	Smith	John	1		04/15/60	265000	35000	10	1
246	Houston	Larry	2	111	05/19/67	150000	10000	40	2
123	Roberts	Sandi	2	111	12/02/91	75000		10	2
433	McCall	Alex	3	543	05/10/97	66500		20	4
543	Dev	Derek	2	111	03/15/95	80000	20000	20	1
200	Shaw	Jinku	5	135	01/03/00	24500	3000	30	
135	Garner	Stanley	2	111	02/29/96	45000	5000	30	5
222	Chen	Sunny	4	123	08/15/99	35000		10	3

DEPT (deptId, DeptName, Location, EmployeeId)

DeptId	DeptName	Location	EmployeeId
10	Finance	Charlotte	123
20	InfoSys	New York	543
30	Sales	Woodbridge	135
40	Marketing	Los Angeles	246

POSITION (PositionId, PosDesc)

PositionId	PosDesc
1	President
2	Manager
3	Programmer
4	Accountant
5	Salesman

SALARYLEVEL (LevelNo, LowerLimit, UpperLimit)

LevelNo	LowerLimit	UpperLimit
1	1	25000
2	25001	50000
3	50001	100000
4	100001	500000

QUALIFICATION (Qualld, QualDesc)

Qualld	QualDesc
1	Doctorate
2	Masters
3	Bachelors
4	Associates
5	High School

Figure 3-10 Sample tables for NamanNavan Corporation's employee database.

DEPENDENT (Employeeld, Dependentld, DepDOB, Relation)

EmployeeId	DependentId	DepDOB	Relation
543	1	09/28/58	Spouse
543	2	10/14/88	Son
200	1	06/10/76	Spouse
222	1	02/84/75	Spouse
222	2	08/23/97	Son
222	3	07/10/99	Daughter
111	1	12/12/45	Spouse

Figure 3-10 Sample tables for NamanNavan Corporation's employee database (*continued*).

The NamanNavan Corporation database contains six tables to describe all employee-related information. The EMPLOYEE table describes each employee in the company. Each employee is identified by a unique EmployeeId, which is the primary key for the table. The basic attributes for the employee include the employee's last name, first name, immediate supervisor, date of hire for keeping track of anniversary and seniority, yearly salary, commission for the year, and other company-related information. This table includes three foreign keys. PositionId is a foreign key that references a lookup POSITION table to retrieve an employee's position/job title in the company. The DeptId is another foreign key to retrieve a department's name, the department's location, and information about the manager. The third foreign key field, QualId, enables the company to keep record of an employee's highest qualification.

The DEPT table, another important table in the database, includes demographic information about the department's name and primary location, and the manager responsible for managing day-to-day operation. Each department is identified by a unique DeptId as a primary key.

The SALARYLEVEL table has different grades based on the salary range as defined by the company. An employee belongs to a certain level or grade based on his/her salary.

Each employee's dependents for purposes of the health plan and payroll taxes are included in the DEPENDENT table. This table does not have a single attribute that can be used as primary key. The EmployeeId and DependentId together make up the composite primary key for the table. Age is not used as an attribute because it does not remain the same. Each dependent's age can be derived using available date-related functions in Oracle.

The POSITION and QUALIFICATION tables are basically lookup tables for the EMPLOYEE table to get descriptions based on foreign keys in the EMPLOYEE table that are primary keys in the POSITION and QUALIFICATION tables.

The EMPLOYEE, DEPENDENT, and DEPT tables can have more attributes, but they are omitted for simplicity. Similarly, another lookup table could have been created to look up relations based on some RelationId attribute in the DEPENDENT table.

ALTERNATE TEXT EDITORS

The SQL*Plus editor is a line editor, similar to EDLIN in MS-DOS. It is no fun working with line editors. The user does not have control over the screen. Line editors do not allow a user to move cursor up and down, and clicking with a mouse is definitely out of the question. You can use an alternate text editor such as Notepad or any other text editor in Windows to type your SQL queries. The query typed in a full-screen text editor can be saved in a file or copied to the clipboard. The query can be loaded from a file or pasted from the clipboard into SQL*Plus to execute it.

The EDIT (or ED) command can be used to invoke alternate text editor from the SQL*Plus command prompt SQL>. The EDIT command invokes an alternate editor with contents from the buffer or with an existing file as shown in Fig. 3-6. The user can make necessary changes to the query and transfer the contents back to SQL*Plus. We will see an illustration in Chapter 4.

ORACLE ONLINE HELP

In the next chapter, you will learn to write and execute SQL queries at the SQL*Plus prompt. If you make a syntax error, Oracle will display an error message showing the line number and the location of error on the line. Oracle places an asterisk (*) at the location of the error and also displays an error code (for example, ORA-009xx) followed by a brief description. Just like any programming language compiler, these error descriptions are not very user friendly. You will get used to some of the common error messages as you start experimenting. Some queries take up a few lines, and for a typist like me, typing mistakes are bound to happen! In any case, to get detailed explanation of an error message, follow these steps:

Click **Start → Programs → Oracle for Windows xx → Oracle 8 Error messages**

Each Oracle product has its own specific help file. Another way to open the help file is by double clicking on **ORAWIN95\MSHELP\ora.hlp** or **ORANT\ MSHELP\ora.hlp.** The help application opens up a window similar to MS-Windows help, where you can click on the Index tab and type the error code (ORA-009xx) of interest. Oracle provides the user with an explanation of the cause of the error and the user action required to rectify it.

Some errors are easy to find; some are not. To fix an error, always start at the line where the error is shown, but keep in mind that the error might not be on that line. Check for common mistakes like misspelled keywords, missing commas, misplaced commas, missing parentheses, invalid user-defined names, or repeated user-defined words. In the next chapter, we will actually go through the entire procedure by entering an erroneous query.

IN A NUTSHELL . . .

- Personal database management systems (DBMSs) are stored on a client computer and are meant for single users.
- A client/server DBMS runs on a server and user applications run on the client computers.
- Personal databases are characterized by heavy hardware demands, heavy network traffic, database corruption, transaction losses, and poor recovery mechanisms.
- Client/server databases have better recovery mechanisms.
- Client/server databases provide automatic tables and record-level locking.
- Client/server databases provide file-based transaction logging for recovery of transactions in case of a failure.
- Oracle 8 is a popular client/server database management system based on the relational model.
- The Oracle 8 environment provides utilities to work with database tables; developing forms, reports, and graphs; managing users and databases; and interfacing the web and databases.
- Structured Query Language (SQL) is a standard nonprocedural language to work with relational database tables.
- SQL*Plus is Oracle's proprietary environment to enter SQL queries.
- SQL is a language with data retrieval, DML, DDL, DCL, and transaction control query statements.
- SQL*Plus is an environment that provides users with editing, file, formatting, execution, and interaction commands.
- The Indo–US College's student database system contains student, faculty, course, course-section, and registration information. It includes the following tables:
  - STUDENT
  - FACULTY
  - COURSE
  - CRSSECTION
  - REGISTRATION

- ROOM
- TERM
- LOCATION
- MAJOR
- DEPARTMENT
- The NamanNavan Corporation's employee database system contains employee, department, and dependent information in the following tables:
  - EMPLOYEE
  - DEPT
  - POSITION
  - SALARYLEVEL
  - QUALIFICATION
  - DEPENDENT

EXERCISE QUESTIONS

1. How are client requests served by a server in a personal database and in a client/server database?
2. How are transactions handled by personal and client/server databases in case of a failure?
3. What are the advantages of client/server databases over personal databases in a multi-user environment?
4. Name various tools provided by Oracle 8 DBMS.
5. What is SQL? What are the different types of query statements a user can write using SQL in Oracle 8?
6. What are the functions of SQL*Plus environment?
7. Give two examples of database applications appropriate for personal database system.
8. Give two examples of database applications appropriate for client/server database system.

LAB ACTIVITY

1. Log in to Oracle Server at your installation. Locate the *plus80w.exe* file on your client computer and double click on it, or click on

   START → Programs → Oracle for Windows95/NT → SQL*Plus 8.0

   Ask your DBA/lab personnel/professor for your login username, password, and database name/host string. Soon, you will get the SQL> prompt in the SQL*Plus environment.

2. You have not learned any query statements or SQL*Plus commands yet. Try the following query at the prompt as given here:

```
SQL> CREATE TABLE dept (DeptId NUMBER (2),
   2                    DeptName VARCHAR2 (15) NOT NULL,
   3                    Location VARCHAR2 (12),
   4                    EmployeeId NUMBER (4),
   5                    CONSTRAINT dept_deptno_pk PRIMARY KEY (deptno));
```

If you type this above given query without any errors, a "Table created" message will be displayed. If you make a mistake by misspelling a keyword or by missing a punctuation mark, use SQL*Plus editing commands to debug errors.

3. Invoke the default full-page editor. What is the default editor?

4. What is displayed in the editor?

5. Use the following SQL*Plus command at the prompt:

DESCRIBE dept

(*Notice:* the SQL*Plus command does not end with a semicolon.) What is displayed by the command?

6. Exit from the SQL*Plus environment.

4

Oracle Tables: Creation and Modification

IN THIS CHAPTER . . .

- You will learn about Data Definition Language queries to work with the structure of an Oracle database table.
- Various data types used in defining attributes in a database table are discussed.
- Integrity and value constraints and their inclusion in a CREATE TABLE query at the attribute and table level are outlined.
- View, modification, and removal of a table's structure are also covered.

In the previous chapters, you learned about relational terminology, database modeling, normalization techniques, the SQL*Plus environment, and its commands. Now is the time to put everything together. In Oracle 8, database tables are objects stored under a user's account in allocated tablespace on an Oracle server's disk. Each table under a user's account must have a unique table name. In the classroom environment, each student is a user with a unique login/username. Each object including a table created by a user is stored under that user's schema. In this and subsequent chapters, you will create and use tables for the Indo–US College and the NamanNavan Corporation. You will learn to create tables using SQL statements at the SQL*Plus prompt. You will also learn the use of alternate editors for easier editing of erroneous queries.

NAMING CONVENTIONS

A table is an object that stores data in an Oracle database. When you create a table, you must specify the table name, the name of each attribute, the data type of each attribute, and the size of each attribute. Oracle provides you with different constraints to specify a primary or a composite key for the table, to define a foreign key in a table that references a primary key in another table, to set data validation rules for each attribute, to specify whether an attribute allows NULL values, and to specify if an attribute should have unique values only.

The table and attribute names can be up to 30 characters long. It is possible to have a table name that is only one character long. In naming tables and attributes, letters (A–Z, a–z), numbers (0–9) and special characters—$ (dollar sign), _(underscore) and # (pound or number sign)—are allowed. The table or attribute name must begin with a letter. The names are case insensitive. Spaces and hyphens are not allowed in a table or an attribute name. An Oracle server reserved word cannot be used as a table or an attribute name. Remember, the most common mistake is the use of a space in naming such things. It is always a good practice to create short but meaningful names. Figure 4-1 shows some valid and invalid table and attribute names.

Valid names	Invalid names (with reason)
STUDENT	STUDENT_COURSE_REGISTRATION_TABLE (more than 30 characters long)
MAJOR_CODE	MAJOR CODE (spaces not allowed)
X	CREATE (reserved word not allowed)
PROJECT2000	PROJECT***2000 (special character * not allowed)
STUDENT#REG#TABLE	#STUDENT (must start with a letter)

Figure 4-1   Valid/invalid table and attribute names.

DATA TYPES

When a table is created, each attribute in the table is assigned a data type. A data type specifies the type of data that will be stored in that attribute. By providing a data type for an attribute, the wrong kinds of data are prevented from being stored in the attribute. For example, a name such as Smith cannot be stored in an attribute with a NUMBER data type and similarly, a job title such as Manager cannot be stored in an attribute with a DATE data type. Data types also help optimize storage space. Some of the Oracle data types are described here.

VARCHAR2

The VARCHAR2 type is a character data type to store variable-length character data in an attribute. A maximum size must be specified for this type. The default and minimum size is 1. The maximum allowable size is 4000 characters in Oracle 8. The maximum size was 200 characters in previous versions. The size is specified within parentheses. If the data are smaller than the specified size, only the data value is stored and trailing spaces are not added to the value. For example, if an attribute NAME is assigned data type VARCHAR2 (25), and the name entered is Steve Jones, only 11 characters are stored. Fourteen spaces are not added to make its length equal to the size of the attribute. If a value longer than the specified size is entered, an error is generated. The longer values are not truncated. VARCHAR2 is the most appropriate type for an attribute whose values do not have a fixed length.

CHAR

The CHAR type is a character data type to store fixed-length character data in an attribute. The default and minimum size is 1. The maximum allowable size is 2000 characters, and was only 255 characters in previous versions. If the value smaller than the specified size is entered, trailing spaces are added to make its length equal to the specified length. If the value is longer than the specified size, an error occurs. The CHAR type is appropriate for fixed-length values. For example, PHONE, SOCIAL_SECURITY_NUMBER, or MIDDLE_INITIAL can use the CHAR type. The phone numbers and social security numbers have numeric values, but they also use special characters, such as hyphens and parentheses. Both of them use fixed-length values, so CHAR is the most appropriate type for them. The CHAR data type uses the storage more efficiently and processes data faster than the VARCHAR2 type.

NUMBER

The NUMBER data type is used to store negative, positive, integer, fixed-decimal, and floating point numbers. The number data type is used for any attribute that is going to be used in mathematical calculations—for example, SALARY, COMMIS-SION, or PRICE. When a number type is used for an attribute, its **precision** and **scale** can be specified. Precision is the total number of digits in the number, both to the left and to the right of the decimal point. The decimal point is not counted in specifying the precision. Scale is the total number of digits to the right of the decimal point. The precision can range from 1 to 38. The scale can range from −84 to 127.

An **integer** is a whole number without any decimal part. To define an attribute with integer values, only scale size is provided. For example, EmployeeId in the EMPLOYEE table has values of 111, 246, 123, 433, and so on. The data type for it would be defined as NUMBER(3), where 3 represents the maximum number of digits. Remember to provide room for future growth when defining the size. If a corporation has up to 999 employees, a size of 3 will work for now. With future growth, the corporation's employee size may rise to 1000 or higher. By using a size of 4, you are providing room for up to 9999 employees.

A **fixed-point** decimal number has a specific number of digits to the right of the decimal point. The PRICE attribute has values in dollars and cents, which requires 2 decimal places—for example, values like 2.95, 3.99, 24.99, and so on. If it is defined as NUMBER (4,2), the first number specifies the precision and the second number specifies the scale. Remember that the decimal place is not counted in the scale. The given definition will allow a maximum price of $99.99.

A **floating-point** decimal number has a variable number of decimal places. The decimal point may appear after any number of digits, and it may not appear at all. To define such an attribute, do not specify the scale or precision along with the NUMBER type. For example, TAXRATE, INTEREST_RATE, and STUDENT_GPA attributes are likely to have variable numbers of decimal places. By defining an attribute as a floating-point number, a value can be stored in it with very high precision.

DATE

The DATE data type is used for storing date and time values. The range of allowable dates is between January 1, 4712 B.C. and December 31, 9999 A.D. The day, month, century, hour, minute, and second are stored in the DATE-type attribute. There is no need to specify size for the DATE type. The default date format is DD-MON-YY, where DD indicates the day of the month, MON represents the month's first three letters capitalized, and YY represents the last two digits of the year. These three values are separated by hyphens. The default time format is HH:MM:SS A.M., representing hours, minutes and seconds in a 12-hour time format. If only a date is entered, the time defaults to 12:00:00 A.M. If only a time is entered, the date defaults to the first day of the current month. For example, HIREDATE for EmployeeId 111 in EMPLOYEE table in the NamanNavan Corporation database is stored as 04-APR-60 12:00:00 A.M.

In a table, it is not advisable to use attributes like AGE because the age changes for all entities, and it changes at different times. An attribute like AGE can become a very high-maintenance attribute. It is advisable to use BIRTHDATE as an attribute. Oracle 8 provides users with quite a few built-in date functions for date manipulation. Simple date arithmetic is enough to calculate age from the birth date! The birth date never changes, so no maintenance on it is necessary.

Other advanced data types used in Oracle are not used in the sample databases discussed in Chapter 3. These advanced data types' definition and use are outlined here for your information only:

LONG. The LONG type is used for variable-length character data up to 2 gigabytes. There can be only one LONG type attribute in a table. It is used to store a memo, invoice, or student transcript in the text format. When defining to LONG type, there is no need to specify its size.

NCHAR. The NCHAR type is similar to CHAR but uses 2-byte binary encoding for each character. The CHAR type uses 1-byte ASCII encoding for each character, giving it the capability to represent 256 different characters. The NCHAR type is useful for character sets such as the Japanese Kanji character set, which has thousands of different characters.

CLOB. The Character Large Object data type is used to store single-byte character data up to 4 gigabytes.

BLOB. BLOB stands for Binary Large Object and stores binary data up to 4 gigabytes.

NCLOB. The character Large Object type, which uses 2-byte character codes.

BFILE. BFILE stands for Binary File and stores references to a binary file that is external to the database and is maintained by the operating system's file system.

RAW or **LONG RAW.** These are used for raw binary data.

Many of the Large Object (LOB) data types are not supported by all versions of Oracle and its tools. These data types are used for storing digitized sounds, for images, or to reference binary files from Excel spreadsheets or Word documents. We will not use LOB data types in this book. Figure 4-2 shows a brief summary of Oracle data types and their use in storing different types of data.

Data Type	Use
VARCHAR2 (size)	Variable length character data—1 to 4000 characters
CHAR (size)	Fixed-length character data—1 to 2000 characters
NUMBER (p)	Integer values
NUMBER (p, s)	Fixed-point decimal values
NUMBER	Floating-point decimal values
DATE	Data and time values (Y2K compliant!)
LONG	Variable-length character data up to 4 gigabytes
NCHAR	Similar to CHAR, uses 2-byte encoding
BLOB	Binary data up to 4 gigabytes
CLOB	Single-byte character data up to 4 gigabytes
NCLOB	Similar to CLOB, supports 2-byte encoding
BFILE	Reference to a external binary file
RAW or LONG RAW	Raw binary data

Figure 4-2 Data types and their use.

CONSTRAINTS

Constraints enforce rules at the table level. An Oracle table can be created with the attribute names, data types, and attribute sizes, which are sufficient just to populate them with actual data. Without constraints no rules are enforced. The constraints make your database a true relational database. We learned the integrity rules in Chapter 1. The constraints are used in Oracle to implement integrity rules of a relational database and to implement data integrity at the individual attribute level. Whenever a row/record is inserted, updated, or deleted from the table, a constraint must be satisfied for the operation to succeed. A table cannot be deleted if there are dependencies from other tables in the form of foreign keys.

Types of Constraints

1. *Integrity constraints*—define the primary key and the foreign keys with the table and primary key it references.
2. *Value constraints*—define if NULL values are disallowed, if UNIQUE values are required, and if only certain values are allowed in an attribute.

Naming a Constraint

Oracle identifies constraints with an internal name. For a user's account, each constraint name must be unique. A user cannot create constraints in two different tables with the same name. There is a general convention used for naming constraints:

<table name>_<attribute name>_<constraint type>

Here *table name* is the name of the table where the constraint is being defined, *attribute name* is the name of the attribute to which the constraint applies, and *constraint type* is an abbreviation used to identify the constraint's type. Figure 4-3 shows popular abbreviations used for the constraint type.

Constraint Type	Abbreviation
Primary Key	pk
Foreign Key	fk
Check	cc or ck
Not Null	nn
Unique	uk

Figure 4-3 Popular constraint abbreviations.

For example, a constraint name *emp_deptno_fk* refers to a constraint in table EMP on attribute DeptNo of type foreign key. A constraint name *dept_deptno_pk* is for a primary key constraint in table DEPT on attribute DeptNo.

If you do not name a constraint, the Oracle server will generate a name for it by using *SYS_Cn* format, where *n* is any unique number. For example, *SYS_C000010* is an Oracle server named constraint. These names are not user friendly like user-named constraints.

Defining a Constraint

A constraint can be created at the same time that the table is created, or it can be added to the table afterward. There are two levels where a constraint is defined:

1. *Column level.* A column-level constraint references a single column/attribute and is defined along with the definition of column/attribute. Any constraint can be defined at column level except for FOREIGN KEY constraint. The general syntax is

   > *Column datatype [CONSTRAINT constraint_name] constraint_type,*

   (In this book, you will see the following convention for syntax: Reserved words will be written in uppercase and user-defined words in lower or mixed case. Optional parts will be within brackets ([ ])).

2. *Table level.* A table-level constraint references one or more columns/attributes and is defined separately from the definitions of the columns/attributes. Normally it is written after all columns, and attributes are defined. All constraints can be defined at the table level except for the NOT NULL constraint. The general syntax is

   > *[CONSTRAINT constraint_name] constraint_type (Column, ...),*

Primary Key Constraint. The primary key constraint is also known as the entity integrity constraint. It creates a primary key for the table. A table can have only one primary key constraint. An attribute or combination of attributes used as a primary key cannot have a null value and it can only have unique values. For example, the DEPT table in the NamanNavan Corporation database used the DeptId column as a primary key. At the column level,

> **DeptId NUMBER (2) CONSTRAINT dept_deptid_pk PRIMARY KEY,**

At the table level,

> **CONSTRAINT dept_deptid_pk PRIMARY KEY (DeptId),**

If a table uses more than one column as its primary key (i.e., a composite key), the key can only be declared at table level. For example, the DEPENDENT table in the NamanNavan database uses two columns for the composite primary key.

> **CONSTRAINT dependent_emp_dep_pk PRIMARY KEY (EmployeeId, DependentId),**

Foreign Key constraint. The foreign key constraint is also known as the referential integrity constraint. It uses a column or columns as a foreign key and establishes a relationship with the primary key of the same table or another table. For example, FacultyId in the STUDENT table in the Indo–US College database references the primary key FacultyId in the FACULTY table. The STUDENT table is known as the dependent or child table, and the FACULTY table is known as the referenced or parent table.

To establish a foreign key in a table, the other referenced table and its primary key must already exist. Foreign key and referenced primary key attributes need not have the same name, but a foreign key value must match the value in the parent table's primary key value or be NULL. For example, the foreign key FacultyId cannot have the value 999 in the STUDENT table, because it does not exist in the FACULTY (parent) table's primary key FacultyId.

Oracle does not keep pointers for relationships, but they are based on constraints and data values within those columns. The relationship is purely logical and not physical in Oracle. At the table level (in the STUDENT table),

CONSTRAINT student_facultyid_fk FOREIGN KEY (FacultyId)
REFERENCES faculty (FacultyId),

Before ending a foreign key constraint, ON DELETE CASCADE can be added to allow deletion of a record/row in the parent table and deletion of the dependent rows/records in the child table. Without the ON DELETE CASCADE clause, the row/record in the parent table cannot be deleted if the child table references it. For example, the row for FacultyId 111 cannot be deleted from the FACULTY table because it is referenced by a row in the STUDENT table.

NOT NULL constraint. The NOT NULL constraint ensures that the column has a value and the value is not a NULL (unknown or blank) value. A space or a numeric zero is not a NULL value. There is no need to use the NOT NULL constraint for the primary key column because it automatically gets a NOT NULL constraint. The foreign key is permitted to have NULL values, but a foreign key is sometimes given the NOT NULL constraint. This constraint cannot be entered at the table level. For example, the name column in FACULTY table is not a key attribute, but you don't want to leave it blank. At the column level, the constraint is defined by

Name VARCHAR2 (15) CONSTRAINT faculty_name_nn NOT NULL,

or

Name VARCHAR2 (15) NOT NULL,

In the second example, the user does not supply the constraint name, so Oracle will name it with SYS_Cn format.

UNIQUE KEY constraint.   The unique key constraint requires that every value in a column or set of columns be unique. If it is applied to single column, the column is known as the **unique key.** If it is applied to a set of columns, the group of columns is known as the **composite unique key.** The unique key constraint allows null values unless NOT NULL is also applied to the column. For example, the DeptName column in DEPT table should not have duplicate values. At the table level, the constraint is defined by

CONSTRAINT dept_dname_uk UNIQUE (DeptName),

and at the column level by

DeptName VARCHAR2 (12) CONSTRAINT dept_dname_uk UNIQUE,

The composite unique key constraint can be defined only at the table level by specifying column names separated by a comma within parentheses. Oracle implicitly creates a unique index on the unique key to enforce the UNIQUE key constraint.

CHECK constraint.   The CHECK constraint defines a condition that every row must satisfy. There can be more than one CHECK constraint on a column, and the CHECK constraint can be defined at the column as well as the table level. At the column level, the constraint is defined by

DeptId NUMBER (2) CONSTRAINT dept_deptid_cc
CHECK ((DeptId >= 10) and (DeptId <= 99)),

and at the table level by

CONSTRAINT dept_deptid_cc
CHECK ((DeptId >= 10) and (DeptId <= 99)),

DEFAULT value (not a constraint).   The DEFAULT value ensures that a particular column will always have a value when a new row is inserted. The default value gets overwritten if a user enters another value. The default value is used if a null value is inserted. For example, if most of the students live in New Jersey, 'NJ' can used as a default value for the State column in the STUDENT table. At the column level, the value is defined by

State CHAR (2) DEFAULT 'NJ',

CREATING AN ORACLE TABLE

A user creates an Oracle table from the SQL*Plus environment. You will run the Oracle Client application from your PC as described in "Logging in to SQL*Plus" in Chapter 3. An Oracle table is created from the SQL> prompt in the SQL*Plus environment. A Data Definition Language (DDL) SQL statement, CREATE TABLE, is used for table creation. A table is created as soon as the CREATE query is executed by the Oracle server. The general syntax of CREATE TABLE query is

```
CREATE TABLE [schema.] tablename
 (column/attribute1 datatype [CONSTRAINT constraint_name] constraint_type...,
  (column/attribute2 datatype [CONSTRAINT constraint_name] constraint_type,
                              ⋮
 [CONSTRAINT constraint_name] constraint_type (column, ... ), ... );
```

In the syntax,

schema is optional, and it is same as the user's name.

tablename is the name of the table given by the user.

column/attribute is the name of a single column/attribute.

Datatype is the column's data type and size.

constraint_name is the name of constraint provided by the user as per the conventions discussed earlier in this chapter.

constraint_type is the integrity or value constraint.

Each column may have zero, one, or more constraints defined at the column level. The table level constraints are normally declared after all column definition.

SQL is not case sensitive. In this textbook, the reserved words are written in capitalized letters and user-defined names in lowercase letters. The spaces, tabs, and carriage returns are ignored. Let us create the STUDENT table in the Indo–US College using the CREATE TABLE query statement. When the query is executed and there are no syntax errors, a "Table Created" message will be displayed on the screen.

The query did not return with a "Table Created" message when executed as shown in Fig. 4-4. Oracle displayed an error message instead. The error messages are not very user friendly. In the query shown, the column definition in line 13 is missing a comma. The error message does not really tell us that! We will discuss error codes and messages later in this chapter.

We will debug the query using SQL*Plus commands. The error is in line 13, and we will perform the following steps (see Fig. 4-5):

1. Go to line 13 (* is displayed next to the current line number)

2. Replace the character) in line 13 with), or append a comma (,) to the line

3. Execute the debugged query using a slash (/)

```
SQL> CREATE TABLE student
  2          (StudentId CHAR(5),
  3           Last      VARCHAR2 (15) NOT NULL,
  4           First     VARCHAR2 (15) NOT NULL,
  5           Street    VARCHAR2 (25),
  6           City      VARCHAR2 (15),
  7           State     CHAR (2),
  8           Zip       CHAR (5),
  9           StartTerm CHAR (4),
 10           BirthDate DATE,
 11           FacultyId NUMBER (3),
 12           MajorId   NUMBER (3),
 13           Phone     CHAR (10)
 14           CONSRAINT student_studentid_pk PRIMARY KEY (StudentID));

CONSRAINT student_studentid_pk PRIMARY KEY (StudentID))
*
ERROR at line 14:
ORA-00907: missing right parenthesis
```

Figure 4-4 CREATE TABLE query with an error.

```
SQL> 13
 13*                        Phone     CHAR (10)
SQL> C/)/),
 13*                        Phone     CHAR (10),
SQL> /

ERROR at line 14:
ORA-00907: missing right parenthesis
```

Figure 4-5 CREATE TABLE query with another error.

As you see in Fig. 4-5, the query still has an error in line 14. We will edit the query with the help of an alternate editor, Notepad. To load an erroneous query and modify it, we perform the following steps:

1. At the SQL> prompt we type **ED** (or **EDIT**) to invoke Notepad.
2. We will edit the word CONSRAINT and change it to CONSTRAINT.

3. We save our query on the floppy using the Save option from the File menu in Notepad, and name our query A:\CREATE. Notepad adds the extension .TXT to the filename.
4. We exit Notepad to go back to the SQL*Plus environment.
5. We can run the saved query with @ or the RUN command.

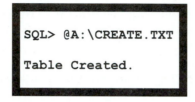

```
SQL> @A:\CREATE.TXT

Table Created.
```

Figure 4-6   Successful CREATE TABLE query.

The "Table Created" message as shown in Fig. 4-6 is displayed when the statement is error-free. At this point, the table is created and its structure is saved. We created the STUDENT table with PRIMARY KEY and NOT NULL constraints only. Once a table is created, more constraints can be added, more attributes can be added, and existing attributes' properties can be changed.

DISPLAYING TABLE INFORMATION

When a user creates a table or many tables in his/her database, Oracle keeps track of them all using its own system database. Oracle has SQL statements and SQL*Plus commands for the user to view that information from Oracle's system objects.

Viewing a User's Table Names

A user types a SQL query to retrieve his/her table names. Often you use it to review information, and often you want to find out what is out there and what is to be created. The query is

SELECT table_name FROM user_tables;

Oracle creates system tables to store information about the users and user objects. USER_TABLES is an Oracle system database table and TABLE_NAME is one of its attributes. The display will include all table names you have created and any other tables that belong to you. The USER_TABLES table has many other attributes. To display all attributes, type the following query:

SELECT * FROM user_tables;

(You will see more information than you need. The display rows will wrap many times to show all attributes/information related to each table)

Viewing a Table's Structure

You can display the structure entered by you in a CREATE TABLE query. If you have made any changes to the table's structure, the changes will also show in the structure's display. Figure 4-7 shows the SQL*Plus command to view a table's structure. The command is DESCRIBE (or DESC), which does not need a semi-colon at the end because it is not a SQL statement. Notice that the default display of column names, the NOT NULL constraint, and data type is in uppercase. You did not add a NOT NULL constraint for the primary key, but by default Oracle adds it for all primary key attributes.

```
SQL> DESCRIBE student
 Name                            Null?     Type
 ------------------------------- --------- ----
 STUDENTID                       NOT NULL  CHAR (5)
 LAST                            NOT NULL  VARCHAR2 (15)
 FIRST                           NOT NULL  VARCHAR2 (15)
 STREET                                    VARCHAR2 (25)
 CITY                                      VARCHAR2 (15)
 STATE                                     CHAR (2)
 ZIP                                       CHAR (5)
 STARTTERM                                 CHAR (4)
 BIRTHDATE                                 DATE
 FACULTYID                                 NUMBER (3)
 MAJORID                                   NUMBER (3)
 PHONE                                     CHAR (10)
```

Figure 4-7   DESCRIBE command and table's structure.

Viewing Constraint Information

Oracle's system table USER_CONSTRAINTS stores information about constraints you have entered for each column. Figure 4-8 shows the query and the result, which includes the constraint's name and type. When you type the query, the table name must be typed in uppercase because Oracle saves table names in uppercase. If you type the table name in lowercase, no constraint names will be displayed.

The constraints named by the user have more meaningful names than the ones named by Oracle. Constraints like NOT NULL are usually not named by the user. Oracle names them using the SYS_Cn format, where n is any number. Constraint type C is displayed for NOT NULL and CHECK constraints. Constraint type P is for primary key, and type R is for foreign key constraints. You will type only the first two lines of the query in Fig. 4-8 to display all constraints in your account.

```
SQL> SELECT CONSTRAINT_NAME, CONSTRAINT_TYPE
  2       FROM USER_CONSTRAINTS
  3       WHERE TABLE_NAME = 'STUDENT';

CONSTRAINT_NAME                       CONSTRAINT_TYPE
----------------------------------    ---------------
SYS_C001675                           C
SYS_C001676                           C
SYS_C001677                           C
STUDENT_STUDENTID_PK                  P
```

Figure 4-8   Constraint information.

You can use the following command to see the constraint names and associated column names:

```
SELECT CONSTRAINT_NAME, COLUMN_NAME
  FROM USER_CONS_COLUMNS
  WHERE TABLE_NAME = 'STUDENT';
```

In this statement, only the table name within single quotes needs to be in upper-case because Oracle stores table names in that case.

ALTERING AN EXISTING TABLE

In a perfect scenario, the table that you create will not need any structural modifications. You must try to plan and design a database that is perfect in all respects. In reality, that is not the case. Even perfect tables need changes. There are certain modifications, that you can make to a table's structure. There are other modifications that you cannot make to an existing table's structure.

Modifications allowed without any restrictions:

- Add a new attribute/column to the table.
- Delete a foreign key constraint from a table.
- Delete a primary key constraint from a table, which also removes any references to it from other tables in the database.
- Increase the size of an attribute. For example, VARCHAR2 (15) can be changed to VARCHAR2 (20).

Modifications allowed with restrictions:

- Adding a foreign key constraint is allowed only if the current values are NULL or exist in the referenced table's primary key.
- Adding a primary key constraint is allowed if the current values are NOT NULL and are unique.

- Changing a column/attribute's data type and size is allowed only if there is no data in it.
- Adding a UNIQUE constraint is possible if the current data values are unique.
- Adding a CHECK constraint is possible if the current data values comply with the new constraint.
- Adding a DEFAULT value is possible if there is no data in the column.

Modifications not allowed:

- Changing a column's name.
- Removing a column/attribute.

In Oracle 8, you are allowed to remove/drop a column from a table or set it as unused. If you already have created a table and there is a need to make a change that is not allowed, you may DROP the table and re-create it. You will also learn in a later chapter that a table can be created using another table with the use of a nested query.

Adding a New Column to an Existing Table

The general syntax to add a column to an existing table is

ALTER TABLE tablename
ADD columnname datatype;

For example, if Indo–US College decides to track a student's social security number along with the student's ID, a new column can be added to the STUDENT table as shown in Fig. 4-9.

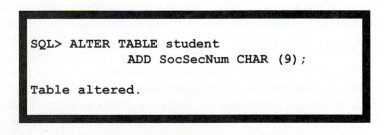

```
SQL> ALTER TABLE student
          ADD SocSecNum CHAR (9);

Table altered.
```

Figure 4-9 Adding a column to a table.

Modifying an Existing Column

The general syntax to modify an existing column is

ALTER TABLE tablename
MODIFY columnname newdatatype;

where *newdatatype* is the new data type or the new size for the attribute. The Indo–US College wants to use a zip code using 5 digits, a dash, and a 4-digit mail code whenever known. The data type can be changed from CHAR (5) to VAR-CHAR2 (10) to accommodate this new format (see Fig. 4-10).

```
SQL> ALTER TABLE student
         MODIFY Zip VARCHAR2 (10);

Table altered.
```

Figure 4-10   Modifying a column.

Adding a Constraint

In this section, we will try to add various constraints in a table using the ALTER TABLE query. As introduced in Chapter 3, the STUDENT table in the Indo–US College's database has a FacultyId attribute, which references the FACULTY table's primary key FacultyId. To add a constraint using ALTER TABLE, the syntax for table level constraint is used. The general syntax of ALTER TABLE is

> **ALTER TABLE tablename**
> **ADD [CONSTRAINT constraint_name] constraint_type (column, ...),**

Let us try to add the foreign key constraint in the STUDENT table as shown in Fig. 4-11.

As you see in Fig. 4-11, this error message is easier to understand. In order to create a foreign key constraint, the parent table, whose primary key attribute is referenced by the child table's foreign key attribute, must already exist in the database. Even the primary key attribute that is referenced must exist in the parent table defined as the primary key. Remember that the two attributes, the foreign key and the primary key that it references, need not have the same name. The best solution to such a situation would be to create all tables first without any foreign key constraints first. Then create tables using a CREATE TABLE query with FOREIGN KEY constraints to reference tables already created. An alternate solution is to create all tables with their constraints except for the foreign key constraint. Once all the tables are created, then use the ALTER TABLE query to add the FOREIGN KEY constraint.

Error Codes

Fig. 4-12 shows the Oracle error help screen that is displayed when you run Oracle 8 error messages. Click on **START → Oracle 8 for Windows NT/95 → Oracle 8**

```
SQL> ALTER TABLE STUDENT
  2     ADD CONSTRAINT student_facultyid_fk FOREIGN KEY(FacultyId)
  3         REFERENCES faculty (FacultyId);

ADD CONSTRAINT student_facultyid_fk FOREIGN KEY (FacultyId)
    REFERENCES faculty (FacultyId)
                    *

ERROR at line 3:
ORA-00942: table or view does not exist
```

Figure 4-11 Unsuccessful ALTER TABLE query.

Figure 4-12 Oracle help screen.

```
┌─────────────────────────────────────────────────────────────────────────┐
│ ❓ Oracle8 Messages and Codes                                   _ □ X    │
├─────────────────────────────────────────────────────────────────────────┤
│ Help Topics │  Back  │  Print  │  Options  │   <<   │   >>   │           │
├─────────────────────────────────────────────────────────────────────────┤
│  ORA-00942                                                                │
├─────────────────────────────────────────────────────────────────────────┤
│  ORA-00942 table or view does not exist                                   │
│                                                                           │
│  Cause      The table or view entered does not exist, a synonym that is   │
│             not allowed here was used, or a view was referenced where a   │
│             table is required. Existing user tables and views can be      │
│             listed by querying the data dictionary. Certain privileges    │
│             may be required to access the table. If an application        │
│             returned this message, the table the application tried to     │
│             access does not exist in the database, or the application     │
│             does not have access to it.                                   │
│                                                                           │
│  Action     Check each of the following:                                  │
│                                                                           │
│             • the spelling of the table or view name.                     │
│                                                                           │
│             • that a view is not specified where a table is required.     │
│                                                                           │
│             • that an existing table or view name exists.                 │
│                                                                           │
│             Contact the database administrator if the table needs to be   │
│             created or if user or application privileges are required to  │
│             access the table.                                             │
│                                                                           │
│             Also, if attempting to access a table or view in another      │
│             schema, make certain the correct schema is referenced and     │
│             that access to the object is granted.                         │
└─────────────────────────────────────────────────────────────────────────┘
```

Figure 4-13   Oracle error code and explanation.

Error Messages. Once the error help screen is displayed, click on the Index tab. Then type the error code received from Oracle in the space provided. When you are done typing, click on the Display button to get an explanation of the error (Fig. 4-13). In the figure, the explanation of the error code is straightforward. The help shows the cause of the error and gives hints for corrective actions.

Now, let us add a NOT NULL constraint and a DEFAULT value to the Start-Term and State columns respectively in the STUDENT table. If a student does not have a start term, it is difficult for an academic department to track the student's class and projected date of graduation. If the college is located in New Jersey area and most of the students are from in-state, it is a good idea to add a DEFAULT value to avoid data entry in to the column. A user can always overwrite the default value, but if it is left blank or null, the default value is used by Oracle. To add such constraints a MODIFY clause is used with an ALTER TABLE query. For example,

```
ALTER TABLE student MODIFY StartTerm CHAR (4)
    CONSTRAINT student_startterm_nn NOT NULL;
ALTER TABLE student MODIFY State CHAR (2)
    DEFAULT 'NJ';
```

Dropping a Column (Oracle 8i Onward)

As you already know, Oracle8 does not allow you to remove a column from the table, but Oracle8i does. Only one column can be dropped at a time. The column may or may not contain any data. When a column is dropped, there must be at least one column left in the table. In other words, you can't remove the last remaining column from a table. It is not possible to recover a dropped column and its data. The general syntax is

ALTER TABLE tablename DROP COLUMN columnname;

Oracle 8i also allows a user to mark columns as unused by using

ALTER TABLE tablename SET UNUSED (columnname);

The unused columns are like dropped columns. This is not a very good feature, because the storage space used by unused columns is not released. They are not displayed with other columns, they are not displayed in table's structure, and the user can drop all unused columns with the following statement.

ALTER TABLE tablename DROP UNUSED COLUMNS;

If no columns are marked as unused, this statement does not return any error messages.

DROPPING A TABLE

When a table is not needed in the database, it can be dropped. Sometimes, the existing table structure has so many flaws, that it is advisable to drop it and re-create it. When a table is dropped, all data and the table's structure are permanently deleted. The DROP operation cannot be reversed. Oracle does not question you with an "Are You Sure?" message. You can drop a table only if you are the owner of the table or have a higher privilege to do so. Many other objects based on the dropped table are affected. All associated indexes are removed. The table's views and synonyms become invalid. The general syntax is

DROP TABLE tablename;

For example,

DROP TABLE sample;

Oracle displays a "Table dropped" message when a table is successfully dropped.

RENAMING A TABLE

You can rename a table provided you are the owner of the table. The general syntax is

RENAME oldtablename TO newtablename;

For example,

RENAME dept TO department;

Oracle will display a "Table renamed" message when this statement is executed. We will not change the DEPT table's name and will still refer to it by its original name later in this textbook. The RENAME statement can be used to change name of other Oracle objects such as a view, synonym, or sequence, which we will cover in the next chapters.

TRUNCATING A TABLE

Truncating a table is removing all records/rows from the table. The structure of the table stays intact. You must be the owner of the table with the DELETE TABLE privilege to truncate a table. The SQL language has a DELETE statement which can be used to remove one or more (or all) rows from a table, that is reversible. The TRUNCATE statement, on the other hand, is not reversible. Truncation releases storage space occupied by the table, but deletion does not. The syntax is

TRUNCATE TABLE tablename;

For example,

TRUNCATE TABLE employee;

Oracle displays a "Table truncated" message on this statement's execution. The EMPLOYEE table is an integral part of the NamanNavan Corporation's database. You do not want to truncate it unless you would like to type all employees' data again!

SPOOLING

Spooling is a very handy feature. During a session, a user can redirect all statements, queries, commands, and results to a file for later review or printout. The spooling method creates a text file of all actions and their results. Everything you see on your screen is redirected to the file, which is saved with an .LST extension.

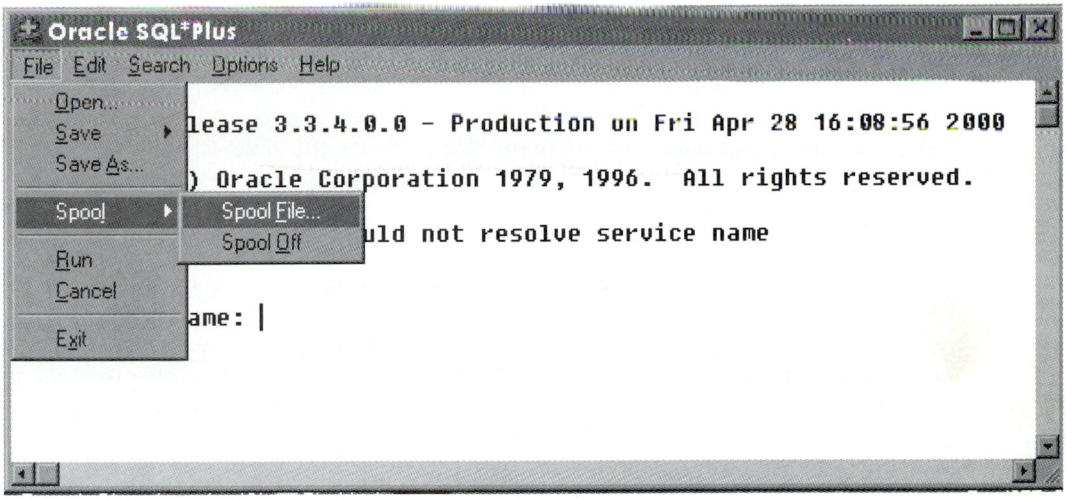

Figure 4-14   Spool menu.

To start spooling, you will go to the File menu in the SQL*Plus window. Then, you will click on Spool and Spool File in subsequent menus (see Fig. 4-14). You will be prompted to enter a filename, which will be created with an .LST extension.

To stop spooling at any point, use the same menu to click on Spool Off (see Fig. 4-14). When spooling is turned off, the file is saved and closed on to the disk. The spooled file can be opened in any text editor such as Notepad for viewing or printing. In the classroom environment, professors can ask students to spool all their work, which includes required queries and their results. The students can submit their disk or the printed hard copy.

In this chapter, you learned all the Data Definition Language (DDL) statements, which enable you to create and modify a table's structure. In the next chapter, you will learn about Data Manipulation Language (DML) statements to populate tables with the INSERT query, modify data using the UPDATE query, and remove data using the DELETE query. We will also learn to retrieve a table's underlying data with the SELECT query and its various clauses.

IN A NUTSHELL . . .

- The Oracle database tables are stored under a user's account in allocated table space on a server's disk.
- The Oracle object names can be up to 30 characters long and can use letters, numbers, and the $, #, and _ characters only. All the names must start with a letter.

- Each attribute in a table is assigned a data type to specify the type of data to be stored in it. Basic data types are CHAR (fixed-length character data), VARCHAR2 (variable-length character data), NUMBER (integer, fixed-decimal point, and floating-decimal-point values) and DATE (date and time values). The data type attribute also includes the size.

- Advanced data types include LONG, NCHAR, CLOB, BLOB, NCLOB, BFILE, and RAW.

- Constraints enforce rules at the table level. Two types of constraints are integrity constraint (primary key and foreign key) and value constraint (check, not null, and unique). The constraints are named either by the user or by Oracle, using a standard convention. A constraint is defined at column or table level using slightly different syntax.

- A DDL statement, CREATE TABLE, is used for table creation. The creation of a table includes attribute names, data types, the sizes of the attributes, and constraint definitions.

- Oracle provides a user with SQL statements and SQL*Plus commands to view the user's tables, table structure, and constraint information.

- The ALTER TABLE statement is used to modify an existing table's structure. The modifications may include addition of a new column, modifying an existing column, or adding a constraint. Oracle 8 does not allow a user to drop a column from a table. There are restrictions imposed for certain modifications.

- A table can be dropped from the database or renamed. A table can be truncated to remove all its rows/records.

- Oracle error messages are displayed with error codes. A user can get more information about the causes of errors and the actions necessary to correct them using Oracle 8 Error messages from Windows environment.

- The spooling method is used to spool all queries, statements, and commands along with their results to a text file.

EXERCISE QUESTIONS

True/False

1. In Oracle 8, a table name cannot be one character long.
2. If a data value entered in a VARCHAR2 type field is longer than the actual size, the value is truncated.
3. The NUMBER data type can be used for integer, fixed-point decimal, and floating-point decimal values.
4. Two tables can have constraints with the same constraint name under a user's database.
5. A foreign key field must reference a primary key field in another table, and both fields must have the same name.

Find the valid/invalid table/attribute names.

1. CRS-SECTION
2. SALARY_LEVEL
3. Employee'sId
4. Employee Id
5. $SALARY
6. Proj2000
7. Qualification_Code_For_Employees

Give the column name, data type, and size for the following attributes.

1. Student's date of birth
2. Social Security number (without dashes)
3. Telephone number (with area code)
4. Employee's gender
5. Employee's picture in a file
6. Link to a word document
7. Customer's last name

Write a constraint definition for the following constraints (use the case-study tables in Chapter 3.)

1. Primary key in the DEPT table
2. Foreign key DeptId in the EMPLOYEE table
3. CHECK constraint for QualId in the EMPLOYEE table
4. NOT NULL constraint for the MajorDesc column in the MAJOR table
5. UNIQUE constraint for DeptName in the DEPT table

Write answers for the following.

1. What is the use of data types? Name four basic data types and state their use.
2. What are two types of constraints? Give two examples of each.
3. How are the constraints named?
4. Does Oracle allow a composite key? If so, how is it defined?
5. Can you change a field's name in an existing table in Oracle 8? Can you delete a field from a table?
6. Is it possible to add any type of constraint to an existing table? Are there any restrictions?
7. What are the differences between SQL and SQL*Plus?

LAB ACTIVITY

1. **(a)** Use SQL statements to create STUDENT, FACULTY, COURSE, CRSSECTION, REGISTRATION, ROOM, TERM, LOCATION, MAJOR, and DEPARTMENT tables in the Indo–US College database tables as given in Chapter 3. Use SQL*Plus commands or Notepad to debug your statements' errors, if there are any.

- Define a primary key constraint for each table. (Do not specify foreign keys yet.)
- Define NOT NULL, DEFAULT, UNIQUE, and CHECK constraints wherever appropriate.

Before running your statements, start spooling to a file named CH4LAB1A.LST. When all tables are created, stop spooling and print the spooled file.

(b) Now, add the required foreign key constraints for each table. Do not add any records yet. Spool your statements and results to the CH4LAB1B.LST file and print it.

(c) Spool to the CH4LAB1C.LST file and print all table names from your account, each table's structures, and constraint information for each table.

2. Use SQL statements to create all six tables from the NamanNavan Corporation database in Chapter 3. If you have already created a DEPT table in Chapter 3's Lab Activity, you will skip it. Define the primary key, foreign key, NOT NULL, DEFAULT, CHECK, and UNIQUE constraints in the CREATE TABLE statement only. (*Remember:* Foreign key constraint requires existence of the referenced table). Spool your statements and results to the CH4LAB2.LST file and print each table's structure and constraints as well.

5

Working with Tables: Data Management and Retrieval

IN THIS CHAPTER . . .

- You will learn how to populate tables using Data Manipulation Language (DML) statements.
- You will also learn to change existing data and to remove unnecessary rows/records.
- Data retrieval queries on single tables are introduced.
- Various clauses are used with data retrieval queries for filtering, sorting, and grouping of data.
- Data is manipulated using single-row functions and group functions.

ADDING A NEW ROW/RECORD

The Data Manipulation Language (DML) statement INSERT is used to insert a new row/record into a table. A user can insert values for all attributes or a selected list of attributes in a record. The general syntax for the INSERT statement is as follows:

INSERT INTO tablename [(column1, column2, column3,...)]
    VALUES (value1, value2, value3,...);

The column names are optional. If column names are omitted from the INSERT statement, you must enter a value for each column/attribute. If you know the order of column names in correct order, you can enter values in the same order following the VALUES keyword. (Use the SQL*Plus command DESCRIBE to display the table's structure to make sure.) If you insert values in incorrect order and a numeric value is entered for a character type attribute, Oracle will not accept new record and will generate an error message. If your statement is accepted, a '1 row created' message is displayed on the screen.

If you do enter column names, they do not have to be in the same order as they were defined in table's structure at the time of creation. Once you enter column names, their respective values must be in the same order as the column names. For example, let us add a new record to STUDENT table in the Indo–US College database.

INSERT INTO student (StudentId, Last, First, Street, City, State, Zip, StartTerm,
BirthDate, FacultyId, MajorId, Phone)
VALUES (`00100', 'Diaz', 'Jose', '1 Ford Avenue #7', 'Hill', 'NJ', '08863',
'WN99', '12-FEB-80', 123, 100, '9735551111');

When entering values, numeric data is not enclosed within quotes. The character and date type values are enclosed within single quotes. How do you enter a character value that contains a single quote character? For example, 'Daddy's Pizza Parlor' will result in an error. You must type two single quotes to enter a single quote character. The solution is 'Daddy''s Pizza Parlor'. The first quotation mark acts as an escape character for the second one.

The default format to enter the date value is 'DD-MON-YY'. If you use the default format, the year will default to the current century. The birth date of '15-APR-60' will be stored with the year as 2060. The student's calculated age will return a negative number! If you want to enter a date in any other format, the TO_DATE function is used for converting a character value to the date equivalent. For example,

TO_DATE ('02/12/1980', 'MM/DD/YYYY')
TO_DATE ('FEB 12, 1980', 'MON DD, YYYY')

Now, let us enter a new record into DEPT table in the NamanNavan Corporation's database without using the column names.

INSERT INTO dept
VALUES (10, 'Finance', 'Charlotte', 123);

The DEPT table contains four attributes, and the values in the previous statement are in correct order. While inserting values, you must remember that the foreign key attributes in a table must either have a NULL value or that value must already exist as a primary key value in the table referenced by the foreign key. In the STUDENT table's INSERT statement, the value for FacultyId and MajorId columns are cross-referenced by Oracle in the FACULTY and MAJOR tables respectively. If you have not populated those two parent tables, your new record in the STUDENT table will not be accepted. The best way is to populate tables without foreign keys first; in other words, the parent tables must be populated before their child tables.

Entering Null Values

NULL values are allowed in non-primary-key attributes, that do not have a NOT NULL constraint. Check the 'Null?' display from the DESCRIBE command before inserting null value.

There are two methods for inserting a NULL value in an attribute.

1. *Implicit Method.* In the implicit method, the column's name is omitted from the column list in an INSERT statement. For example,

INSERT INTO dept (DeptId, DeptName)
VALUES (50, 'Production');

In this example, the Location and EmployeeId columns are not included. The new record will be inserted into the table with no values for those two columns. It is allowed only if the NOT NULL constraint is not used for them.

2. *Explicit Method.* In the explicit method, the value NULL is used as a value for numeric column, and an empty string ('') is used for date or character columns. For example,

INSERT INTO dept (DeptId, DeptName, Location, EmployeeId)
VALUES (60, 'Personnel', 'Chicago', NULL);

You will insert null in EmployeeId if you do not know the manager's EmployeeId for newly created Personnel department in Chicago.

Often you do not know the value of an attribute and decide to use a null value for it. If your table has records with null values, you have to update those records once actual values are known. That is additional data entry. One way to avoid null values is by using a DEFAULT value on columns.

Substitution Variables

Inserting rows into a table is a very tedious task. In real-life tables, we are talking about thousands of rows per table! There are screen designers, form creators, and so on. An SQL statement does not have those fancy controls or buttons. The SQL language does have substitution variables, which enable you to create interactive

```
SQL> INSERT INTO dept (DeptId, DeptName, Location, EmployeeId)
  2     VALUES (&dept_id,'&dept_name','&location', &emp_id);

Enter value for dept_id: 70
Enter value for dept_name: Testing
Enter value for location: Miami
Enter value for emp_id: NULL

1 row created.
```

Figure 5-1 Substitution variables.

SQL script. When you execute the script, Oracle prompts you to enter a value for the substitution variable. The ampersand (&) character is used before the substitution variable in the query. The substitution variables for character and date type columns are enclosed within a pair of single quotation marks. Figure 5-1 shows the use of substitution variables and the interactive prompts displayed by Oracle.

> **Question:** You just ran the SQL statement in Fig. 5-1. How will you insert the next record using the same statement?
>
> **Answer:** The last SQL statement is in the buffer, so you will type a slash (/) to re-execute the statement from the buffer. If you stored the statement in a file, you can execute the same file again with the RUN or @ command.

CUSTOMIZED PROMPTS

The substitution variable prompts are standard. Oracle displays 'Enter the value for' followed by the name of the substitution variable. The SQL*Plus command ACCEPT is used for customized prompts. The ACCEPT command does not use an ampersand in front of the variable name. ACCEPT in fact accepts values for substitution variables that can be used later in other statements. If an ACCEPT statement is used for a variable, the value of that variable, once entered, is remembered during the session. You might not want to use the ACCEPT statement for a variable to be used later in more than one INSERT statement. The general syntax is

ACCEPT variablename PROMPT 'prompt message'

For an example, see Fig. 5-2.

```
ACCEPT dept_id PROMPT `Please enter a department number (10 to 99): `
ACCEPT dept_name PROMPT `Please enter department name: `
ACCEPT location PROMPT `Please enter location city: `
ACCEPT emp_id PROMPT `Please enter manager Id: `


INSERT INTO dept (DeptId, DeptName, Location, EmployeeId)
VALUES (&dept_id, `&dept_name`, `&location`, &emp_id);
```

Figure 5-2 Custom prompt with ACCEPT.

UPDATING EXISTING ROWS/RECORDS

Once data are added to the tables for various entities, it may not stay the same forever. A female employee gets married and changes her last name, a student changes his/her major, a customer/vendor moves to a new location, or an employee gets a salary increment. These are real-life possibilities. When you create tables, you should use attributes that are not very high maintenance. For example, you should not use an attribute called AGE. The age changes every year for an individual, and it changes on different days for almost everybody.

In SQL, the UPDATE statement is used for such modifications to data. Only one table can be updated at one time. It is possible to change more than one attribute at a time. The general syntax is

> *UPDATE tablename*
> > *SET column1 = newvalue [, column2 = newvalue,...]*
> > *[WHERE condition];*

The condition is optional, but in most cases you would need to use it. If the condition is not used with UPDATE, all rows will be updated. The conditions are created using column names, relational operators, and values. You already know that Oracle is case sensitive as far as the values in single quotation marks are concerned. The relational operators are shown in Fig. 5-3.

Relational Operator	Meaning
=	Equal to
<>	Not equal to
>	Greater than
>=	Greater than or equal to
<	Less than
<=	Less than or equal to

Figure 5-3 Relational operators.

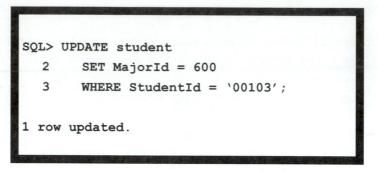

Figure 5-4   Successful UPDATE statement.

Suppose a student with ID '00103' in the Indo–US College's database switches major from BS—Computer Science to BS—Telecommunications. We will write an update statement to change the student's MajorId in the STUDENT table. Figure 5-4 shows a successful update operation. The same UPDATE statement without the WHERE clause would result in updating all students' MajorId to 600.

Question: Can we change a student's MajorId to 700?

Answer: The obvious answer is Why not? The correct answer is No. A student may not have MajorId = 700 because it is a foreign key attribute, that references the primary key in the MAJOR table. Oracle cross-references every foreign key value with the referenced primary key values. The parent table does not have the value 700, so the child table cannot use that value.

Let us try it in Fig. 5-5 and check out Oracle's message. Oracle will not allow you to use MajorId = 700 in the child table STUDENT because it references

```
SQL> UPDATE student
  2      SET MajorId = 700
  3      WHERE StudentId = '00103';



UPDATE student
      *
ERROR at line 1:
ORA-02291: integrity constraint (NSHAH.STUDENT_MAJORID_FK)
violated - parent key not found
```

Figure 5-5   Unsuccessful UPDATE statement.

a parent table MAJOR (MajorId). The parent key attribute does not contain the value 700. There are other operators for writing conditions like AND, OR, BETWEEN–AND, IN, and LIKE. We will learn more about them later in this chapter.

DELETING EXISTING ROWS/RECORDS

Deletion is another data maintenance operation. When employees leave the company or students enroll but never start college, you might want to remove their information from your database. In Oracle, the SQL statement DELETE is used for deleting unwanted rows. Its general syntax is

DELETE [FROM] tablename
[WHERE condition];

The keyword FROM is optional. The WHERE clause adds a condition to the DELETE statement. Once again, the condition is optional, but it is necessary. You normally would delete only those records that meet a criterion. The DELETE statement without a condition will result in a table with no records. A DELETE statement without a WHERE clause has same effect as a TRUNCATE statement. The only difference is that the DELETE operation can be undone, but the TRUNCATE operation makes the change permanent. Figure 5-6 shows successful execution of a DELETE query. If a row with department number 60 exists, it is deleted.

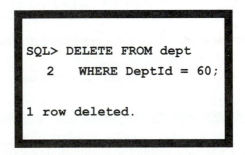

```
SQL> DELETE FROM dept
  2      WHERE DeptId = 60;


1 row deleted.
```

Figure 5-6 Successful DELETE statement.

If you try to delete a record from a table whose primary key value is used in another table's foreign key attribute, Oracle will display an 'Integrity constraint . . . violated–child record found' error message. The parent record that is referenced by a child record cannot be removed. See Figure 5-7 for an unsuccessful DELETE operation. In such cases, you may drop a constraint or temporarily disable it. A dropped constraint is removed permanently, whereas a disabled constraint can be enabled later.

```
SQL> DELETE FROM dept
  2    WHERE DeptId = 20;
```

```
DELETE FROM dept
            *
ERROR at line 1:
ORA-02292: integrity constraint (NSHAH.EMPLOYEE_DEPTID_FK)
violated - child record found
```

Figure 5-7   Unsuccessful DELETE statement.

DROPPING A CONSTRAINT

You can view constraint information from a USER_CONSTRAINT table, which has CONSTRAINT_NAME, TABLE_NAME, CONSTRAINT_TYPE, and COLUMN_NAME attributes. A dropped constraint is no longer enforced by Oracle, and it does not show up in the list of USER_CONSTRAINTS. The general syntax is

> *ALTER TABLE tablename*
> *DROP PRIMARY KEY/UNIQUE (columnname) /*
> *CONSTRAINT constraintname [CASCADE];*

For example,

> *ALTER TABLE major*
> *DROP PRIMARY KEY CASCADE;*

This statement drops the primary key constraint from the MAJOR table. The CASCADE clause drops the dependent foreign key constraints, if any. You can drop a constraint by using its name, which is why it is important to name all constraints with a standard naming convention. For example,

> *ALTER TABLE employee*
> *DROP CONSTRAINT employee_deptid_fk;*

DISABLING/ENABLING CONSTRAINTS

A disabled constraint does not need re-creation. It can be enabled again. The CASCADE option can be used while disabling a constraint to disable dependent integrity constraints also. The general syntax is

ALTER TABLE tablename
DISABLE CONSTRAINT constraintname [CASCADE];

For example,

ALTER TABLE student
DISABLE CONSTRAINT student_studentid_pk CASCADE;

The ENABLE CONSTRAINT clause reactivates a disabled constraint. All the data must "obey" the constraint, because the constraint applies to all data in the table. Enabling a PRIMARY KEY or UNIQUE constraint automatically creates an index. The general syntax is

ALTER TABLE tablename
ENABLE CONSTRAINT constraintname;

There is no CASCADE clause with ENABLE. The DISABLE and ENABLE clauses can also be used in CREATE TABLE statement.

RETRIEVING DATA FROM A TABLE

The main purpose of the SQL language is for querying the database. You have already learned to create, alter, insert, update, and delete by using SQL statements. The most important statement or query is the SELECT query. A user retrieves data from the underlying table or tables with a SELECT query. The output can be sorted, it can be grouped, and information can be derived with the use of mathematical expressions and built-in functions. In Chapter 1 we covered nine relational operations. Now is the time to test those operations. The general syntax is

SELECT columnlist
FROM tablename;

The columns can be listed in any order. They do not have to be in the order given by the DESCRIBE command. For example, Fig. 5-8 shows output from a SELECT query.

As you see, the column names are displayed in uppercase. In the STUDENT table, the attribute Last comes before the attribute First, but the output displays them in the order given in the SELECT query. By default, character data is displayed with left justification and numeric data with the right justification.

```
SQL> SELECT first, last FROM student;

FIRST              LAST
---------------    ---------------
Jose               Diaz
Mickey             Tyler
Rajesh             Patel
Deborah            Rickles
Brian              Lee
Amir               Khan


6 rows selected.
```

Figure 5-8   Output from a SELECT query.

Wild Card (*)

If you want to see all attributes in a table, you do not have to list them all. You can use wild card asterisk (*) in place of the column list, and all columns will be displayed in the same order as the underlying table structure. Fig. 5-9 depicts the use of the wild card*.

Two problems with displaying all rows and all columns are the screen's default line size and page size. After 80 columns, the row display wraps to the next line. After displaying 11 rows under column headings, column headings are repeated for more rows. The default number of columns used for a NUMBER column is nine. You can change these values from the Options menu in the SQL*Plus environment.

The environment variables can be changed by clicking on the Options menu in SQL*Plus, then by selecting Environment from it. Soon an Environment window will pop up and you can select *linesize* from the list of environment variables. Then, change the value from Default to Current and type in the new value. The default value for line size is 80. Similarly, *pagesize* and other variables can be set (see Fig. 5-10 for an illustration). Alternately, you can type SET commands at the SQL> prompt.

DISTINCT Clause

The DISTINCT clause is used to suppress duplicate values from a result. The word *DISTINCT* is used right after the keyword SELECT and before the column name.

```
SQL> SELECT *
  2    FROM course;


COURSEID TITLE                      CREDITS
-------- -------------------- ---------

EN100    Basic English              0
LA123    English Literature         3
CIS253   Database Systems           3
CIS265   Systems Analysis           3
MA150    College Algebra            3
AC101    Accounting                 3


6 rows selected.
```

Figure 5-9 Wild card asterisk (*).

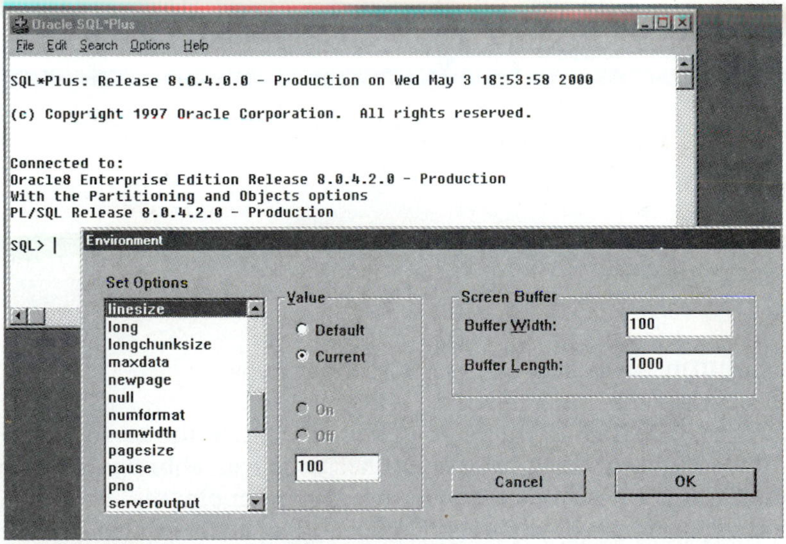

Figure 5-10 Setting Environment variable.

Let us see the difference in result from two SELECT queries, with and without the DISTINCT clause. Figure 5-11 shows the SELECT statement without DISTINCT, which outputs 11 rows with duplicate values on the left.

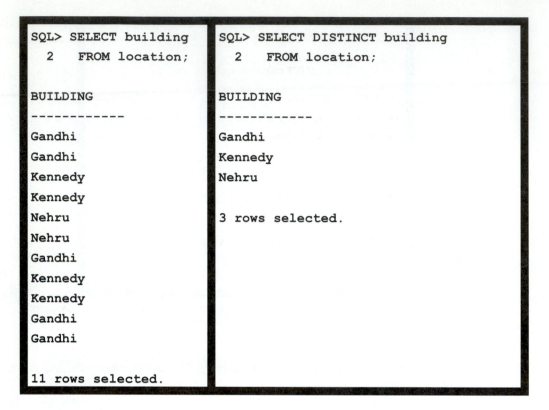

```
SQL> SELECT building          SQL> SELECT DISTINCT building
  2    FROM location;           2     FROM location;


BUILDING                       BUILDING
------------                   ------------

Gandhi                         Gandhi

Gandhi                         Kennedy

Kennedy                        Nehru

Kennedy

Nehru                          3 rows selected.

Nehru

Gandhi

Kennedy

Kennedy

Gandhi

Gandhi


11 rows selected.
```

Figure 5-11   SELECT, with and without DISTINCT.

On the right, using DISTINCT eliminates duplicate values and returns three unique values.

Column Alias

When a SELECT query is executed, SQL*Plus uses the column's name as the column heading. Normally the user gives abbreviated names for columns, and they are not very descriptive. For example, the attribute name Lname is used for an employee's last name and DepDOB is used for a dependent's date of birth.

Column aliases are useful because they let you change the column's heading. When a calculated value is displayed, the mathematical expression is not displayed as the column heading but the column alias is displayed. The column alias is written right after the column name with an optional keyword AS in between. The alias heading appears in uppercase by default. If an alias includes spaces or special characters, or if you want to preserve its case, you must enclose it in double quotation marks (" "). The general syntax is

SELECT columnname [AS] alias...

In the example in Fig. 5-12, LastName is an alias for Last and FirstName is an alias for First. Notice that the word AS is omitted the second time, because it is an optional word. The headings will look like

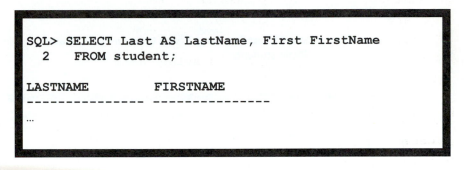

Figure 5-12   Column alias.

Now let us look at another example, one where the alias uses spaces and special characters. We also want to display it in mixed case, not in uppercase. The column heading looks exactly the way it is typed in the statement (see Fig. 5-13).

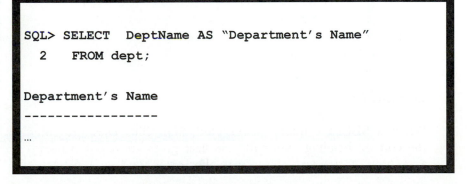

Figure 5-13   Column alias—case preserved.

Concatenation

The word *concatenation* is a common word in computer jargon, but in daily life it is seldom used. Concatenation means joining or linking. In SQL, concatenation joins a column or a character string to another column. The result is a column, which is a string or a series of characters. Two vertical bars or pipe symbols (||) are used as concatenation operator. The symbol appears on your keyboard with the backslash (\) character. You will need to depress the SHIFT key to enter the character. Figure 5-14 shows the result of concatenating two columns in the EMPLOYEE table. The two column's values are joined without any space separating them. In Fig. 5-15, we have altered the output so that the names are displayed with the last name and first name separated by a comma and a space. We need to use a character string to accomplish it.

Now try this:

```
SELECT First || ' ' || Last || 'was born on ' || Birthdate
FROM student;
```

```
SQL> SELECT Lname || Fname As "Employee Name"
  2    FROM employee;


Employee Name
------------------------------
SmithJohn
HoustonLarry
RobertsSandi
McCallAlex
DevDerek
ShawJinku
GarnerStanley
ChenSunny

8 rows selected.
```

Figure 5-14 Concatenation.

ARITHMETIC OPERATIONS

The arithmetic expressions are used to display mathematically calculated data. These expressions use columns, numeric values, and arithmetic operators (see Fig. 5-16).

```
SQL> SELECT Lname || ', ' || Fname As "Employee Name"
  2    FROM employee;


Employee Name
-----------------------------
Smith, John
Houston, Larry
Roberts, Sandi
McCall, Alex
Dev, Derek
Shaw, Jinku
Garner, Stanley
Chen, Sunny

8 rows selected.
```

Figure 5-15 Concatenation with a character string.

Operator	Use
*	Multiplication
/	Division
+	Addition
-	Subtraction

Figure 5-16 Arithmetic operators.

When arithmetic operators are used with columns in the SELECT query, the underlying data is not changed. The calculations are for output purposes only.

Order of Operation

- Multiplication and division have higher priority than addition and subtraction.
- If more than one operator of the same priority is present, the operators are performed from left to right.
- Whatever is in parentheses is done first.

```
SQL> SELECT Lname, Salary+Commission
  2    FROM employee;


LNAME                  SALARY+COMMISSION
---------------        -----------------
Smith                            300000
Houston                          160000
Roberts
McCall
Dev                              100000
Shaw                              27500
Garner                           50000
Chen


8 rows selected.
```

Figure 5-17   Arithmetic operation and NULL values.

As you see in Fig. 5-17, if the column alias is not used, the expression is displayed as the column heading. It is optional to leave a space on both sides of an arithmetic operator. One other peculiar thing is the total of Salary and Commission. When a Salary value is added to a NULL value in the Commission column, the total is a NULL value. The expression can be changed to salary + NVL (Commission, 0), where NVL is a function that substitutes a NULL value with second argument in parentheses, a zero, for arithmetic operation. We will revisit the NVL function shortly.

RESTRICTING DATA WITH A WHERE CLAUSE

When we used the SELECT query in Fig. 5-8, we restricted the number of columns to only two. It was an example of a *projection* operation. In Fig. 5-9, we basically displayed all attributes. In both cases, all rows from the table were displayed. Many times you don't want to see all the rows from a table, but you want to see only those rows that meet a criteria. A WHERE clause is used with a SELECT query to restrict the rows picked. It is the implementation of a *selection* operation. A WHERE clause uses a simple condition or a compound condition. The rows, which satisfy supplied conditions, are displayed in the output. The syntax of SELECT changes a little with an added WHERE clause. The general syntax of the WHERE clause is

SELECT columnlist
FROM tablename
[WHERE condition(s)];

The conditions are written using column names; relational (Fig. 5-3), logical (Fig. 5-18), and other comparison operators (Fig. 5-19); literal values; mathematical expressions; and built-in functions.

Logical Operator	Meaning
AND	Returns TRUE only if both conditions are true.
OR	Returns TRUE if one or both conditions are true.
NOT	Returns TRUE if the condition is false.

Figure 5-18   Logical operators.

AND	OR
TRUE AND TRUE = TURE	TRUE OR TRUE = TRUE
TRUE AND FALSE = FALSE	TRUE OR FALSE = TRUE
FALSE AND TRUE = FALSE	FALSE OR TRUE = TRUE
FALSE AND FALSE = FALSE	FALSE OR FALSE = FALSE
NULL AND TRUE = NULL	NULL OR TRUE = TRUE
NULL AND FALSE = FALSE	NULL OR FALSE = NULL
NULL AND NULL = NULL	NULL OR NULL = NULL

Figure 5-19   AND and OR.

You are familiar with the arithmetic operators and relational operators already. The logical operators AND and OR work with two conditions, whereas NOT works on one condition only. All three return a TRUE or FALSE result. The table in (Fig. 5-19) shows the working of AND and OR operators.

There are other special comparison operators, which are given in Fig. 5-20. The IS NULL operator checks for a NULL value. It returns TRUE for the NULL value and FALSE for the NOT NULL value. The BETWEEN. . .AND operator checks for a range of values using lower and upper limits. The IN operator is an alternate and shorter way of writing OR conditions. The LIKE operator is used with the wild cards for pattern matching.

Operator	Meaning
IS NULL	Is a null value.
BETWEEN...AND	Between a range of values (both included).
IN	Match any value from a list (An alternate way to write OR).
LIKE	Match a value using wild cards.

Figure 5-20   Other comparison operators.

In this section, we will give many examples of restricted data retrieval. The Indo–US College database has a few thousand students. The administration wants to identify students who started in the Winter 2000 term. We have used a few sample records in each table for simplicity. Based on the records entered, we will get output as given in Fig. 5-21.

The sample STUDENT table has six rows, but only two StartTerm values match 'WN00'. When character values are tested in conditions, Oracle is case sensitive about it. The character and date values are enclosed within single quotation marks.

In Fig. 5-22 no rows are selected from the query, though there is one department in the NamanNavan Corporation database located there. The problem here

```
SQL> SELECT StudentId, Last, First
  2     FROM student
  3     WHERE StartTerm = 'WN00';


STUDENTID LAST             FIRST
--------- ---------------- ----------------
00102     Patel            Rajesh
00105     Khan             Amir

2 rows selected.
```

Figure 5-21   Data retrieval with a WHERE clause.

```
SQL> SELECT *
  2     FROM dept
  3     WHERE Location = 'WOODBRIDGE';


no rows selected.
```

Figure 5-22 Case sensitivity.

is the all uppercase value in the query. The actual data is in proper case. We will learn character functions soon to avoid these types of problems.

Let us try another relational operator in the condition. The president of the NamanNavan Corporation wants to find out the name and department number of all employees who make $100,000 or more in salary only. The president will be surprised if he does not see his name in the list in Fig. 5-23.

Let us say that it is time to schedule courses for the next term. The Accounting department wants to schedule a course in a classroom that accommodates 40 to 45 students. We can perform this query by using two conditions with the AND operator

```
SQL> SELECT Lname, Fname, Salary, DeptId
  2     FROM employee
  3     WHERE Salary >= 100000;

LNAME               FNAME               SALARY    DEPTID
---------------     ---------------     --------  ---------

Smith               John                265000         10
Houston             Larry               150000         40

2 rows selected.
```

Figure 5-23 Relational operator >=.

```
SQL> SELECT Building, RoomNo, Capacity, RoomType
  2     FROM location
  3     WHERE Capacity BETWEEN 40 AND 45;


BUILDING     ROOMNO   CAPACITY  ROOMTYPE
--------   ---------  ---------  --------
Nehru          309        45 C
Kennedy        206        40 L


2 rows selected.
```

Figure 5-24 BETWEEN...AND operator.

or by using the BETWEEN...AND operator. Figure 5-24 uses a BETWEEN...AND operator with 40 as the lower limit and 45 as the upper limit. The same condition can be written as a compound condition with the logical operator AND as given in Fig. 5-25.

When the relational and logical operators are used together, the order of precedence is as follows if all operators exist:

- Whatever is in parentheses is performed first.
- Relational operators are performed first.
- The NOT operator is performed next.
- The AND operator is performed third.
- The OR operator is performed last.

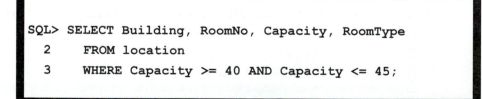

```
SQL> SELECT Building, RoomNo, Capacity, RoomType
  2     FROM location
  3     WHERE Capacity >= 40 AND Capacity <= 45;
```

Figure 5-25 Compound condition with AND.

In the previous two figures, we displayed Room Type also. The department is looking for a classroom, not a lab. We can further restrict data by adding another condition to check for the classroom (see Fig. 5-26).

```
SQL> SELECT Building, RoomNo, Capacity
  2     FROM location
  3     WHERE Capacity BETWEEN 40 AND 45
  4     AND RoomType = 'C';


BUILDING ROOMNO  CAPACITY
-------- ------  ---------
Nehru       309        45


1 row selected.
```

Figure 5-26 Compound condition using two columns.

The NamanNavan Corporation is conducting a study regarding their employees' qualifications. The company wants to identify all employees with bachelors', masters', and doctorate degrees. The corresponding qualification codes are 3, 2, and 1. The most appropriate operator is OR, because the employee has to have one of the three codes (see Fig. 5-27). The same result can be obtained by using the IN operator in place of three conditions and two OR conjunctions, for example,

WHERE QualId IN (3, 2, 1);

Similarly, if we want to find out the names of all students in the Indo–US College database who are from New York and New Jersey, we can use the OR

```
SQL> SELECT Lname, Fname, DeptId, QualId
  2     FROM employee
  3     WHERE QualId = 3 OR QualId = 2 OR QualId = 1;
```

Figure 5-27 OR operator.

```
SQL> SELECT Last, First, State
  2      FROM student
  3      WHERE State IN ('NY', 'NJ', 'CT', 'DE', 'PA');
```

Figure 5-28   IN operator.

operator. What if we are looking for students from New York, New Jersey, Connecticut, Delaware, and Pennsylvania? With OR we will need five conditions. In such a case, the IN operator is preferable.

In the EMPLOYEE table, there is information about the employee's immediate supervisor to whom he/she reports. Is there any employee who does not have a supervisor? If so, then either the information is missing or the employee has the highest position in the company. Let us search for such employees in Fig. 5-29.

Fortunately, there is only one employee without supervisor information, who happens to hold the president's position. If more such records were found, data entry personnel would have to UPDATE that information. Similarly, we can check for rows with no null value in a column. In other words, we would like to see rows with a value in a column. For example, the REGISTRATION table in the college database has rows with final grade and also has rows with a null value

```
SQL> SELECT Lname, Fname, Supervisor
  2      FROM employee
  3      WHERE Supervisor IS NULL;


LNAME               FNAME              SUPERVISOR
---------------     ---------------    ----------
Smith               John


1 row selected.
```

Figure 5-29   IS NULL operator.

```
SQL> SELECT StudentId, CsId, Final
  2     FROM registration
  3     WHERE Final IS NOT NULL
  4     AND StudentId = '00100';


STUDENTID        CSID FINAL
---------   --------- -----
00100            1101 F
00100            1102 B
00100            1104 A


3 rows selected.
```

Figure 5-30 IS NOT NULL operator.

for the final grade. Student '00100' has course sections with and without final grades (see Fig. 5-30).

Wild Cards

You have already seen examples with a search for a string value. There are times when you do not know the exact string value. You can select rows that match a pattern of characters. Such a search is known as a wild card search. There are two wild cards for a pattern search. Figure 5-31 explains the use of these wild cards.

Wild Card	Use
%	Represents 0 or more characters.
_(Underscore)	Represents any 1 character.

Figure 5-31 Wild cards.

A search with the wild cards requires you to use the LIKE operator. In the college's database, we want to see the information about faculty members, whose names start with the letter *C*. All faculty names start with an uppercase letter. Oracle is case sensitive, so 'c' in place of 'C' will not return any faculty names. Figure 5-32 has a query that searches for such faculty names.

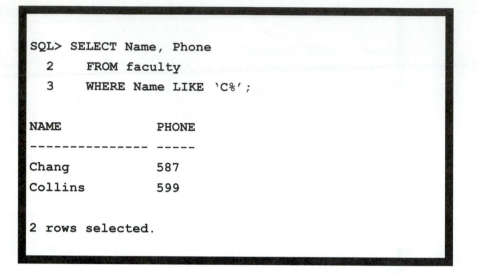

```
SQL> SELECT Name, Phone
  2     FROM faculty
  3     WHERE Name LIKE 'C%';


NAME              PHONE
---------------   -----
Chang             587
Collins           599


2 rows selected.
```

Figure 5-32   The wild card %.

Similarly, if we want to find out the names of employees hired during the 1960s, we can look for the hire date that falls between Jan. 1, 1960 and Dec. 31, 1969. Would the BETWEEN...AND operator be the best choice for it? Not really! We can use a combination of both wild cards to achieve the same result. We have two employees in with hire dates in the 1960s. Figure 5-33 uses '%6_' which means that the date starts with any characters, the second to last character is a 6, and the

```
SQL> SELECT Lname, Fname
  2   FROM employee
  3   WHERE HireDate LIKE '%6_';


LNAME             FNAME
---------------   ---------------
Smith             John
Houston           Larry


2 rows selected.
```

Figure 5-33   The % and _ operators.

last character could be anything. In the two case study databases, none of the tables use a value that actually uses the character % or_.

> **Question:** How do you look for a value that has a wild card character embedded in it?
>
> **Answer:** You use an escape character. SQL does not provide any particular character as an escape character, but you can specify one for the query. The WHERE clause will look like this:

WHERE column LIKE '%/_%' ESCAPE '/';

The first % means the column value starts with any characters in the beginning. The second % means the value ends with any characters. The characters /_ mean that there is a _ character in the value. The character / is used as the escape character, which changes the meaning of _ from a wild card to the underscore character.

SORTING

The order of rows in a table does not matter. You can insert rows in any order. When you type a SELECT query, the order of rows is not defined. You may want to see rows in a specific order based on a column or columns. It is not necessary to display a sort column in the SELECT clause. For example, you may want to see employees in alphabetical order by their name, view employees with the highest-paid employee first and lowest-paid employee last, or display students by their major in alphabetical order.

The ORDER BY clause is used with the SELECT query to sort rows in a table. The rows can be sorted in ascending or descending order. The rows can be sorted based on one or more columns. The expanded syntax of SELECT given here uses an ORDER BY clause, which is always used last in the statement. The general syntax is

SELECT columnlist
 FROM tablename
 [WHERE condition(s)]
 [ORDER BY column/expression [ASC/DESC]];

In the syntax, ASC stands for ascending order. The default order is ascending, so there is no need to type ASC for ascending order. The keyword DESC stands for descending or reverse order.

In an ascending sort, numeric values are displayed from the smallest to the largest value, character values are displayed in alphabetical order, and date values

Type of Value	Ascending Sort Order
Numeric	Lowest in highest value.
Character	Alphabetical order.
Date	Earliest date first.

Figure 5-34   Ascending sort order.

are displayed with the earliest date first (see Fig. 5-34). The NULL values are displayed last in ascending order. In descending order, the effect is reversed for all type of values. The NULL values are displayed first in the descending order.

In the next four examples, we will perform ascending sort by one column (Fig. 5-35), descending sort by one column (Fig. 5-36), sort by column alias (Fig. 5-37), and sort by multiple columns (Fig. 5-38). First let us display all faculty members in alphabetical order. The ORDER BY clause will use the Name column

```
SQL> SELECT Name, Phone
  2      FROM faculty
  3      ORDER BY Name;


NAME                 PHONE
---------------- -----
Chang                587
Collins              599
Jones                525
Mobley               529
Rivera               544
Sen                  579
Vajpayee             577
Williams             533


8 rows selected.
```

Figure 5-35   Single column sort.

```
SQL> SELECT Lname, Fname, Salary
  2     FROM employee
  3     WHERE DeptId = 30
  4     ORDER BY Salary DESC;


LNAME               FNAME               SALARY
---------------     ---------------     ---------
Garner              Stanley               45000
Shaw                Jinku                 24500


2 rows selected.
```

Figure 5-36 Descending order sort.

as the sort field (see Fig. 5-35). In this example, the word ASC can be added to the ORDER BY clause. Then the sort clause will look like this:

ORDER BY Name ASC;

Now, let us find out all employees with their salaries in descending order. The employee with the highest salary will be at the top, and the employee with the lowest salary will be at the bottom. We will restrict it to employees belonging to department 30 only. There are only two employees in department 30, and the result shows the employee with the higher salary first.

Next, let us use an expression in the SELECT statement and give it a column alias. We will use the column alias as our sort column. The alias *monthlysalary* represents the monthly salary of each employee, and it is also used for sorting data (see Fig. 5-37).

In our next example of sorting, we will sort by two different columns and each column will be sorted in a different order. In case of a sort by multiple columns, the first column is the primary sort column and the second column is the secondary sort column. The rows are sorted based on the primary sort column first; then the rows with same value in the primary sort columns are sorted within their group using the secondary sort column. For example, in sorting the LOCATION table using Building as the primary sort column and Capacity as the secondary sort column, first buildings will be sorted. Then, within each building, rows are sorted based on the capacity (see Fig. 5-38).

```
SQL> SELECT Lname || ', ' || Fname AS fullname,
  2         Salary / 12 AS monthlysalary
  3     FROM employee
  4     WHERE DeptId = 10
  5     ORDER BY monthlysalary;


FULLNAME                        MONTHLYSALARY
------------------------------- -------------
Chen, Sunny                       2916.666666
Roberts, Sandi                           6250
Smith, John                      22083.333333


3 rows selected.
```

Figure 5-37 Sort by an alias.

```
SQL> SELECT Building, RoomNo, Capacity
  2     FROM location
  3     WHERE Building IN ('Nehru', 'Kennedy')
  4     ORDER BY Building, Capacity DESC;

BULDING ROOMNO CAPACITY
------- ------ --------
Kennedy 204        50
Kennedy 206        40
Kennedy 202        35
Kennedy 210        30
Nehru   301        50
Nehru   309        45


6 rows selected.
```

Figure 5-38 Multiple-column sort.

106

We restricted our query to two buildings because the Clanc
with a capacity of two each. The building names are in ascendi
followed by Nehru. Within each building, the room numbers a
on capacity in descending order: Kennedy's four rooms in desc
pacity, followed by two rooms in Nehru in descending order by then ~-ₚ

BUILT-IN FUNCTIONS

The built-in functions provide a powerful tool and enhancement of a basic query.
A function takes zero or more arguments and returns back a single value. Just like
other software and programming languages, the functions covered in this section
are specific to Oracle. Functions are used for performing calculations on data, converting data, modifying individual data, manipulating a group of rows, and formatting columns. In Oracle's SQL, there are two types of functions:

1. *Single-row functions* work on individual columns from individual rows and
   return one result per row.
2. *Group functions* manipulate data in a group of rows and return single
   results.

Single-Row Functions

The single row functions take different types of arguments, work on a data item
from each row, and return one value back for each row. The arguments are in the
form of a constant value, variable value, column, and/or expression. The value returned by a function may be of a different type than the argument(s) supplied. The
general syntax is

Function (column / expression [, argument1, argument2,...])

where function is the name of the function, column is a column from a table, expression is a character string or a mathematical expression, and the arguments are
any argument(s) used by the function.

There are various types of single-row functions:

- *Character functions* take a character string or character-type column as an
  argument and return a character or numeric value.
- *Number functions* take a number or number-type column as an argument
  and return a numeric value.
- *Date functions* take a date value or date-type column as an argument, and
  return date-type data. (*Exception:* The MONTHS_BETWEEN function
  returns a numeric value.)
- *Conversion functions* convert value from one data type to another.
- *General functions*.

Character functions.   The character functions perform case conversion or character manipulation. Figure 5-39 has a list of character functions and their use. The case conversion character functions change a string or character-type column data's case. For example,

UPPER ('Oracle')   → 'ORACLE'
LOWER ('DaTaBaSe SyStEmS') → 'database systems'
INITCAP ('DaTaBaSe SyStEmS') → 'Database Systems'

Character Function	Use
UPPER (column / expr)	Converts each letter to uppercase.
LOWER (column / expr)	Converts each letter to lowercase.
INITCAP (column / expr)	Converts character value to the proper case (i.e., first character of each word is converted to uppercase and the rest to lowercase.)
CONCAT (column / expr, column / expr)	Joins the first value to the second value. Similar to the ‖ operator discussed earlier.
SUBSTR (column / expr, x, y)	Returns a substring, starting at character position x, returns y number of characters.
INSTR (column / expr, c)	Returns position of the supplied character.
TRIM ('c' FROM column / expr)	Removes leading and trailing characters.
LENGTH (column / expr)	Returns number of characters.
LPAD (column / expr, n, 'str')	Pads value with 'str' to the left to total width of n.

Figure 5-39   Character functions.

Often more than one data entry person will populate a table. One person enters names in all uppercase and the other uses proper case. This could become a

```
SQL> SELECT UPPER (First || ' ` || Last) ||
  2      ` lives in ` || INITCAP (city) AS EMPINFO
  3      FROM student
  4      WHERE MajorId = 600;


EMPINFO
-------------------------------------------------
BRIAN LEE lives in Hope

1 row selected.
```

Figure 5-40   Case conversion functions.

nightmare for data retrieval query writers, if it were not for functions. Functions are very useful in the WHERE clause's conditions as well. For example,

```
SELECT*
    FROM student
        WHERE UPPER (Last) = 'PATEL';
```

This query takes the last-name value for each row, converts it to uppercase, and then checks it against the all uppercase value 'PATEL'. Irrespective of the case used in the table, the query will work.

The character manipulation functions manipulate character type value to return another character- or numeric-type result. For example,

```
CONCAT ('New', 'York')    → 'NewYork'
SUBSTR ('HEATER', 2, 3)   → 'EAT'
INSTR ('abcdefg', 'd')    → 4
TRIM (' 'FROM ' Fords ')  → 'Fords'
LENGTH ('Oracle 8')       → 8
LPAD (Salary, 9, '*')     → ***265000
```

Number functions. The number functions take numeric value(s) and return a numeric value. The ROUND function rounds the value, expression, or column to n decimal places. If n is omitted, 0 decimal place is assumed. If n is negative, rounding takes place to the left side of the decimal place. For example,

$$ROUND (25.465, 2) = 25.47$$
$$ROUND (25.465, 0) = 25$$
$$ROUND (25.465, -1) = 30$$

The TRUNC function truncates the value, expression or column to n decimal places. If n is not supplied, 0 decimal place is assumed. For negative n, truncation takes place to the left side of the decimal place. For example,

$$TRUNC (25.465, 2) = 25.46$$
$$TRUNC (25.465, 0) = 25$$
$$TRUNC (25.465, -1) = 20$$

Number Function	Use
ROUND (column / expr, [n])	Rounds the column or expression to n decimal places.
TRUNC (column / expr, [n])	Truncates the column or expression to n decimal places.
POWER (n, p)	Returns n raised to power p (n^p).
ABS (n)	Returns the absolute value of n.
MOD (x, y)	Returns the integer remainder of x/y.

Figure 5-41a Number functions.

The POWER function finds the power of a number (n^p). For example,

POWER (2, 4) = 16
POWER (5, 3) = 125

The ABS function returns the absolute value of a column, expression, or value. For example,

ABS (−1) = 1

The MOD function finds the integer remainder of x divided by y. It ignores the quotient. For example,

MOD (5, 2) = 1
MOD (3, 5) = 3
MOD (8, 4) = 0

Date functions.   We already know that Oracle stores dates internally with day, month, century, hour, minute, and second information. The default date format is DD-MON-YY. There is a very useful date function called SYSDATE that does not take any arguments. SYSDATE returns the system's current date. Oracle also has a dummy table called DUAL. The DUAL table is owned by user SYS and it is available to all users. The DUAL table is useful when you want to find the outcome of a function and the argument is not taken from any table. For example,

SELECT SYSDATE
FROM DUAL;

This query will display the current date. Similarly, the DUAL table can be used to display the outcome of any of the character and number functions.

The DATE-type column is very important. You can derive a lot of information from date columns by performing 'date arithmetic.' As you see in Fig. 5-41b, you can add or subtract a number of days to or from a date to get a new resulting date. You can also add a number of hours to a date. If you have two dates, you can find the gap in days between them.

Date Expression	Result
Date + number	Adds a number of days to a date.
Date − number	Substracts a number of days from a date.
Date + number / 24	Adds a number of hours to a date.
Date1 − Date2	Gives the number of days between two dates.

Figure 5-41b   Date arithmetic.

```
SQL> SELECT Last, First, (SYSDATE - Birthdate) / 365 AGE
  2    FROM student;


LAST              FIRST                AGE
--------------    --------------    ---------
Diaz              Jose              20.245132
Tyler             Mickey            21.151984
-
6 rows selected.
```

Figure 5-42   Age calculation from birth date.

In Fig. 5-42, we have an expression (SYSDATE − BirthDate) that finds the difference in days. Then we divide the number of days by 365 to convert it to years. To consider leap years, we can divide by 365.25 days instead of 365. The resulting age has a decimal value. You can truncate (TRUNC) the result to 0 decimal places, and the age will be a whole number. The modified expression will look like this:

TRUNC ((SYSDATE − BirthDate) / 365.25)

Similarly, we can find the number of months or number of weeks by dividing days by 30 or 7 respectively.

The common date functions and their use are given in Fig. 5-43. The function MONTHS_BETWEEN returns a number. If *date1* is later than *date2,* the result is positive; otherwise the result is negative. The decimal part in the result is due to the portion of the month or extra days of the month. It is useful in finding the delay between delivery date and payment date. For example,

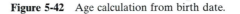
MONTHS_BETWEEN ('01-DEC-01', '11-JAN-01') → 10.677

Date Function	Use
MONTHS_BETWEEN (date1, date2)	Find number of months between two dates.
ADD_MONTHS (date, m)	Adds calender months to a date.
NEXT_DAY (date, 'day')	Finds next occurrence of a day from given date.
LAST_DAY (date)	Returns last day of the month.
ROUND (date [, 'format'])	Rounds date to nearest day, month, or year.
TRUNC (date [, 'format'])	Truncates date to nearest day, month, or year.

Figure 5-43   Date functions.

The function ADD_MONTHS adds the number of months supplied as a second argument. The number must be an integer value. It can be positive or negative. For example, if an item is shipped today and payment is due in three months, what is the payment date?

ADD_MONTHS ('06-SEP-00', 3) → '06-DEC-00'

The function NEXT_DAY returns the next occurrence of a day of the week following the date supplied. The second argument could be a number in quotes or a day of the week. For example,

NEXT_DAY ('06-SEP-00', 'SUNDAY') → '10-SEP-00'
NEXT_DAY ('06-SEP-00', 'WEDNESDAY') → '13-SEP-00'

The function LAST_DAY finds the last date of the month for the date supplied as an argument. If something is due by the end of this month, what is that date? For example,

LAST_DAY ('06-SEP-00') → '30-SEP-00'

The ROUND function rounds a date based on the format specified. If a format is missing, rounding is to the nearest day. For example,

ROUND ('20-NOV-00', 'MONTH') → '01-DEC-00'

Here, the date is nearest to December 1. In the next example the date is nearest to the first of next year.

ROUND ('20-NOV-00', 'YEAR') → '01-JAN-01'

The TRUNC function truncates the date to the nearest format specified. Truncation to the nearest month returns the first day of the date's month, and truncation to the nearest year returns the January 1 of the date's year. For example,

TRUNC ('20-OCT-00', 'MONTH') → '01-OCT-00'
TRUNC ('20-OCT-00', 'YEAR') → '01-JAN-00'

Other functions.   The NVL function converts a null value to actual value supplied as an argument. The second argument is enclosed within the single quotation marks for columns with DATE, CHAR, or VARCHAR2 data types. The general syntax is

NVL (column, value)

If the value in a column is null, convert it to a specified value. For example,

NVL (Commission, 0)
NVL (HireDate, '01-JAN-00')
NVL (MidTerm, 'No Grade entered)

If the commission amount is null, convert it to 0. If HireDate is not entered, use '01-JAN-00' for it.

Now, we will revisit our query in Fig. 5-17, where we tried to add Salary and Commission columns. The total was blank for employees without a value in the Commission column. Remember, any number plus NULL is equal to null. Let us rewrite the same query using the NVL function (see Fig. 5-44).

```
SQL> SELECT Lname, Salary+NVL (Commission, 0) TOTSAL
  2     FROM employee;

LNAME                 TOTSAL
---------------   ---------
Smith                 300000
Houston               160000
Roberts                75000
McCall                 66500
Dev                   100000
Shaw                   27500
Garner                 50000
Chen                   35000

8 rows selected.
```

Figure 5-44   Arithmetic with the NVL function.

The DECODE function is a conditional statement type of function. If you are familiar with any programming language like Visual Basic 6 (If-ElseIf or Select-Case structures) or C (if-else if or switch-case structures), you will understand the function with ease. The DECODE function tests a column or expression, and for each of its matching value provides an action. The general syntax is

DECODE (column / expr, value1, action1,
[value2, action2, ...,]
[, default]);

The default action is provided for any value that does not match values checked within the function. If the default value is not used, a null value is returned for nonmatching values. For example, we are displaying new salary for all employees based on their PositionId. PositionId 1 gets a 20% raise, 2 gets 15%, 3 gets 10%, 4 gets 5%, and others get no increment at all. If the last default salary is not included in the statement, the new salary for employees with PositionId 5 is displayed as null.

```
SELECT Lname, Salary, DECODE (PositionId, 1, Salary * 1.2,
                                        2, Salary * 1.15,
                                        3, Salary * 1.1,
                                        4, Salary * 1.05,
                                        Salary) "New Salary"
FROM employee;
```

Conversion functions.   The conversion functions convert data from one data type to another. The Oracle server follows some rules to convert data type implicitly. For example, if you enter a character string that includes a valid number, the Oracle server can successfully convert CHAR data to NUMBER data. If you enter a date as string and use the default date format 'DD-MON-YY', the Oracle server can perform CHAR to DATE conversion successfully. It is advisable to use explicit data conversion functions for successful and reliable queries. The three conversion functions in Fig. 5-45 are used for explicit data type conversion in queries.

The TO_CHAR function converts a number or date value to its character equivalent. The format argument is enclosed in single quotation marks, and the

Conversion Function	Use
TO_CHAR (number / date [, format])	Converts a number or a date to VARCHAR2 value based on format provided.
TO_NUMBER (char [, format])	Converts a character value with valid digits to number using format provided.
TO_DATE (char [, format])	Converts a character value to date value based on format provided. Default format is DD-MON-YY.

Figure 5-45   Conversion functions.

format value is case sensitive. Figures 5-46 to 5-49 describe common formats for number and date with examples. In Fig. 5-49, fm is used to remove unnecessary spaces or zeroes in the front or in the middle.

Nested Functions

The single-row functions can be nested within each other in an expression. In nested functions, the innermost function is evaluated first and then evaluation moves outward. The outermost function is evaluated last. There is no limit on layers of nesting for single-row functions. Evaluate the following expression:

NEXT_DAY (ADD_MONTHS (TRUNC (TO_DATE
('05/06/2000', 'MM-DD-YYYY'), 'MONTH'), 2), 'TUESDAY')

(Did you get July 4, 2000 in date format?)

Number Format	Meaning
9	Number of 9s to determine width. Ex. 99999
0	Displays leading zeroes. Ex. 099999
$	Displays floating dollar sign. Ex. $99999
.	Displays decimal point in specified location. Ex. 99999.99
,	Displays comma in specified location. Ex. 99,999
PR	Puts negative numbers in parenthesis. Ex. 99999PR

Figure 5-46   Number formats.

```
SQL> SELECT Lname, Fname,
  2     TO_CHAR (Salary, '$999,999') AS SALARY,
  3     FROM employee;


LNAME            FNAME            SALARY
--------------- ---------------- ---------
Smith            John             $265,000
Houston          Larry            $150,000
...


11 rows selected.
```

Figure 5-47   TO_CHAR with number format.

Date/Time Format	Meaning
YYYY	Four-digit year.
Y, YY, or **YYY**	Last one, two, or three digits of the year.
YEAR	Year spelled out.
Q	Quarter of the year.
MM	Two-digit month.
MON	First three letters of the month.
MONTH	Month name using nine characters. Left characters padded with spaces.
RM	Month in Roman numerals.
WW or **W**	Week number of year or month.
DDD, DD, or **D**	Day of year, month, or week.
DAY	Name of day using nine characters. Left charactes padded with blanks.
DY	Three letter abbreviated name of day.
DDTH	Ordinal number such as seventh.
DDSP	Spelled out number.
DDSPTH	Spelled out ordinal number.
HH, HH12, or **HH24**	Hour of day, or hour (0–12), or hour (0–23)
MI	Minute (0–59).
SS	Second (0–59).
SSSSS	Seconds from midnight (0-86399)
"of"	String in quotes is displayed in the result.

Figure 5-48   Date/time formats.

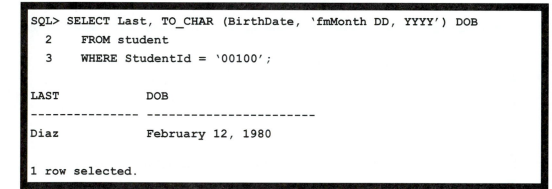

```
SQL> SELECT Last, TO_CHAR (BirthDate, 'fmMonth DD, YYYY') DOB
  2     FROM student
  3     WHERE StudentId = '00100';


LAST              DOB
--------------    ----------------------
Diaz              February 12, 1980


1 row selected.
```

Figure 5-49   TO_CHAR with date format.

Group Functions

The group functions perform an operation on a group of rows and return one result. Look at the EMPLOYEE and STUDENT tables.

- Who makes the lowest salary?
- Who got the maximum commission?

- What is the company's total payroll?
- How many students started in the Winter 2000 semester?

It is easy to look through small tables and find answers. In a real-life situation, most tables have hundreds and thousands of records. It is efficient to look through them with simple queries and group functions.

While using the functions described in Fig. 5-50, the keywords DISTINCT or ALL can be used before listing the argument in parenthesis. The keyword ALL, which means use all values including duplicate values, is the default. DISTINCT tells the function to use nonduplicate values only.

Let us write a query to find the total, average, highest, and lowest salaries from the EMPLOYEE table. Figure 5-51 shows use of group functions on a number column Salary.

Now we will try the MAX and MIN functions on a date field. Which student from the STUDENT table was born first and who was born last? Check out Fig. 5-52. The MAX of a date returns the latest date, and the MIN of a date returns the earliest date. If you use the function on a character column, MAX will return the last name alphabetically and MIN will return the first name alphabetically.

Group Function	Use
SUM (column)	Finds sum of all values in a column, ignores null values.
AVG (column)	Finds average of all values in a column, ignores null values.
MAX (column / expression)	Finds maximum value and ignores null values.
MIN (column / expression)	Finds minimum value and ignores null values.
COUNT (* / column / expression)	Counts number of rows including nulls for *. Counts non-null values if column or expression is used as argument.

Figure 5-50   Group functions.

```
SQL> SELECT SUM (Salary), AVG (Salary), MAX (Salary), MIN (Salary)
  2     FROM employee;

SUM(SALARY) AVG(SALARY) MAX(SALARY) MIN(SALARY)
----------- ----------- ----------- -----------
     741000       92625      265000       24500
```

Figure 5-51   Group functions on a number column.

```
SQL> SELECT MAX (BirthDate) AS YOUNGEST, MIN (BirthDate) AS OLDEST
  2    FROM student;


YOUNGEST   OLDEST
--------- ---------
12-DEC-82 20-OCT-70
```

Figure 5-52   Group function on a date column.

In Figs. 5-53 and 5-54, uses of the COUNT function on an entire row and a column are given. When rows are counted in the EMPLOYEE table, all eight employees' rows are counted. When Commission column values are counted, the null values are ignored, giving us only commissioned employees. We can change that using the NVL function:

COUNT (NVL (Commission, 0))

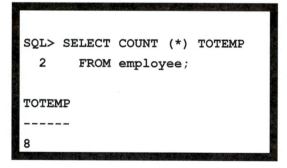

```
SQL> SELECT COUNT (*) TOTEMP
  2    FROM employee;


TOTEMP
------
8
```

Figure 5-53   COUNT all rows.

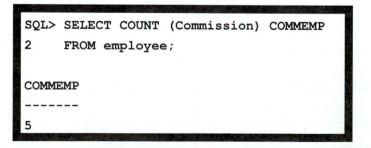

```
SQL> SELECT COUNT (Commission) COMMEMP
  2    FROM employee;


COMMEMP
-------
5
```

Figure 5-54   COUNT values in a column.

Null values in Commission columns are replaced with 0 in the query, and an 8 is returned from the query.

Question: Which of the following queries will return a higher average from the Commission column?

SELECT AVG (Commission) FROM EMPLOYEE;
SELECT AVG (NVL (Commission, 0) FROM EMPLOYEE;

Answer: The first query, because it adds all commissions and divides the total by 5, whereas the second query divides the total by 8.

GROUPING DATA

The rows in a table can be divided into different groups to treat each group separately. The group functions can be applied to individual groups in the same fashion they are applied to all rows. The GROUP BY clause is used for grouping data. The general syntax is

```
SELECT column, groupfunction (column)
    FROM tablename
    [WHERE condition(s)]
    [GROUP BY column/expression]
    [ORDER BY column/expression [ASC/DESC]];
```

- When you include a group function and the GROUP BY clause in your query, the individual column(s) appearing in SELECT must also appear in GROUP BY.
- The WHERE clause can still be used to restrict data before grouping.
- The WHERE clause cannot be used to restrict groups.
- A column alias cannot be used in a GROUP BY clause.
- The GROUP BY column does not have to appear in a SELECT query.
- When a column is used in the GROUP BY clause, the result is sorted in ascending order by that column by default. In other words, GROUP BY has an implied ORDER BY. You can still use an ORDER BY clause explicitly to change the implied sort order.

In the next few figures, you will see the effect of a GROUP BY clause on queries with group functions.

As you see in Fig. 5-55, the DeptId column is automatically sorted because it is used in the GROUP BY clause. The DeptId column is not necessary in the SELECT clause, but it is a good idea to include it there so that the counts make sense.

```
SQL> SELECT DeptId, COUNT (*)
  2     FROM employee
  3     GROUP BY DeptId;


  DeptId COUNT(*)
--------- --------
      10        3
      20        2
      30        2
      40        1
```

Figure 5-55   COUNT rows by group.

The WHERE clause can be used to restrict rows, but it cannot be used to restrict groups, as you see in Fig. 5-56. In Fig. 5-56, we are trying to see buildings with four or more rooms. We can fix this problem with a new clause, which is used to restrict groups.

```
SQL> SELECT Building, COUNT (*)
  2       FROM location
  3       WHERE COUNT (*) >= 4
  4       GROUP BY Building;

WHERE COUNT (*) >= 4
      *
ERROR at line 3:
ORA-00934: group function is not allowed here
```

Figure 5-56   Invalid WHERE clause.

HAVING Clause

The HAVING clause can restrict groups. The WHERE clause restricts rows; the GROUP BY clause groups remaining rows; the Group function works on each group, and the HAVING clause keeps the groups that match the group condition.

In the following sample query (Fig. 5-57), the WHERE clause filters out the building named Kennedy, the rest of the rows are grouped by the building names Gandhi and Nehru, the groups function COUNT counts the number of rows in each

```
SQL> SELECT Building, COUNT (*) AS ROOMS
  2      FROM location
  3      WHERE UPPER (Building) <> 'KENNEDY'
  4      GROUP BY Building
  5      HAVING COUNT (*) >= 4;


BUILDING ROOMS
-------- -----
Gandhi         5
```

Figure 5-57 HAVING Clause

group, and the HAVING clause keeps groups with four or more rows, that is, the Gandhi building with five rows/rooms.

NESTING GROUP FUNCTIONS

The single-row functions can be nested to many levels, but the group functions can only be nested to two levels. For example,

> **SELECT SUM (ActualCount) FROM crssection GROUP BY CourseId;**

will find the total enrollment for each CourseId. If you use this output for an outer function in a nested scenario as follows, you will get a different answer.

> **SELECT MAX (SUM (ActualCount)) FROM crssection GROUP BY CourseId;**

The answer returned by this query is 85, because the outer query takes totals by each CourseId and finds the one with the largest value.

REVISITING SUBSTITUTION VARIABLES

The substitution variables can be used in queries other than the INSERT query. They can substitute for column names, table names, expressions, or text. Their use is to generalize queries by inserting them

- In the SELECT statement in place of a column name.
- In the FROM clause in place of a table name.

- In the WHERE clause as column expression or text.
- As an entire SELECT statement.

If a variable is to be reused within a query without getting a prompt again for the same variable, double-ampersand (&&) substitution variable is used. The user gets only one prompt for the variable with &&, and the value of the variable is then used for more than one time. In Fig. 5-58, the variable *columnname* is used twice, once in the SELECT statement in column list and then again as the sort column in ORDER BY clause. The user gets only one prompt for the variable.

```
SQL> SELECT Lname, Fname, &&columnname
  2     FROM employee
  3     WHERE DeptId = 30
  4     ORDER BY &columnname;


Enter value for columnname: Salary


LNAME           FNAME           SALARY
--------------- --------------- ---------
Shaw            Jinku              24500
Garner          Stanley            45000

2 rows selected.
```

Figure 5-58   The && substitution variable.

DEFINE COMMAND

A variable can be defined at the SQL>Prompt. The variable is assigned a value that is held until the user exits from SQL*Plus or the user undefines it. The general syntax is

DEFINE variable [= value]

For example,

DEFINE last = Shaw

The variable *last* gets the value *Shaw*, which can be used as a substitution variable in a query. For example,

SELECT * FROM employee WHERE Lname = '&last';

DEFINE last will return the value of the variable if it already has a value, otherwise Oracle will display an "UNDEFINED" message.

The variable's value can be erased with the UNDEFINE command. For example,

UNDEFINE last

The variable is valid during a session only. If you want to use a variable every time you log in, it can be defined in your login script file (login.sql).

IN A NUTSHELL . . .

- The Data Manipulation Language (DML) statements INSERT, UPDATE, and DELETE are used for data maintenance.
- Date and character values are enclosed in single quotation marks. Oracle is case sensitive about character values and format sensitive about date values. The default date format is DD-MON-YY. Number values are not enclosed in quotation marks.
- To use a character value with a single quotation mark, use the single quotation mark twice in succession.
- Null values can be entered implicitly or explicitly. A null value is an unknown and undefined value.
- A foreign key value in a child table is allowed only if the value exists in the parent table's primary key.
- A user can create interactive scripts by using substitution variables and the ACCEPT command.
- The UPDATE statement is used to change existing data.
- Conditions use column, value, relational, logical, and other special operators.
- Every INSERT, DELETE, and UPDATE command is successful provided integrity constraints are not violated.
- A constraint can be dropped permanently or disabled temporarily using the ALTER TABLE statement. The disabled constraint can be enabled later.
- The SELECT query is used to retrieve data from the existing tables.
- The wild card * is used to display all columns with the SELECT query.

- The DISTINCT clause in front of a column name returns nonduplicate values only.
- A column alias is used for more descriptive column headings because the column names are abbreviated. By default, column names are displayed as column headings in data retrieval.
- A column alias can also be used for expressions. A column alias is enclosed in double quotation marks to preserve case or to use special characters.
- The concatenation characters ‖ join a column or a character string to another column.
- The arithmetic operations are performed on number data types for data manipulation. Whatever is in parentheses is performed first. Operators * and / have higher precedence than + and − operators.
- Use of a null value in an arithmetic expression returns a null result.
- The logical operators AND and OR are used to evaluate multiple conditions.
- The special comparison operator LIKE is used when wild cards % and _ are used for pattern matching. The wild card % represents 0 or more characters. The wild card _ represents one character only.
- The order of rows in a table is undefined. The rows can be displayed in a sorted order with the ORDER BY clause in the SELECT statement. The default sort order is ascending. The DESC keyword is used for sorting in descending order.
- Single-row functions work on each row individually. They include character functions, number functions, date functions, data conversion functions, and other general functions. All functions take 0 or more arguments and return one value back.
- The NVL function converts a null value to another specified value provided as its second argument.
- The DECODE function is similar to the if-else if or case structures in the programming languages.
- In an expression with nested single-row functions, the innermost function is performed first and the outermost function is done last.
- The SYSDATE function is an Oracle function that returns the current date from the system. SYSDATE is very useful in date arithmetic.
- The group functions work on a group of rows to return one result per group. The rows can be grouped together by using the GROUP BY clause with a SELECT query.
- The WHERE clause is used to restrict rows; similarly, the HAVING clause is used to restrict groups.
- The group functions can be nested like single-row functions. The nesting is limited to two functions for group functions.

- The && substitution variable is used to reuse a variable's value without getting prompted again.
- The DEFINE and UNDEFINE commands are used at the SQL*Plus prompt to assign and erase a variable's value.

EXERCISE QUESTIONS

True/False:

1. In Oracle, character values are enclosed in single quotation marks, but date and number values are not.
2. The default date format is DD-MM-YYYY.
3. A null value is not defined or not known.
4. The UPDATE statement without the WHERE clause can update all rows in the table.
5. A column alias is enclosed in double quotation marks to display a column name in uppercase only.
6. The AND operator returns a TRUE result if one of the two conditions is true.
7. Only two single-row functions can be nested in an expression.
8. The WHERE clause restricts individual rows, but the HAVING clause restricts groups.
9. There is no restriction in deleting a row from a parent table.
10. The DELETE statement without a WHERE clause has the same effect as TRUNCATE.

List output from the following queries. (Use the tables created in the Chapter 4 Lab Activity.)

1. SELECT FIRST || " || LAST "Name", BIRTHDATE FROM STUDENT;
2. SELECT DISTINCT (MAJORID) FROM STUDENT;
3. SELECT * FROM LOCATION ORDER BY BUILDING, CAPACITY DESC;
4. SELECT LNAME, FNAME, (SYSDATE − HIREDATE) DAYS FROM EMPLOYEE ORDER BY DAYS;
5. SELECT BUILDING, AVG (CAPACITY)
   FROM LOCATION
   GROUP BY BUILDING
   HAVING AVG (CAPACITY) > 25;

Which of the following queries will result in an error message? Why? (Use the tables created in the Chapter 4 Lab Activity.)

1. SELECT LASTNAME, FIRSTNAME FROM STUDENT;
2. SELECT DEPTID, COUNT (*) FROM EMPLOYEE;
3. INSERT INTO DEPT VALUES (90, RESEARCH, NULL, NULL);
4. SELECT DEPTID, SUM (SALARY)
   FROM EMPLOYEE

GROUP BY DEPTID
WHERE SUM (SALARY) > 200000;
5. DELETE FROM DEPT WHERE DEPTID = 10;

LAB ACTIVITY

Write queries for the following. (Use tables created in Chapter 4 Lab Activity.)
1. Display all employee names (last name and first name separated by a comma and a space) and salary with appropriate column aliases.
2. Display all employees who do not get any commission.
3. Display unique building names from LOCATION (see Fig 3-9).
4. Count the total number of rooms in LOCATION.
5. Count the distinct building names in LOCATION.
6. Find course sections in the Spring 2001 term where enrollment has not reached the maximum.
7. Display all student names and birth dates. Display birth dates with the format '20 OCTOBER, 1970'.
8. Find the total, average, highest, and lowest salaries by each department.
9. Display the total number of dependents for each employee for employees who have at least two dependents.
10. Give a 10% raise to employee number 111.
11. Delete department number 30 from the department table. If it is not successful, write down your suggestion to make it work.
12. Display only the year value from each employee's hire date.
13. Find average employee commission. (a) Ignore nulls. (b) Do not ignore nulls.
14. Add 12 months to each employee's hire date to find his/her first anniversary date.
15. For each course ID, display the actual enrollment in descending order.

6

Multiple Tables:
Joins and Sub-queries

IN THIS CHAPTER . . .

- You will learn to design queries based on multiple tables.
- You will retrieve related data from various tables in a database.
- Different types of table joins are discussed.
- Independent query results are combined together by using set operators.
- Subqueries or nested queries are introduced for data retrieval.
- Subqueries are used with other data management and data definition language statements.

In Chapter 5, you learned data retrieval techniques to obtain data from a single table with the SELECT query. You also learned the use of various clauses and functions used in SELECT statements. In this chapter, we will expand on what we have learned in the previous chapter. You will learn to create queries where data is retrieved from more than one table or more than one single query. For example, a student's demographic information is in the STUDENT table and a student's faculty advisor's information is in the FACULTY table. An employee's name is in the EMPLOYEE table, but an employee's department's information ID is in the DEPT table, an employee's dependents are in the DEPENDENT table, and an employee's salary grade is in the SALARYLEVEL table. Sometimes, you can accomplish tasks by joining two or more tables, by joining a table to itself, or by using an output from one query as data in another query. A majority of the relational algebraic operations are covered in this chapter to see how they are implemented in Oracle 8.

JOIN

When the required data exist in more than one table, related tables are joined using a join condition. The join condition combines a row in one table with a row in another table based on the same values in the common attributes. In most cases, the common attributes are the primary key in one table and a foreign key in another. In this section, you will be introduced to different types of joins based on the join condition used.

Product

The product is also known as a Cartesian product. A product results from a multitable query where the join condition is not used or is not valid. The product operation joins each row in the first table with each and every row in the second table. The product normally results in an output with a large number of rows and is not very useful. Whenever retrieving data from more than one table, you must use a valid join condition to avoid a product! You would perform a product operation if you were looking to find all possible combinations of rows from two tables. In Fig. 6-1, you will see an example of a product where all students and faculty members are matched unconditionally. The last name is selected from the STUDENT table and a name is selected from the FACULTY table. There is no join condition provided. The result is 48 rows because the product of two tables with m and n rows respectively returns $m \cdot n$ rows. The STUDENT table has 6 rows, and the FACULTY table has 8 rows, hence the result ($6 \cdot 8 = 48$ rows). If you were looking for each student's last name and his/her faculty advisor's name, you would use a join condition using the STUDENT table's foreign key FacultyId and the FACULTY table's primary key FacultyId to find matching rows.

The Cartesian product is covered in this section, but it is not a join operation. There is no join without a join condition. There are four types of joins:

- Equijoin
- Nonequijoin
- Outer join
- Self-join

```
SQL> SELECT Last, Name
  2      FROM student, faculty;


LAST                NAME
---------------     ---------------
Diaz                Jones
Tyler               Jones
Patel               Jones
...
Diaz                Williams
Tyler               Williams
Patel               Williams
...


48 rows selected.
```

Figure 6-1   Cartesian product.

Equijoin

The equijoin is a join with a join condition involving common attributes from two tables. If you need to get information about a student from the STUDENT table and corresponding information about the faculty advisor from the FACULTY table, you would use the following syntax:

> *SELECT columnnames*
> *FROM tablenames*
> *WHERE join condition;*

The column names include columns from both tables separated by commas, table names are all table names separated by commas, and the join condition is a condition that includes common attributes/columns from each table. The join condition normally (but not always) includes a foreign key attribute from one table and a referenced primary key column from the other table. Suppose you want to get a student's last name, the student's first name, the faculty advisor's name, and the faculty advisor's phone number. You would get them from the STUDENT and FACULTY tables. The common attribute in both tables is FacultyId, which is the foreign key in the child STUDENT table and the primary key in the parent FACULTY table. The join condition will return the requested information from rows in two tables where the FacultyId value is same. The row without a match is not selected by the query. Figure 6-2 shows the result from an equijoin.

In Fig. 6-2, you see that all students are picked from the STUDENT table, but faculty members are picked based on the FacultyId in the student rows. The faculty member *Collins* (FacultyId = 333) is not selected because there is no match in the STUDENT table. On the other hand, *Chang* (FacultyId = 555) is picked twice because it appears twice as a value in the foreign key attribute of STUDENT table.

The Cartesian product is rarely useful, but Equijoin is a very important operation in the database querying. Another thing to be noted is the use of *tablename.columnname*. When columns are retrieved from more than one table, the use of a table name qualifier in front of the column name tells Oracle to retrieve that column from the table specified. Oracle is pretty smart about it. If a

```
SQL> SELECT student.Last, student.First,
  2         faculty.Name, faculty.Phone
  3    FROM student, faculty
  4   WHERE student.FacultyId = faculty.FacultyId;

LAST             FIRST             NAME             PHONE
---------------  ----------------  ---------------  -----
Diaz             Jose              Mobley           529
Tyler            Mickey            Chang            587
Patel            Rajesh            Jones            525
Rickles          Deborah           Chang            587
Lee              Brian             Sen              579
Khan             Amir              Williams         533

6 rows selected.
```

Figure 6-2 Equijoin.

column exists in only one of the two tables involved in the query, it is not necessary to use a table name as a qualifier. If a column exists in both tables involved, you must use the table name qualifier. The join condition in an equijoin will have the table name qualifier. Because the join condition usually has the same column names from two tables, without a qualifier the column names become ambiguous. The qualifier actually improves performance because you are telling the Oracle server where to go to find that column. Remember that the two join columns need not have the same name.

Sometimes the required information is in more than two tables. The FROM clause will have all tables needed, and the WHERE clause will have more than one join condition. If you need to join n tables, you would need $n - 1$ join conditions. In our NamanNavan Corporation database, an employee's demographic information is in the EMPLOYEE table. The EMPLOYEE table has three foreign keys: PositionId, referencing the POSITION table; QualId, referencing the QUALIFICATION table, and DeptId, referencing the DEPT table. You would need to join 4 tables to retrieve information from all those tables. That means the query will have $4 - 1 = 3$ join conditions. The query will look like the one in Fig. 6-3. For simplicity, we will join 3 tables using 2 join conditions. (*Note:* There

```
SQL> SELECT employee.Lname, employee.Fname,          name of colum and qualifier
  2          dept.DeptName, position.PosDesc
  3     FROM employee, dept, position      — name of table
  4    WHERE employee.DeptId = dept.DeptId  — condition
  5      AND employee.PositionId = position.PositionId;

LNAME             FNAME             DEPTNAME        POSDESC
---------------   ---------------   ------------    ----------
Smith             John              Finance         President
Houston           Larry             Marketing       Manager
Roberts           Sandi             Finance         Manager
McCall            Alex              InfoSys         Programmer
Dev               Derek             InfoSys         Manager
Shaw              Jinku             Sales           Salesman
Garner            Stanley           Sales           Manager
Chen              Sunny             Finance         Accountant

8 rows selected.
```

Figure 6-3 Multiple joins.

is a limit on the number of join conditions within a query. Try joining 4 tables and you will receive a "No rows selected" message.)

The multiple-join example selects information from 3 tables using a query with 2 join conditions. If you look at the query, the table qualifiers are used quite a few times. There is a way to shorten and simplify this query.

Table Aliases

In Chapter 5 you learned about column aliases, which are used for renaming column headings in a query. Table aliases are used to avoid using lengthy table names over and over again in a query. A table alias can be from 1 to 30 characters long. Normally, very short alias names are used to shorten the query and save some keystrokes. The table alias appears in the FROM clause of the SELECT query. A table name is written followed by a space, and then a table alias is supplied. Though they appear after the SELECT clause, alias names can be used as qualifiers for column names. All table aliases are valid only in the SELECT query, where they are named and used. In Fig. 6-4, you will see the same query you saw

```
SQL> SELECT e.Lname, e.Fname,
  2         d.DeptName, p.PosDesc
  3     FROM employee e, dept d, position p
  4     WHERE e.DeptId = d.DeptId
  6     AND e.PositionId = p.PositionId;


LNAME              FNAME             DEPTNAME        POSDESC
---------------    ---------------   ------------    ----------
Smith              John              Finance         President
Houston            Larry             Marketing       Manager
Roberts            Sandi             Finance         Manager
McCall             Alex              InfoSys         Programmer
Dev                Derek             InfoSys         Manager
Shaw               Jinku             Sales           Salesman
Garner             Stanley           Sales           Manager
Chen               Sunny             Finance         Accountant

8 rows selected.
```

Figure 6-4 Table aliases.

in Fig. 6-3 with table aliases. The results obtained from queries in Fig. 6-3 and Fig. 6-4 are exactly the same, but the query in Fig. 6-4 is shortened by the use of table aliases.

Additional Conditions

In addition to join conditions, you may use additional conditions using the AND operator to restrict information. Suppose you want to see the information of Fig. 6-4 for employees belonging to department number 10 only. Fig. 6-5 shows the use of additional condition with the AND operator, where the information is displayed for DeptId = 10 only. The three tables are joined for employees in department 10, which results in 3 rows instead of all 8 employee rows.

```
SQL> SELECT e.Lname, e.Fname,
  2          d.DeptName, p.PosDesc
  3     FROM employee e, dept d, position p
  4     WHERE e.DeptId = d.DeptId
  5     AND e.PositionId = p.PositionId
  6     AND e.DeptId = 10;


LNAME             FNAME            DEPTNAME       POSDESC
---------------   --------------   ------------   ----------
Smith             John             Finance        President
Roberts           Sandi            Finance        Manager
Chen              Sunny            Finance        Accountant

3 rows selected.
```

(handwritten annotation: definition)

Figure 6-5 Additional condition with join.

Nonequijoin

There is no matching attribute in the SALARYLEVEL table for the Salary attribute in the EMPLOYEE table. The only possible relationship between two tables is between the Salary attribute of the EMPLOYEE table and the LowerLimit and UpperLimit attributes in the SALARYLEVEL table. The join condition for these tables can be written using any operator other than the = operator. That is why it is called the nonequijoin. Fig. 6-6 is an example of a nonequijoin.

```
SQL> SELECT e.Lname, e.Fname, s.LevelNo
  2    FROM employee e, salarylevel s
  3    WHERE e.Salary BETWEEN s.LowerLimit AND s.UpperLimit;


LNAME            FNAME             LEVELNO
--------------   ---------------   ---------
Smith            John                 4
Houston          Larry                4
Roberts          Sandi                3
McCall           Alex                 3
Dev              Derek                3
Shaw             Jinku                1
Garner           Stanley              2
Chen             Sunny                2

8 rows selected.
```

Figure 6-6   Nonequijoin.

The Nonequijoin condition of Fig. 6-6 could have been written as

e.Salary >= s.LowerLimit AND e.Salary <= s. Upper Limit;

If you look at the SALARYLEVEL table, none of the salaries appears in more than one level. In other words, there is no overlapping. None of the employees makes a salary that is not included in the range of salaries. Due to these two reasons, each employee appears once in the result. Note that none of the columns are ambiguous, so table aliases are not necessary (but they are used in the query here).

Outer Join

You saw in the equijoin that the rows from two tables are selected only if the common attribute values are same in both tables. If a value in one table does not have a matching value in the other table, it is not joined. Fig. 6-2 displayed all students from the STUDENT table and their advisors from the FACULTY table. Some of the faculty members are not any student's advisor, so they did not get picked. Suppose you also want to see all those faculty advisor names. You would change your query's join condition and create a join known as an outer join.

The table that does not contain the matching value is known as the deficient table. In our case the deficient table is the STUDENT table because it does not contain all faculty ID. The outer join uses the (+) operator in the join condition on the deficient side. The (+) operator can be used on any side of the join condition, but it can't be used on both sides in one condition. The general syntax is

> *SELECT tablename1.columnname, tablename2.columnname*
> *FROM tablename1, tablename2*
> *WHERE tablename1.columnname (+) = tablename2.columnname;*

The join condition will look different if the (+) operator is used on the right hand side. For example,

> *WHERE tablename1.columnname = tablename2.columnname (+);*

Figure 6-7 shows an outer join using STUDENT and FACULTY tables. The outer join operator (+) is used on the STUDENT side because it is the deficient table. Compare the output in Fig. 6-7 with the output in Fig. 6-2. The outer join also includes three faculty members who are not advisors to any students.

```
SQL> SELECT student.Last || ', ' || student.First AS STUDENT,
  2          faculty.Name AS ADVISOR
  3     FROM student, faculty
  4    WHERE student.FacultyId (+) = faculty.FacultyId;


STUDENT                             ADVISOR
--------------------------------    ----------------
Diaz, Jose                          Mobley
Tyler, Mickey                       Chang
Patel, Rajesh                       Jones
Rickles, Deborah                    Chang
Lee, Brian                          Sen
Khan, Amir                          Williams
                                    Vajpayee
                                    Rivera
                                    Collins


9 rows selected.
```

Figure 6-7 Outer join.

Self-Join

A self-join is joining a table to itself. It sounds meaningless, but think about it using this scenario. In the EMPLOYEE table, EmployeeId is the primary key attribute that describes each entity. For example, EmployeeId 200 represents employee Shaw, Jinku. The table also has another attribute called Supervisor, which has the ID of an employee's supervisor. How can you find the name of the supervisor for an employee? You can look up the supervisor ID, go to the EmployeeId column to find its match, and then read the name. This is easier said than done. A self-join is one join that is not so easy to understand.

When a table is joined to itself, two copies of the same table are created. They are treated like any two tables, and a join is produced from those two copies. Let us explain that by using the EMPLOYEE table. The following operations are performed in a self-join of Fig. 6-8:

- Two copies of EMPLOYEE tables are created, *e* and *s*.
- An employee's last name is picked from the *e* table and the corresponding Supervisor ID is retrieved.

```
SQL> SELECT e.Lname || ' reports to ' || s.Lname
  2    FROM employee e, employee s
  3    WHERE e.Supervisor = s.EmployeeId


E.LNAME||' reports to '||S.LNAME
-------------------------------
Houston reports to Smith
Roberts reports to Smith
McCall reports to Dev
Dev reports to Smith
Shaw reports to Garner
Garner reports to Smith
Chen reports to Roberts

7 rows selected.
```

Figure 6-8 Self-join.

- The matching EmployeeId is found from the *s* table. The first employee in the *e* table does not have a supervisor and so is not picked.
- The last name from the *s* table is retrieved based on the EmployeeId.

In short, the table is looked at twice, once for the employee and once for the supervisor.

SET OPERATORS

In Chapter 1, you learned about union, intersection, and difference operations. If you recall, these operations are possible on "union compatible" tables. The implementation of these operations is through the use of set operators. The union compatibility is achieved or the set operations are performed on results from two independent queries. The output from both queries must return same number of columns and respective columns must have similar domain. Figure 6-9 lists all set operators and their use.

Set Operator	Use
UNION	It returns all rows from both queries, but duplicate rows are not displayed.
UNION ALL	It returns all rows from both queries and displays all duplicate rows.
INTERSECT	It returns all rows that appear in both queries' results.
MINUS	It returns rows that are returned by the first query minus rows returned by the second query.

Figure 6-9   Set operators.

The general syntax for any set operation is

> *SELECT Query1*
> *Set operator*
> *SELECT Query2;*

where *Set operator* is one of the four set operators described in Fig. 6-9.

We will use the STUDENT table from the Indo–US College database, which has all student records. Now, we will use another temporary table called WORKER (Fig. 6-10), which contains staff members of the college and also student workers.

UNION

The UNION operator takes output from two queries and returns all rows from both results. The duplicate rows are displayed only once. All six student's rows are

WORKER (Workerld, Last, First)

Workerld	Last	First
00110	Ward	Tim
00111	Turner	Jackie
00103	Rickles	Deborah
00113	Malone	Teresa
00105	Khan	Amir
00107	Feliciano	Donna

Figure 6-10   Temporary table WORKER.

selected from the first query and four rows are selected from the second query. Two rows from the second query are duplicate rows, and they are not repeated (ID 00103 and ID 00105). Figure 6-11 lists all students and staff members in the result.

```
SQL> SELECT StudentId ID, Last, First
  2      FROM student
  3  UNION
  4  SELECT WorkerId ID, Last, First
  5      FROM worker;


ID    LAST             FIRST
----- ---------------- ----------------
00100 Diaz             Jose
00101 Tyler            Mickey
00102 Patel            Rajesh
00103 Rickles          Deborah
00104 Lee              Brian
00105 Khan             Amir
00110 Ward             Tim
00111 Turner           Jackie
00113 Malone           Teresa
00107 Feliciano        Donna
```

Figure 6-11   UNION operation.

UNION ALL

The UNION ALL operation is similar to the UNION operation. The only difference is that UNION ALL operation displays duplicate rows also. If you find UNION ALL of the STUDENT and WORKER tables, you will get six rows from the first query and six rows from the second query (see Fig. 6-12).

```
SQL> SELECT StudentId ID, Last, First
  2    FROM student
  3  UNION ALL
  4    SELECT WorkerId ID, Last, First
  5    FROM worker;


ID    LAST             FIRST
----- ---------------- ----------------
00100 Diaz             Jose
00101 Tyler            Mickey
00102 Patel            Rajesh
00103 Rickles          Deborah
00104 Lee              Brian
00105 Khan             Amir
00110 Ward             Tim
00111 Turner           Jackie
00103 Rickles          Deborah
00113 Malone           Teresa
00105 Khan             Amir
00107 Feliciano        Donna
```

Figure 6-12 UNION ALL operation.

INTERSECT

The INTERSECT operation works on output from two separate queries and returns rows that appear in both outputs. In the student and worker example, INTERSECT will return students who are also workers in the college.

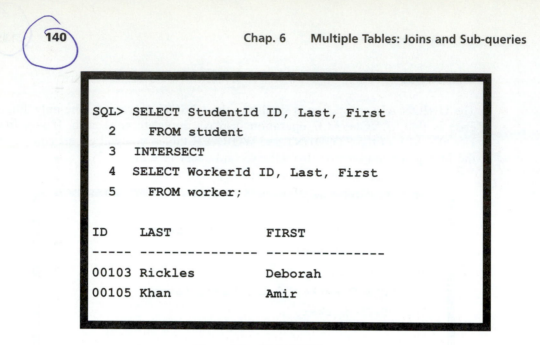

```
SQL> SELECT StudentId ID, Last, First
  2      FROM student
  3   INTERSECT
  4   SELECT WorkerId ID, Last, First
  5      FROM worker;


ID     LAST             FIRST
-----  ---------------  ---------------
00103  Rickles          Deborah
00105  Khan             Amir
```

Figure 6-13 INTERSECT operation.

In Fig. 6-13, you see only two student rows, which are the only ones in the WORKER table.

MINUS

The MINUS operation is same as the difference operation covered in Chapter 1. When MINUS is performed on outputs from two queries, the result is the rows in the first query's result that are not in the second query's result. Remember that the STUDENT table minus the WORKER table is not same as the WORKER table minus the STUDENT table. Figure 6-14 is an example of a minus operation in which the result includes students who are not workers. Figure 6-15 shows workers who are not students.

SUB-QUERY

Sub-queries are also known as nested queries. A sub-query is normally a SELECT query within one of the clauses in another SELECT query. Very powerful queries can be designed by using simple sub-queries. A sub-query is very useful when a query based on a table depends on the data in that table itself. The sub-query can be used within a WHERE, HAVING, or FROM clause of another SELECT query. The subqueries are of two types:

- Single-row sub-query: a sub-query that returns only one row of data.
- Multiple-row sub-query: a sub-query that returns more than one row of data.

```
SQL> SELECT StudentId ID, Last, First
  2     FROM student
  3   MINUS
  4   SELECT WorkerId ID, Last, First
  5     FROM worker;

ID    LAST             FIRST
----- ---------------- ----------------
00100 Diaz             Jose
00101 Tyler            Mickey
00102 Patel            Rajesh
00104 Lee              Brian
```

Figure 6-14 MINUS operation.

```
SQL> SELECT WorkerId ID, Last, First
  2     FROM worker
  3   MINUS
  4   SELECT StudentId ID, Last, First
  5     FROM student;

ID    LAST             FIRST
----- ---------------- ----------------
00110 Ward             Tim
00111 Turner           Jackie
00113 Malone           Teresa
00107 Feliciano        Donna
```

Figure 6-15 MINUS operation.

Single-Row Sub-query

The general syntax is

> SELECT columnlist
> FROM tablename
> WHERE columnname operator
> (SELECT columnlist
> FROM tablename
> WHERE condition);

There are certain rules you have to follow while creating a sub-query:

- The sub-query must be enclosed within a pair of parentheses.
- The ORDER BY clause cannot be used in a sub-query.
- The sub-query is used on the right-hand-side of the condition.

When a statement is written with a sub-query, the inner query is executed first. The inner query returns a value or a set of values to the outer query. Next the outer query is executed with the result from the inner query.

In Fig. 6-16, you see a sub-query based on two tables. It returns a result similar to the one in Fig. 6-5. The sub-query example is substituted for a join condition and an additional condition of Fig. 6-5. The inner query finds the DeptId 10 from the DEPT table based on DeptName = 'FINANCE'. The result is used in the condition of the outer query, which returns employees in DeptId = 10.

```
SQL> SELECT e.Lname, e.Fname,
  2     FROM employee e
  3     WHERE e.DeptId =
  4          (SELECT DeptId
  5            FROM dept WHERE UPPER (DeptName) = 'FINANCE');


LNAME            FNAME
---------------  ---------------
Smith            John
Roberts          Sandi
Chen             Sunny

3 rows selected.
```

Figure 6-16 Sub-query using two tables.

A sub-query can be based on one table. Suppose you want to find out names of employees who make more salary than employee McCall (EmployeeId = 433). You will find out the salary for the employee in the inner query and then use it in the outer query. For example,

```
SELECT Lname, Fname, Salary
    FROM employee
    WHERE Salary > (SELECT Salary
                        FROM employee WHERE EmployeeId = 433);
```

Creating a Table Using a Sub-Query

You can create a table by using a nested SELECT query. The query will create a new table and populate it with the rows selected from the other table. The general syntax is

```
CREATE TABLE tablename
AS
SELECT query;
```

When a new table is created with a sub- or nested query, the primary key constraint is not transferred to the new table from the existing table. The NOT NULL constraint does get transferred to the new table. For example,

```
CREATE TABLE depart20
AS
SELECT EmployeeId, Lname, Fname, Salary
FROM employee
WHERE DeptId = 20;
```

In this example, the new table DEPART20 is created. The SELECT query selects all employees belonging to department 20. The new table contains only four attributes as selected by the inner query.

INSERT Using a Sub-Query

An existing table can be populated with a sub-query. The table must already exist to insert rows into it. The general syntax is

```
INSERT INTO tablename [(column aliases)]
SELECT columnnames FROM tablename WHERE condition;
```

For example,

> INSERT INTO depart30 (Empno, Last, First)
> SELECT EmployeeId, Lname, Fname
> FROM employee WHERE DeptId = 30;

In the example, all employees in department 30 are selected and the other table is populated with those employees only. The VALUE clause is not used with the sub-query. The column aliases from INSERT are optional. The column aliases can be used with columns in the SELECT query itself.

UPDATE Using a Sub-Query

Another use of a sub-query is in updating of data. If an employee is leaving and his/her position, supervisor, and salary information are to be given to another existing employee, UPDATE can be performed with a sub-query. The general syntax is

> *UPDATE tablename*
> *SET (columnnames) =*
>   *(SELECT-FROM-WHERE sub-query)*
> *WHERE condition;*

For example,

> UPDATE employee
> SET (PositionId, Supervisor, Salary) =
>   (SELECT PositionId, Supervisor, Salary
>   FROM employee WHERE EmployeeId = 135)
> WHERE EmployeeId = 200;

In the example above, Jinku Shaw (EmployeeId = 200) gets the position, supervisor, and salary of Stanley Garner (EmployeeId = 135). The inner query returns three values, which are assumed by three columns in the outer query. You must be careful with the order of columns in both inner and outer queries. The order of columns must be same in both queries.

DELETE Using a Sub-Query

A row or rows from a table can be deleted based on a value returned by a sub-query. The general syntax is

> *DELETE FROM tablename*
> *WHERE Columnname =*
>   *(SELECT-FROM-WHERE sub-query);*

For example, if a corporation decides to close the Marketing department in Los Angeles and all employees in the department are to be removed from the database, you will use a DELETE statement with a sub-query:

```
DELETE FROM employee
    WHERE DeptId =
        (SELECT DeptId FROM dept
            WHERE UPPER (DeptName) = 'MARKETING');
```

Multiple-Row Sub-Query

A multiple-row sub-query returns more than one row. The operators used in single-row sub-queries ($=, <>, >, >=, <$ and $<=$) cannot be used with multiple-row sub-queries. Figure 6-17 shows special operators used with multiple-row sub-queries.

Operator	Use
IN	Equal to any of the values in a list.
ALL	Compare the given value to every value returned by the sub-query.
ANY	Compare the given value to each value returned by the sub-query.

Figure 6-17   Multiple-row sub-query operators.

Let us look at examples of sub-queries returning more than one row.

```
SELECT StudentId, Last, First
    FROM student
    WHERE FacultyId IN (SELECT FacultyId
        FROM faculty WHERE DeptId = 1);
```

The inner query returns two values (111, 123). You cannot use the $=$ operator, but the IN operator is more appropriate.

The ANY operator can be used in combination with other relational operators.

- $<$ANY means less than the maximum value
- $=$ANY is similar to IN
- $>$ANY means more than the minimum value

The ALL operator can also be used with other relational operators.

- $>$ALL means more than the maximum value
- $<$ALL means less than the minimum value

For example,

```
SELECT EmployeeId, Lname, Fname, Salary
    FROM employee
    WHERE Salary >ANY
        (SELECT Salary FROM employee WHERE PositionId = 2)
    AND PositionId <> 2;
```

The inner query returns (150000, 75000, 80000, 45000). >ANY means more than the minimum salary 45000 with PositionId not equal to 2. Rows with EmployeeId 111 and 433 are selected.

Another example is

```
SELECT EmployeeId, Lname, Fname, Salary
    FROM employee
    WHERE Salary <ALL
        (SELECT AVG (Salary) FROM employee GROUP BY DeptId);
```

The inner query returns values (125000, 73250, 34750, 150000). <ALL means the employee with salary less than the minimum in the list of values. From the original table in Chapter 3, only one row, and EmployeeId 200 and salary of 24500, would be picked.

TOP-N ANALYSIS

Top-N queries are used to sort rows in a table and then find the first N largest values or first N smallest values. For example, you want to find out the bottom 5 salaries in a company, the top 3 room capacities, or the last 10 employees hired by a company.

The Top-N query uses an ORDER BY clause to sort rows in ascending or descending order. The sorted rows are numbered with a pseudo-column named ROWNUM. If the rows are sorted in ascending order by the Top-N column, the smallest value of the Top-N column is at the top of the list. The largest value of the Top-N column is at the top of the list if the rows are sorted in descending order by the Top-N column. You can display the required number of rows based on the ROWNUM.

In Fig. 6-18, Capacity is the Top-N column. The rows in the LOCATION table are sorted in descending order to get largest capacity at the top of the list. The condition ROWNUM <= 5 selects row numbers 1 through 5, the top 5 capacities. The inner SELECT statement in the FROM clause is used as the data source for the outer SELECT statement. Such a sub-query is known as an **inline view.** The inline view is a sub-query that can be given an alias name that you can use in a SQL statement, just like a table alias. An inline view is not stored as an object like the other views created with a CREATE VIEW statement (covered in Chapter 7). A sub-query may not use the ORDER BY clause, but an inline view may.

In Fig. 6-19, SALARY is the Top-N column. The rows in the EMPLOYEE table are sorted in ascending order, bringing the lowest salaries to the top. The condition ROWNUM <= 3 retrieves the three lowest salaried employees.

```
SQL> SELECT ROWNUM, Building, RoomNo, Capacity
  2     FROM (SELECT Building, RoomNo, Capacity FROM location
  3            ORDER BY Capacity DESC)
  4     WHERE ROMNUM <= 5;


  ROWNUM BUILDING    ROOMNO  CAPACITY
--------- ----------  ------  ---------
       1 Kennedy     204         50
       2 Nehru       301         50
       3 Nehru       309         45
       4 Kennedy     206         40
       5 Kennedy     202         35

5 rows selected.
```

Figure 6-18 Top-N analysis.

```
SQL> SELECT ROWNUM, Lname, Fname, Salary
  2     FROM (SELECT Lname, Fname, Salary FROM employee
  3            ORDER BY Salary)
  4     WHERE ROMNUM <=3;

ROWNUM LNAME             FNAME               SALARY
------ ---------------- ---------------- ---------
     1 Shaw              Jinku                24500
     2 Chen              Sunny                35000
     3 Garner            Stanley              45000

3 rows selected.
```

Figure 6-19 Top-N analysis.

Important Note about Top-N Analysis

Top-N analysis is explained here in a way that is consistent with the Oracle on-line training documentation. If you cannot perform this analysis with the inline view, which contains an ORDER BY clause in the inner query, the alternate way to perform the analysis is by creating a view with the GROUP BY clause in the SELECT query. The GROUP BY clause contains an implicit ORDER BY operation in the ascending order. You will be able to select the Top N rows from the view based on the ROWNUM pseudo-column. The limitation is that only < and <= operators are allowed with the pseudo-column ROWNUM. As the implied sort is in the ascending order, the lowest values get moved to the top and you will be able to get only the bottom N values. The views are covered in the next chapter.

Here is an alternate Solution for the problem in Fig 6-19:

```
CREATE VIEW empsal_vu
AS
SELECT Lname, Salary
GROUP BY Salary, Lname;

SELECT ROWNUM AS Rank, Lname, Salary
FROM empsal_vu
WHERE ROWNUM <= 3;
```

IN A NUTSHELL . . .

- Two tables can be joined with a common attribute. Usually, the common attributes are a foreign key in one table and the primary key in the other table that is referenced.
- If a join condition is not used in a multiple-table query, it results in a Cartesian product.
- Four types of joins in Oracle are equijoin, nonequijoin, outer join, and self-join.
- It is possible to join more than two tables in a database. You need $n - 1$ conditions to join n tables.
- Table aliases are used in a query to avoid typing long table names in a query. The table aliases are known only in the query where they are defined.
- An additional condition is used along with the join condition to filter out some rows.
- A nonequijoin has a join condition that does not use the equality (=) operator.
- An outer join is achieved by using the (+) operator on the deficient table's side in the join condition. The outer join also selects rows without a matching row in another table involved in join operation.
- A self-join joins a table with itself.
- The set operators UNION, UNION ALL, INTERSECT, and MINUS are used to connect output from two individual SELECT queries. Both

query outputs must return the same number of columns with similar domains.

- The sub-queries are also known as nested queries. In a nested query, the inner query is executed first. The output from the inner query is used by the outer query.
- A single-row sub-query returns one row of data, whereas a multiple-row sub-query returns more than one row of data.
- The inner query in the sub-query is enclosed within parentheses, and it cannot use the ORDER BY clause.
- A sub-query can be used with the SELECT statement. It also is used with CREATE to create a table and populate it with rows in another table.
- A sub-query is also used with INSERT, DELETE, and UPDATE data manipulation queries.
- The multiple-row sub-queries use the special operators IN, ALL, and ANY.
- Top-N analysis is used to sort rows in ascending or descending order and then to find the top N rows for the N highest or lowest values. The inline view is used for a Top-N analysis.

EXERCISE QUESTIONS

True/False:
1. You need at least two different tables for a join.
2. If a table has three rows and another table has four rows, their product will have seven rows.
3. The common attribute in two tables must have same name in order to join them.
4. A table alias is known in the query in which it is created.
5. In an outer join, the (+) operator can be used on any side of the = sign. It cannot be on both sides of a join condition.
6. The set operator UNION does not repeat duplicate rows, but UNION ALL does.
7. TableA MINUS TableB is same as TableB MINUS TableA all the time.
8. A sub-query uses a SELECT query as the inner query.
9. =ANY means IN.
10. >ALL means greater than the minimum value.

Define the following terms and give one example of each.
1. Equijoin
2. Outer join
3. Self-join
4. Top-N query
5. Product

Answer the following questions.

1. How does a Top-N query work?
2. In which situations would you use a self-join?
3. When is it appropriate to use an outer join?
4. State various uses of a sub-query.
5. How would you join five tables in a database theoretically?

LAB ACTIVITY

1. Use the NamanNavan Corporation database tables to design the following queries.
   (Use the spooling method to capture all queries and results in the CHAP6SP1.LST file.)
   (a) Display all employee names and their department names.
   (b) Find the name of the supervisor for employee number 433.
   (c) Find all employees' full names (lastname, firstname format) and their supervisor's name.
   (d) Find each employee's salary information and level based on the salary.
   (e) Display each employee's name, department name, position description, and qualification description. Do you find any problem here?
   (f) Find all employees in the sales department by using a nested query.
   (g) Display employee names and qualification description using an outer join.
   (h) Find out the names and hire dates of the two employees who have been in the company the longest.
   (i) Create a new table, EMP30, and populate it, using an existing table and a sub-query.
   (j) Who is the department manager for the Sales department? Use a nested query.

2. Use the Indo–US College database tables to design the following queries.
   (Use the spooling method to capture all queries and results in the CHAP6SP2.LST file)
   (a) Display a student's full name along with his/her advisor's name.
   (b) Get a student's name, major description, and faculty advisor's name.
   (c) Get all Spring 2001 course IDs with course title and actual enrollment for courses that have reached the maximum allowable enrollment.
   (d) Get Spring 2001 course sections with the faculty member assigned to teach the class. Include course sections without faculty assigned to them.
   (e) Find Spring 2001 course sections with the top three enrollment counts.
   (f) Find all information regarding classrooms using a nested query.
   (g) Create a new table, SP01SECT, for Spring 2001 semester course sections using a sub-query.

7

Advanced Features: Objects, Transactions, and Control

IN THIS CHAPTER . . .

- You will learn about various Oracle objects.
- You will use syntax to create, use, and remove views, sequences, synonyms, and indexes.
- Advantages of transaction control are discussed.
- Users, roles, and privileges for data control are covered.

You have learned to create, modify, remove, use and manipulate an Oracle object called a table. In this chapter, you will learn about other objects such as a view, sequence, synonym, and index. Some of these objects are based on the underlying Oracle tables, and some of them are independent objects. In this chapter, you will also learn about transactions and their advantages. You will be able to grant and revoke rights on your own objects to other users.

VIEWS

A view is an Oracle object that gives the user a logical view of data from an underlying table or tables. You can restrict what users can view by allowing them to see only a few attributes/columns from a table. When a view is created from more than one table, the user can view data from the view without using join conditions

Simple View	Complex View
It is based on one table.	It is based on one or more tables.
It does not contain functions.	It may contain functions.
It does not contain grouped data.	It may contain grouped data.
Data manipulation is possible from a simple view.	Data manipulation is not always possible with a complex view.

Figure 7-1 Types of views.

and complex conditions. The application programs can access data with data independence. Same data can be viewed differently with different views. In short, a view is a logical representation of a subset of data from one or more tables. A view is stored as a SELECT statement in the data dictionary. There are two types of views: simple and complex.

Figure 7-1 shows the difference between simple and complex views. A simple view is based on one table, it does not contain functions or grouped data, and data manipulation is always possible through it. On the other hand, a complex view is based on one or more tables, it may contain functions and/or grouped data, and data manipulation is not always possible through it.

Creating a View

The general syntax is

```
CREATE [OR REPLACE] [FORCE/NOFORCE] VIEW viewname
    [column aliases]
AS SELECT-sub-query
[WITH CHECK OPTION [CONSTRAINT constraintname]]
[WITH READ ONLY];
```

A view is created with a SELECT sub-query. The sub-query cannot use an ORDER BY clause, but a view can.

In the syntax, OR REPLACE replaces an existing view with the same name, if it already exists. The FORCE option creates a view even if the underlying table does not exist. The default is NOFORCE, which does not create a view if the underlying table does not exist. The column aliases are used for the columns selected by the sub-query. The number of aliases must match the number of columns selected by the sub-query. The SELECT sub-query can use all clauses except for the ORDER BY clause. The WITH CHECK OPTION applies to the WHERE clause condition in the sub-query. It allows insertion and update of rows based on the condition that satisfies the view. The CHECK OPTION can also be given an optional constraint name. The WITH READ ONLY option is to make sure that the data in the underlying table are not changed.

```
SQL> CREATE VIEW stuvu500
  2     (StuId, LastName, FirstName, Advisor, MajorNum)
  3      AS SELECT StudentId, Last, First, FacultyId, MajorId
  4         FROM student
  5      WHERE MajorId = 500
  6      WITH CHECK OPTION;
View created.


SQL> SELECT * FROM stuvu500;

STUID LASTNAME            FIRSTNAME           ADVISOR  MAJORNUM
----- ---------------     ----------------    -------- ---------
00101 Tyler               Mickey                  555       500
00103 Rickles             Deborah                 555       500


2 rows selected.
```

Figure 7-2 Simple view.

Figure 7-2 shows creation and use of a simple view. View *stuvu500* is based on the STUDENT table for students with MajorId = 500. The column aliases are given for all four columns selected by the sub-query. The user with access to the view can use it like any other table. The user does not even know the existence of the STUDENT table and other attributes in it. A user sees what you let him/her see!

In Fig. 7-3, you will see a complex view that is created from two tables, EMPLOYEE and DEPT. It uses group functions and derived data. It is not possible to modify data through this view. Notice that the column aliases are given by the sub-query and not by the outer CREATE VIEW statement. If a view by the name *deptsalvu* already existed, this statement would have overwritten the previous view.

There are more rules related to the data manipulation on a view:

- No data manipulation on derived columns.
- No data manipulation on the ROWNUM pseudocolumn.
- No insertion if the base table contains columns with the NOT NULL constraint, which is not selected by the view.
- No insertion if derived columns exist in the view.

```
SQL> CREATE OR REPLACE VIEW deptsalvu
  2     AS SELECT d.DeptName DEPARTMENT, MIN (e.salary) LOWEST,
  3               MAX (e.salary) HIGHEST, AVG (e.Salary) AVERAGE
  4        FROM employee e, dept d
  5        WHERE e.DeptId = d.DeptId
  6        GROUP BY d.DeptName;
View created.


SQL> SELECT * FROM deptsalvu;

DEPARTMENT      LOWEST    HIGHEST   AVERAGE
------------ --------- --------- ---------
Finance          35000    265000    150000
InfoSys          66500     80000     73250
Marketing        24500     45000     34750
Sales           150000    150000    150000

4 rows selected.
```

Figure 7-3   Complex view.

Figure 7-2 has a simple view with a WITH CHECK OPTION clause. It applies to the WHERE condition in the sub-query. The user cannot change the MajorNum because the view accesses rows with MajorId = 500 only. The UPDATE of MajorNum to any other value will result in

ORA-01402: view WITH CHECK OPTION where-clause violation.

Similarly, data manipulation on a view with a WITH READ ONLY clause results in an Oracle server error.

A user can list names of views under his/her ownership by using

SELECT view_name FROM user_views;

Removing a View

A user who owns a view or has the privilege to remove it, can remove a view. The removal of a view does not affect data in the underlying table. When a view is removed, a "View dropped" message is displayed. The general syntax is

DROP VIEW viewname;

For example,

DROP VIEW stuvu500;

SEQUENCES

A sequence is an Oracle object that is used to create sequence of numbers. Many times you create a table with surrogate key attribute such as StudentId, FacultyId, or EmployeeId. These attributes have a numeric data type. Sequencing is a perfect solution for generating values for such numeric attributes. These values can be unique or recycled again, depending upon the attribute. If a sequence is used for a primary key attribute, it better be unique! A sequence is not limited to the primary key values but can be used on any numeric attribute. The general syntax is

```
CREATE SEQUENCE sequencename
    [INCREMENT BY n]
    [START WITH s]
    [MAXVALUE x / NOMAXVALUE]
    [MINVALUE m / NOMINVALUE]
    [CYCLE / NOCYCLE]
    [CACHE c / NOCHACHE] [ORDER / NOORDER];
```

In this syntax, note the following:

INCREMENT BY n	The increment value for the number generation is n. The default increment is 1.
START WITH s	The starting value for the sequence is s. The default start value is 1.
MAXVALUE x	The maximum value for the generated number is x.
NOMAXVALUE	The sequence will keep generating until the maximum allowable value $1 \cdot 10^{27}$ is generated in the ascending order. NOMAXVALUE is -1 for a sequence with descending order (default).
MINVALUE m	The minimum value for the generated number is m.
NOMINVALUE	The minimum value is 1 for a sequence in ascending order and -10^{26} for a sequence in descending order (default).
CYCLE	The sequence continues generating after reaching the maximum or minimum value.
NOCYCLE	No more generation after maximum or minimum value is reached (default).
CACHE c	The oracle server generates numbers in advance and stores them in a cache memory area for improved system performance. The default value for c is 20. If the user provides a number, the server will store that many numbers in the cache memory.
NOCACHE	The server does not store any sequence numbers in memory in advance.

ORDER   The numbers are generated in chronological order.

NOORDER   The numbers are not generated in chronological order.

Suppose you want to create a sequence to generate EmployeeId values in the EMPLOYEE table. The last EmployeeId in the table is 543. You want to start at 544, and the numbers will be incremented by 1 for every new employee (see Fig. 7-4A).

```
SQL> CREATE SEQUENCE employee_EmployeeId_seq
2         INCREMENTED BY 1
3         START WITH 544
4         NOMAXVALUE
5         NOCACHE;
Sequence created.
```

Figure 7-4A   Sequence.

Let us create another sequence to generate MajorId numbers. If you view the table, the last used value is 600 and each value is in steps of 100. In the future, you want to add numbers in steps of 10, starting with 610. The data type of the attribute is NUMBER (3), so the maximum allowable value should be 999 (see Fig. 7-4B).

```
SQL> CREATE SEQUENCE major_MajorId_seq
2         INCREMENTED BY 10
3         START WITH 610
4         MAXVALUE 999
5         NOCACHE;
Sequence created.
```

Figure 7-4B   Sequence.

You can get information about sequences you have created by using the following query:

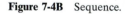

```
SELECT sequence_name, last_number,
        max_value, min_value, increment_by FROM user_sequences;
```

There are pseudo-columns named CURRVAL and NEXTVAL to reference sequence values. The NEXTVAL column returns the next available number in the sequence. It always returns a unique value. The CURRVAL column gives the current sequence value. The NEXTVAL column is used with the sequence name (e.g. *sequencename.NEXTVAL*) to generate the next sequence number. When the new sequence number is generated, the current number is stored in the CURRVAL. The NEXTVAL must be used at least once in order to get the value from CURRVAL.

```
SQL> INSERT INTO major (MajorId, MajorDesc)
  2       VALUES (major_MajorId_seq.NEXTVAL,
  3              'MS - Computer Science');
1 row created.
```

Figure 7-5 Using a sequence.

As the sequence *major_MajorId_seq* is used for the first time in Fig. 7-5, the first value generated is the starting value defined for the sequence. The new major will get value 610. You can check it with the pseudo-column CURRVAL from Oracle's dummy table DUAL. For example,

SELECT major_MajorId_seq.CURRVAL FROM dual;

The number returned by CURRVAL is 610, which is the last value generated by NEXTVAL.

Let us try to find the current value in the *employee_EmployeeId_seq* sequence. Remember that the sequence is created, but it is not used yet.

SELECT employee_EmployeeId_seq.CURRVAL FROM dual;

The query will result in an error message because CURRVAL does not have a value yet, and it is not defined.

When you create a sequence and specify an increment value, you still may find gaps in the values generated. The gaps are created due to one of the following reasons:

- You generated sequence values in an INSERT statement and a rollback occurred.
- You used the CACHE option, and the system crashed. The numbers brought to memory in advance are lost.
- A sequence is used in more than one table or used on more than one attribute.
- The rows are deleted from a table.

Modifying a Sequence

You can modify a sequence if you own it or you have the ALTER privilege. The modified sequence does not affect past numbers, only numbers generated in the future. Modification of the sequence does not allow you to change the START WITH option. The sequence has to be removed and re-created to change the starting value. The maximum value cannot be set to a number less than the current number. You can change the increment, maximum value, minimum value, CYCLE/NOCYCLE, ORDER/NOORDER, and CACHE/NOCACHE options while modifying a sequence. The general syntax is

```
ALTER SEQUENCE sequencename
    [INCREMENT BY n]
    [MAXVALUE x / NOMAXVALUE]
    [MINVALUE m / NOMINVALUE]
    [CYCLE / NOCYCLE]
    [CACHE c / NOCHACHE]
    [ORDER / NOORDER];
```

For example, see the sequence modification in Fig. 7-6.

```
SQL> ALTER SEQUENCE employee_EmployeeId_seq
  2        INCREMENT BY 1
  3        MAXVALUE 9999
  4        NOCACHE;
Sequence altered.
```

Figure 7-6   Modifying a sequence.

Dropping a Sequence

You can drop a sequence with the DROP SEQUENCE statement. A removed sequence cannot be used anymore. For example,

```
DROP SEQUENCE major_MajorId_seq;
```

SYNONYMS

Sometimes object names are very long. If a query uses the object's name more than once, the user has to type that long name that many times. You already know the use of table aliases to shorten table names. Table aliases are useful, but they are only known in the query where they are created. They are not stored as separate objects in your database. The synonyms are Oracle objects, which are used to create alternative names for tables, views, sequences, and other objects. Even when you have privilege to use another user's table, you have to qualify the table name with the user's name. You can create a synonym for *username.tablename*. The general syntax is

**CREATE [PUBLIC] SYNONYM SynonymName
For ObjectName;**

A synonym name must be different than all other objects owned by the user. For example, Fig. 7-7 creates a synonym for a sequence.

```
SQL> CREATE SYNONYM emp_id
  2   FOR employee_EmployeeId_seq;
Synonym created.
```

Figure 7-7   Synonym.

If you have rights equivalent to a Database Administrator DBA, you can create a public synonym. A public synonym is available to all users. For example,

**CREATE PUBLIC SYNONYM reg
FOR nshah.registration;**

A short synonym REG is used for table REGISTRATION owned by user *nshah*.
A synonym can be removed by using DROP SYNONYM statement. Only a DBA privilege allows you to remove a public synonym. For example,

DROP SYNONYM emp_id;

INDEX

An index is another Oracle object that is used for faster retrieval of rows from a table. An index can be created explicitly by using the CREATE INDEX statement or implicitly by Oracle. Once an index exists for a table, the user does not have to open or use the index with a command or a statement. The Oracle server uses the index to search for a row rather than scanning through the entire table. Indexing reduces the search time and disk I/O. All indexes are maintained separately from the table they are based on. Creating and removing an index does not affect the table at all. When a table is dropped, all indexes based on that table are also removed.

Implicit indexes are created when PRIMARY KEY or UNIQUE constraints are defined. Such an index gets the name of the constraint. A user can create explicit indexes based on non-primary-key or nonunique columns for faster row access. The general syntax is

> *CREATE INDEX indexname*
> *ON tablename (columnname1 [, columnname2]...);*

For example, Fig. 7-8 creates an index based on student's last name to speed up searching of student information when the search involves last name as a secondary key.

```
SQL> CREATE INDEX student_Last_idx
  2    ON student (Last);
Index created.
```

Figure 7-8   Explicit index.

You would create an index based on a column if a column is used often in querying or joining, has a big domain of values, or contains many NULL values. When an index is created, it does not store NULL values, so the searching would eliminate those rows. Do not create an index for a very small table, a column not used often in queries, or a table that gets updated often. Every insert and delete in a table updates the index.

TRANSACTIONS

Oracle groups your queries into transactions. A transaction consists of a series of Data Manipulation Language (DML) statements, one Data Definition Language (DDL) statement, or one Data Control Language (DCL) statement. Due to transaction control, Oracle guarantees data consistency. The transaction control statements give you flexibility to undo transactions or write transactions to the disk. Transactions provide consistency in case of a system failure.

In Oracle, your transactions start with the first SQL statement you type. The transaction ends when one of the following occurs:

- A COMMIT or ROLLBACK transaction control statement is used.
- A DDL (CREATE, ALTER, DROP, RENAME, or TRUNCATE) statement is executed (automatic commit).
- A DCL (GRANT or REVOKE) statement is executed (automatic commit).
- A user properly exits (commit).
- The system crashes (rollback).

Once a transaction ends, the new transaction starts with your next statement.

Transaction Control Statement	Action
COMMIT	Ends the current transaction and writes all changes permanently to the disk.
SAVEPOINT n	Marks a point in the current transaction.
ROLLBACK [TO SAVEPOINT n]	Ends the current transaction by undoing all changes if a TO SAVEPOINT clause is not used. It rolls back to the save point if the clause is used, removing the save point and any changes after the save point.

Figure 7-9   Transaction control statements.

There is an environment variable AUTOCOMMIT. By default, it is set to OFF. A user can set it to ON by typing

SET AUTOCOMMIT ON

When AUTOCOMMIT is set to ON, every DML statement is written to the disk as soon as it is executed, every DML statement is committed implicitly, and there is no rollback with AUTOCOMMIT. AUTOCOMMIT can be toggled back to OFF for an explicit COMMIT. If the system crashes, any statements after the last COMMIT are rolled back, so partial changes to tables are not permanently written.

When a user is in the middle of a transaction, he/she can review all DML statements' results by using SELECT queries. After reviewing the results, the user can decide to roll back or commit. The user is getting results from database's temporary storage area. The other users with privileges on the same table cannot view the results of the DML queries until the user commits the changes. Until the user commits all the changes, the rows with DML statements are locked. Other users cannot change the data in the locked rows. By committing, the user changes become permanent, all users can view the results, locks are released, save points are removed, and other users can manipulate affected rows.

In Fig. 7-10, you see a transaction with five DML statements. The transaction has started right after the first COMMIT and the user is at the end of fifth DML

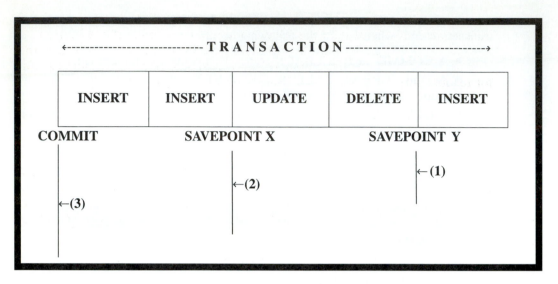

Figure 7-10   Transaction control.

statement. If user types COMMIT, all five DML statements' results are written to the disk permanently. If the user types ROLLBACK TO SAVEPOINT Y, one INSERT after SAVEPOINT Y is rolled back and save point Y is removed [see (1) in the figure]. If the user types ROLLBACK TO SAVEPOINT X, save point Y is removed along with save point X. Three DML statements—UPDATE, DELETE, and INSERT—are rolled back [see (2) in the figure]. If the user types ROLL-BACK, the entire transaction is rolled back and a new transaction begins with the new statement [see (3) in the figure].

- **Question:** If you typed a DML statement that failed during execution, is it still part of your transaction? Is it committed? Is it rolled back?
- **Answer:** The statement is rolled back, and it is not part of your transaction anymore.

Read Consistency and Locking

Oracle implements read consistency. When any DML statement is issued for a database, the old copy of the database before changes is written into a rollback segment. The user who is making changes with DML statements can see the changes with SELECT query from the database. All other users see the snapshot of the database before changes from the rollback segment. The data is consistent to all other users. When the changes are committed, the changes are available to all users as the rollback segment copy is removed and the space is freed for another use later. If the changes are rolled back, the old copy of the database is loaded into the rollback segment again.

A user does not have to write any explicit statements to lock tables. Oracle uses automatic locking with the least restrictions to provide sharing of data with integrity. Two share modes used by Oracle are *exclusive* and *share lock*. Exclusive lock prevents sharing a resource until lock is released. Share lock allows sharing for reading purposes. Oracle also allows a manual lock on data.

LOCKING ROWS FOR UPDATE

When a user supplies a SELECT query, the rows are not locked. Oracle does not lock rows for viewing. As you know, the rows with DML query changes are locked if the changes are not committed. Suppose you want to view rows and also change them. You would want to lock those rows for future changes. You would use SELECT–FOR UPDATE statement for such manual locks. The general syntax is

> *SELECT columnnames*
> *FROM tablenames*
> *WHERE condition*
> *FOR UPDATE OF columnnames*
> *[NOWAIT];*

The use of *columnnames* in FOR UPDATE OF does not mean that the locking is at the column level. The entire row is locked. The column names are used just for information. The NOWAIT clause, which tells the user instantaneously if another user has already locked the row, is optional. If you do not use NOWAIT in the statement, you will have to wait for the row's release. You will not be able to do any processing on it until then.

Figure 7-11 shows the display of a row in the EMPLOYEE table and its locking. Once the row is locked, you can proceed to change the employee's salary and

```
SQL> SELECT Lname, Fname, Salary, Commission
  2     FROM employee
  3     WHERE EmployeeId = 111
  4     FOR UPDATE OF Salary, Commission
  5     NOWAIT;


LNAME            FNAME              SALARY COMMISSION
---------------- ---------------- --------- ----------
Smith            John                265000      35000
```

Figure 7-11   SELECT–FOR UPDATE OF.

commission. If another user tries to update this row, he/she will have to wait for you to release the lock by committing.

CONTROLLING ACCESS

A user's access needs to be controlled in a shared and multiuser Oracle environment. A user's access to the database can be restricted, and a user may or may not be allowed to use certain objects in the database. The security is classified into two types:

1. *System security* defines access to the database at the system level. It is implemented by assigning a username and password, allocating disk space, and providing a user with the ability to perform system operations.
2. *Database security* defines a user's access to various objects and the tasks a user can perform on them.

The Database Administrator (DBA) is the most trusted user, and a DBA has all the privileges. A DBA can create users, assign them privileges, and even drop users.

User, Role, and System Privileges

The DBA can create a user by using a CREATE USER statement. Once a user is created and a password is assigned, the user needs privileges to do anything. The general syntax is

CREATE USER username
IDENTIFIED BY password;

The statement in Fig. 7-12 creates a user and assigns a password. A user can change his/her own password with an ALTER USER statement. For example,

ALTER USER riley IDENTIFIED BY houston;

```
SQL> CREATE USER riley
  2    IDENTIFIED BY basket;
User created.
```

Figure 7-12   Creating a user.

```
SQL> GRANT create table, create sequence, create view
  2    TO riley;
Grant succeeded.
```

Figure 7-13 Granting privileges.

There is a pool of 90 system privileges available for the DBA to grant them to users. The DBA assigns privileges based on the level of a user. Figure 7-13 shows privileges assigned to user *riley*. The general syntax is

GRANT privilege1 [, privilege2...]
TO username1 [, username2...];

Once user *riley* gets privileges to go with the user name and password, he/she can use those privileges immediately. Some users can be assigned more or fewer privileges than the other users.

In a company, there are many users of different levels. Many of them from the same level need the same privileges. It is easier to assign privileges to each level and then assign users to that level. The levels are called roles. A role is similar to a group used by network operating systems. A DBA creates a role by using a CREATE ROLE statement. Then the privileges are granted to the role, and at last the role is granted to the users. For example, Fig. 7-14 has statements to grant privileges to a newly created role and then to grant that role to users.

```
SQL> CREATE ROLE enduser;
Role created.


SQL> GRANT create table, create view, create sequence
  2     TO enduser;
Grant succeeded.


SQL> GRANT enduser TO riley, miller, carter;
Grant succeeded.
```

Figure 7-14 Using roles.

Object Privileges

An object privilege specifies what a user can do with a database object such as a table, a sequence, or a view. There are eight object privileges, and each object has a set of privileges out of the total of eight privileges. The following is a list of all object privileges:

- ALTER
- INSERT
- UPDATE
- DELETE
- SELECT
- REFERENCES
- INDEX
- EXECUTE

A user has his/her objects in his/her own schema. An owner has all possible privileges on the owner's objects. A user can grant privileges on objects from the user's own schema to other users or roles. The grantee can also be given further rights to grant the same privileges to other users on your object. The general syntax is

```
GRANT objectprivileges [(columnnames)] / ALL
    ON objectname
    To user/role/PUBLIC
    [WITH GRANT OPTION];
```

Where *objectprivileges* are some of the eight privileges. If all privileges are to be granted, ALL can be used instead of specifying each privilege separately. Columns on which privileges are granted are specified by *columnnames*. The keyword PUBLIC grants privileges to all users. The WITH GRANT OPTION clause allows the grantee to grant privileges to other users and roles.

Figure 7-15 illustrates two GRANT statements. The first statement gives only *select* privileges on table *student* to user *riley*. The second statement gives *select, insert,* and *update* privileges on table *employee* to two users, *jgundy* and *riley*. The second statement also gives two users privilege to pass those privileges to other users. If user *nshah* is granting these privileges, the grantee will have to qualify the table name with a user name to use it. For example, *nshah.employee*

The user *vgundy* can use table *employee* with the following query:

```
SELECT * FROM nshah.employee;
```

Another approach will be to create a synonym for the table. For example,

```
CREATE SYNONYM emp FOR nshah.employee;
```

```
SQL> GRANT select
  2     ON student
  3     TO riley;
Grant succeeded.



SQL> GRANT select, insert, update
  2     ON employee
  3     TO jgundy, riley
  4     WITH GRANT OPTION;
Grant succeeded.
```

Figure 7-15 Granting object privileges.

The privileges can be granted, and they can be taken away. If a user granted privileges with a WITH GRANT OPTION to another user and that user passed on those privileges, the REVOKE statement takes privileges not only from the grantee but also from users who are granted privileges by the grantee. The general syntax is

> REVOKE privilege1 [, privilege2...] / ALL
> ON objectname
> FROM users/role/PUBLIC
> [CASCADE CONSTRAINTS];

The user with the REFERENCES privilege in the GRANT statement can reference the table. CASCADE CONSTRAINTS removes any foreign key or referential integrity constraints made to the object. In Fig. 7-16, user *riley* loses privileges on the *employee* table from user *nshah*. If user *riley* has passed privileges on the *employee* table to any other users, their privileges are also revoked.

```
SQL> REVOKE select, insert, update
  2     ON employee
  3     FROM riley;
Revoke succeeded.
```

Figure 7-16 Revoking object privileges.

IN A NUTSHELL . . .

- The Oracle objects view, sequence, index, and synonym are stored in a user's schema.
- A view is of two types: simple and complex.
- A simple view is based on a single table, and does not contain function or grouped data. The manipulation of data is always possible from a simple view.
- A complex view is based on one or more tables and may contain functions and grouped data. Manipulation of data is not always possible from a complex view.
- A sequence is an Oracle object that is used to generate a sequence of numbers. The sequence number may start at any number with any increment value, in chronological order or unordered.
- A sequence object can be modified with some restrictions. The gap may occur in sequence values because of a system crash, a deletion of rows, an update operation, or use of a sequence on more than one attribute.
- A synonym is used to use a shortened name for an object.
- Oracle creates an index object for all primary key and unique constraints. A user can create an index based on another column for faster access of rows based on that column.
- The transactions in Oracle give a user more flexibility and consistency in data. A user can COMMIT or ROLLBACK transactions.
- Oracle provides read consistency and automatic locking. A user can manually lock rows for updating.
- A database administrator (DBA) has all privileges. There are 90 system privileges and 8 object privileges. The DBA creates users and roles, and grants them privileges.
- A user can grant privileges to other users on any object in the user's own schema, and can also revoke those privileges.

EXERCISE QUESTIONS

True/False:

1. A simple view is based on a single table.
2. A complex view is always based on two or more tables.
3. In a sequence, to get the current value with CURRVAL, at least one number must be generated first by using NEXTVAL.
4. If a table is dropped, all indexes based on that table are automatically dropped.
5. When a system crashes, it results in automatic COMMIT.

6. The DML statements cannot be rolled back once committed.
7. Any user can create another user with same privileges.
8. A user cannot pass on privileges to other users on objects from the user's own schema unless the WITH GRANT OPTION is used with a GRANT statement.
9. The SELECT statement has an implied lock on rows.
10. When the DML statements are not committed, other users cannot modify the rows involved.

Answer the following questions.
1. Name any five Oracle objects.
2. What are the differences between simple and complex views?
3. When does the automatic commit occur?
4. What is the advantage of creating the following objects?
    (a) Index
    (b) Sequence
    (c) View
    (d) Synonym
5. How is transaction control important in a shared environment?
6. Name eight object privileges. What is used to grant all object privileges? What is used to grant privileges to everybody?

LAB ACTIVITY

Use case study databases for the following queries.
1. Create a view to include all employee information, but hide salary and commission.
2. Create a view to include department name and average salary by department.
3. Create an index to search students faster based on their major ID.
4. Create a sequence to add room IDs and then insert a new room into LOCATION table using the newly created sequence. What is the CURRVAL after the new row is inserted?
5. GRANT the SELECT privilege to another user on your TERM table.
6. INSERT a new Winter 2002 term in the TERM table. Use a SELECT query to see the result. Ask the user with the SELECT privilege (from activity 5) to view your TERM table. COMMIT your transaction and ask the same user to view the table again.
7. Lock student ID 00101 for update of major to 600. Update the row and commit it.

SQL Review:

Supplementary Examples

In this section, a new database is introduced with four tables. This review section is added at this point in the text to review all the statements covered in Chapters 3 through 7. The scripts for creating all four tables and inserting rows into them is also provided after illustrations of the tables. The script is followed by various problems and their solutions with the SQL statements. The sample tables:

CUSTOMER. A table with customers' demographic information.
ITEM. A table with information about the items offered by the company.
INVOICE. A table with individual invoices produced for customers.
INVITEM. A composite entity with invoices and items ordered.

CUSTOMER (<u>CustNo</u>, CustName, State, Phone)

CustNo	CustName	State	Phone
211	Garcia	NJ	732-555-1000
212	Parikh	NY	212-555-2000
225	Eisenhauer	NJ	973-555-3333
239	Bayer	FL	407-555-7777

ITEM (<u>ItemNo</u>, ItemName, Price, QtyOnHand)

ItemNo	ItemName	ItemPrice	QtyOnHand
1	Screw	2.25	50
2	Nut	5.00	110
3	Bolt	3.99	75
4	Hammer	9.99	125
5	Washer	1.99	100
6	Nail	0.99	300

INVOICE (<u>InvNo</u>, InvDate, CustNo)

InvNo	InvDate	CustNo
1001	05-SEP-00	212
1002	17-SEP-00	225
1003	17-SEP-00	239
1004	18-SEP-00	211
1005	21-SEP-00	212

170

INVITEM (InvNo, ItemNo, Qty)

InvNo	ItemNo	Qty
1001	1	5
1001	3	5
1001	5	9
1002	1	2
1002	2	3
1003	1	7
1003	2	1
1004	4	5
1005	4	10

SCRIPTS FOR CREATION OF TABLES

```
CREATE TABLE customer (CustNo NUMBER (3),
        CustName VARCHAR2 (10),
        State CHAR (2) DEFAULT 'NJ',
        Phone CHAR (12),
        CONSTRAINT customer_custno_pk PRIMARY KEY (CustNo));


CREATE TABLE item (ItemNo NUMBER (2),
        ItemName VARCHAR2 (6),
        ItemPrice NUMBER (3,2),
        QtyOnHand NUMBER (3),
        CONSTRAINT item_itemno_pk PRIMARY KEY (ItemNo),
        CONSTRAINT item_qtyonhand_ck CHECK (QtyOnHand >= 0));

CREATE TABLE invoice (InvNo NUMBER (4),
        InvDate DATE,
        CustNo NUMBER (3) NOT NULL,
        CONSTRAINT invoice_invoiceno_pk PRIMARY KEY (InvoiceNo),
        CONSTRAINT invoice_custno_fk FOREIGN KEY (CustNo)
                REFERENCES customer (CustNo));

CREATE TABLE invitem (InvNo NUMBER (4),
        ItemNo NUMBER (2),
        Qty NUMBER (2) NOT NULL,
        CONSTRAINT invitem_invno_itemno_pk PRIMARY KEY (InvNo, ItemNo),
        CONSTRAINT invitem_itemno_fk FOREIGN KEY (ItemNo)
                REFERENCES item (ItemNo));
```

SCRIPTS FOR INSERTION OF ROWS INTO THE TABLES

```
INSERT INTO customer VALUES (211, 'Garcia', 'NJ', '732-555-1000');
INSERT INTO customer VALUES (212, 'Parikh', 'NY', '212-555-2000');
```

```
INSERT INTO customer VALUES (225, 'Eisenhauer', 'NJ', `973-555-3333');
INSERT INTO customer VALUES (239, 'Bayer', 'FL', '407-555-7777');

INSERT INTO item VALUES (1, 'Screw', 2.25, 50);
INSERT INTO item VALUES (2, 'Nut', 5.00, 110);
INSERT INTO item VALUES (3, 'Bolt', 3.99, 75);
INSERT INTO item VALUES (4, 'Hammer', 9.99, 125);
INSERT INTO item VALUES (5, 'Washer', 1.99, 100);
INSERT INTO item VALUES (6, 'Nail', 0.99, 300);

INSERT INTO invoice VALUES (1001, TO_DATE ('05-09-2000', 'dd-mm-yyyy'), 212);
INSERT INTO invoice VALUES (1002, TO_DATE ('17-09-2000', 'dd-mm-yyyy'), 225);
INSERT INTO invoice VALUES (1003, TO_DATE ('17-09-2000', 'dd-mm-yyyy'), 239);
INSERT INTO invoice VALUES (1004, TO_DATE ('18-09-2000', 'dd-mm-yyyy'), 211);
INSERT INTO invoice VALUES (1005, TO_DATE ('21-09-2000', 'dd-mm-yyyy'), 212);

INSERT INTO invitem VALUES (1001, 1, 5);
INSERT INTO invitem VALUES (1001, 3, 5);
INSERT INTO invitem VALUES (1001, 5, 9);
INSERT INTO invitem VALUES (1002, 1, 2);
INSERT INTO invitem VALUES (1002, 2, 3);
INSERT INTO invitem VALUES (1003, 1, 7);
INSERT INTO invitem VALUES (1003, 2, 1);
INSERT INTO invitem VALUES (1004, 4, 5);
INSERT INTO invitem VALUES (1005, 4, 10);
```

INSERTION OF ROWS WITH SUBSTITUTION VARIABLES (ALTERNATE METHOD)

```
INSERT INTO customer VALUES (&customer_no, '&customer_name', '&state', '&phone');
INSERT INTO item VALUES (&item_no, '&item_name', &price, &qty_on_hand);
INSERT INTO invoice VALUES (&inv_no, TO_DATE ('&inv_date', 'dd-mm-yyyy'), &cust_no);
INSERT INTO invitem VALUES (&invoice_no, &item_no, &qty);
```

DISPLAY ALL CUSTOMER INFORMATION

```
        SELECT *
        FROM customer;
```

DISPLAY ALL ITEM NAMES AND THEIR RESPECTIVE UNIT PRICE

```
        SELECT ItemName, ItemPrice
        FROM item;
```

DISPLAY UNIQUE INVOICE NUMBERS FROM THE INVITEM TABLE

```
        SELECT DISTINCT InvNo
        FROM invitem;
```

DISPLAY ITEM INFORMATION WITH APPROPRIATE COLUMN ALIASES

```
SELECT ItemNo "Item Number", ItemName "Name of Item", ItemPrice "Unit Price"
    FROM item;
```

DISPLAY ITEM NAME AND PRICE IN SENTENCE FORM USING CONCATENATION

```
SELECT ItemName || ' has a unit price of $' || ItemPrice FROM item;
```

FIND TOTAL VALUE OF EACH ITEM BASED ON QUANTITY ON HAND

```
SELECT ItemName, ItemPrice * QtyOnHand "Total Value"
    FROM item;
```

FIND CUSTOMERS WHO ARE FROM THE STATE OF FLORIDA

```
SELECT *
    FROM customer
    WHERE UPPER (State) = 'FL';
```

DISPLAY ITEMS WITH UNIT PRICE OF AT LEAST $5

```
SELECT UPPER (ItemName), ItemPrice
    FROM item
    WHERE ItemPrice >= 5;
```

WHICH ITEMS ARE BETWEEN $2 AND $5?

```
SELECT *
    FROM item
    WHERE ItemPrice BETWEEN 2 and 5;
```

or

```
SELECT *
    FROM item
    WHERE ItemPrice >= 2 AND ItemPrice <= 5;
```

WHICH CUSTOMERS ARE FROM THE TRISTATE AREA OF NJ, NY, AND CT?

```
SELECT *
    FROM customer
    WHERE State IN ('NJ', 'NY', 'CT');
```

FIND ALL CUSTOMERS WHOSE NAMES START WITH THE LETTER E

```
SELECT *
    FROM customer
    WHERE CustName LIKE 'E%';
```

FIND ITEMS WITH A *W* IN THEIR NAME

```
SELECT *
    FROM item
    WHERE ItemName LIKE '%w%';
```

SORT ALL CUSTOMERS ALPHABETICALLY

```
SELECT *
    FROM customer
    ORDER BY CustName;
```

SORT ALL ITEMS IN DESCENDING ORDER BY THEIR PRICE

```
SELECT *
    FROM item
    ORDER BY ItemPrice DESC;
```

SORT ALL CUSTOMERS BY THEIR STATE AND ALSO ALPHABETICALLY

```
SELECT *
    FROM customer
    ORDER BY State, CustName;
```

DISPLAY ALL THE CUSTOMERS FROM NEW JERSEY ALPHABETICALLY

```
SELECT *
    FROM customer
    WHERE UPPER (State) = 'NJ'
    ORDER BY CustName;
```

DISPLAY ALL ITEM PRICES ROUNDED TO THE NEAREST DOLLAR

```
SELECT ItemName, ROUND (ItemPrice, 0)
    FROM item;
```

**THE PAYMENT IS DUE IN TWO MONTHS FROM THE INVOICE DATE.
FIND THE PAYMENT DUE DATE**

```
SELECT InvNo, CustNo, InvDate, ADD_MONTHS (InvDate, 2) "Payment Due"
    FROM invoice;
```

or

```
SELECT InvNo, CustNo, InvDate, InvDate + 60 "Payment Due"
    FROM invoice;
```

DISPLAY INVOICE DATES IN 'SEPTEMBER 05, 2000' FORMAT

```
SELECT InvNo, TO_CHAR (InvDate, 'fmMonth DD, YYYY') "Invoice Date"
    FROM invoice;
```

FIND THE TOTAL, AVERAGE, HIGHEST, AND LOWEST UNIT PRICE

```
SELECT SUM (ItemPrice), AVG (ItemPrice), MAX (ItemPrice), MIN (ItemPrice)
    FROM item;
```

HOW MANY DIFFERENT ITEMS ARE AVAILABLE FOR CUSTOMERS?

```
SELECT COUNT (*)
    FROM item;
```

COUNT THE NUMBER OF ITEMS ORDERED IN EACH INVOICE

```
SELECT InvNo, COUNT (ItemNo) "Items Ordered"
    FROM invitem
    GROUP BY InvNo;
```

FIND INVOICES IN WHICH THREE OR MORE ITEMS ARE ORDERED

```
SELECT InvNo, COUNT (ItemNo) "Items Ordered"
    FROM invitem
    GROUP BY InvNo
    HAVING COUNT (ItemNo) >= 3;
```

FIND ALL POSSIBLE COMBINATIONS OF CUSTOMERS AND ITEMS (CARTESIAN PRODUCT)

```
SELECT c.*, t.*
    FROM customer c, item t;
```

DISPLAY ALL ITEM QUANTITIES AND ITEM PRICES FOR INVOICES

```
SELECT  a.InvNo,  a.ItemNo,  b.ItemName,  a.Qty,  b.ItemPrice,  a.Qty  *  b.ItemPrice
        "qty*price"
    FROM invitem a, item b
    WHERE a.ItemNo = b.ItemNo;
```

FIND THE TOTAL PRICE AMOUNT FOR EACH INVOICE

```
SELECT a.InvNo, , SUM(a.Qty * b.ItemPrice) "Total Amount"
    FROM invitem a, item b
    WHERE a.ItemNo = b.ItemNo
    GROUP BY a.InvNo;
```

USE AN OUTER JOIN TO DISPLAY ITEMS ORDERED AS WELL AS NOT ORDERED SO FAR

```
SELECT x.ItemNo, y.InvNo
    FROM item x, invitem y
    WHERE x.ItemNo = y.ItemNo (+);
```

DISPLAY INVOICES, CUSTOMER NAMES, AND ITEM NAMES TOGETHER (MULTIPLE JOINS) (THE JOIN OF FOUR TABLES MIGHT NOT RETURN ANY ROWS IN ORACLE!)

```
SELECT a.InvNo, b.CustName, c.ItemName, d.Qty
    FROM invoice a, customer b, item c, invitem d
    WHERE a.CustNo = b.CustNo AND a.InvNo = d.InvNo AND c.ItemNo = d.ItemNo;
```

FIND INVOICES WITH *HAMMER* AS AN ITEM

```
SELECT v.InvNo, t.ItemName, v.Qty
    FROM invitem v, item t
    WHERE v.ItemNo = t.ItemNo AND UPPER (t.ItemName) = 'HAMMER';
```

FIND INVOICES WITH *HAMMER* AS AN ITEM BY USING A SUB-QUERY INSTEAD OF A JOIN

```
SELECT InvNo, Qty "Hammers ordered"
    FROM invitem
    WHERE ItemNo =
    (SELECT ItemNo FROM item WHERE UPPER (t.ItemName) = 'HAMMER');
```

DISPLAY THE NAMES OF ITEMS ORDERED IN INVOICE NUMBER 1001 (USE A SUB-QUERY)

```
SELECT ItemName
    FROM item
    WHERE ItemNo IN
    (SELECT ItemNo FROM invitem WHERE InvNo = 1001);
```

FIND ITEMS THAT ARE CHEAPER THAN *NUT*

```
SELECT ItemName, ItemPrice
    FROM item
    WHERE ItemPrice <
        (SELECT ItemPrice FROM item WHERE UPPER (ItemName) = 'NUT');
```

CREATE A TABLE FOR ALL THE NEW JERSEY CUSTOMERS BASED ON THE EXISTING CUSTOMER TABLE

```
CREATE TABLE nj_customer
AS
SELECT CustNo, CustName, Phone
    FROM customer
    WHERE UPPER (State) = 'NJ';
```

COPY ALL NEW YORK CUSTOMERS TO THE TABLE WITH NEW JERSEY CUSTOMERS

```
INSERT INTO nj_customer
    SELECT CustNo, CustName, Phone
    FROM customer
    WHERE UPPER (State) = 'NY';
```

RENAME THE *NJ CUSTOMER* TABLE TO *NYNJ_CUSTOMER*

```
RENAME nj_customer TO nynj_customer;
```

FIND CUSTOMERS WHO ARE IN NOT FROM NY OR NJ (USE SET OPERATOR)

```
SELECT CustName, State
    FROM customer
MINUS
SELECT CustName, State
    FROM nynj_customer;
```

DELETE ROWS FROM THE *CUSTOMER* TABLE THAT ARE ALSO IN THE *NYNJ_CUSTOMER* TABLE

```
DELETE FROM customer
    WHERE CustNo IN
        (SELECT CustNo FROM nynj_customer);
```

FIND THE ITEMS WITH THE TOP THREE PRICES

```
SELECT ROWNUM, ItemName, ItemPrice
    FROM (SELECT ItemName, ItemPrice FROM item
        ORDER BY ItemPrice DESC)
WHERE ROWNUM <=3;
```

FIND TWO ITEMS WITH THE LOWEST QUANTITY ON HAND

```
SELECT ROWNUM, ItemName, ItemPrice, QtyOnHand
    FROM (SELECT ItemName, ItemPrice, QtyOnHand FROM item
        ORDER BY QtyOnHand;
WHERE ROWNUM <=2;
```

CREATE A SIMPLE VIEW WITH ITEM NAMES AND ITEM PRICES ONLY

```
CREATE OR REPLACE VIEW item_vu (Name, Price)
AS
SELECT ItemName, ItemPrice
    FROM item;
```

CREATE A VIEW THAT WILL DISPLAY INVOICE NUMBER AND CUSTOMER NAMES FOR NJ CUSTOMERS

```
CREATE OR REPLACE VIEW nj_cust_vu
AS
SELECT InvNo, CustName
    FROM invoice, customer
    WHERE invoice.CustNo = customer.CustNo
    AND UPPER (State) = 'NJ';
WITH CHECK OPTION;
```

**CREATE A SEQUENCE THAT CAN BE USED TO ENTER NEW ITEMS
INTO THE ITEM TABLE**

```
CREATE SEQUENCE itemnum_seq
    INCREMENT BY 1
    START WITH 7
    MAXVALUE 99
    NOCYCLE
    NOCACHE
    ORDER;
```

ADD A NEW ITEM INTO THE ITEM TABLE WITH THE SEQUENCE JUST CREATED

```
INSERT INTO item
    VALUES (itemnum_seq.NEXTVAL, 'Scissors', 7.95, 100);
```

CREATE A SYNONYM FOR THE INVITEM TABLE

```
CREATE SYNONYM ii
    FOR invitem;
```

CREATE AN INDEX FILE TO SPEED UP A SEARCH BASED ON CUSTOMER'S NAME

```
CREATE INDEX customer_name_idx
    ON customer (CustName);
```

**LOCK CUSTOMER BAYER'S RECORD TO UPDATE THE STATE
AND THE PHONE NUMBER**

```
SELECT *
    FROM customer
    WHERE UPPER (CustName) = 'BAYER'
    FOR UPDATE OF State, Phone
    NOWAIT;
```

GIVE EVERYBODY SELECT AND INSERT RIGHTS ON YOUR ITEM TABLE

```
GRANT select, insert
    ON item
    TO public;
```

REVOKE THE INSERT OPTION ON THE ITEM TABLE FROM USER *BOND*

```
REVOKE insert
ON item
FROM bond;
```

8

PL/SQL: Programming Language Basics

IN THIS CHAPTER . . .

- You will learn about the basics of the PL/SQL programming language.
- The PL/SQL anonymous block is introduced.
- The topics include variables, constants, data types, and declarations.
- The assignment statement and the use of arithmetic operators are covered.
- The scope and use of various types of variables are shown in sample programs.
- You will be prepared to write simple PL/SQL blocks.

In Part 2 you learned Oracle's nonprocedural language SQL and its various statements to interface with the Oracle server. SQL is a great query language, but it has its limitations. Oracle Corporation has added a procedural language extension to SQL, which is known as Programming Language/Structured Query Language (PL/SQL). It is Oracle's proprietary language for data access of relational table data. PL/SQL is like any other high-level compiler language out there. If you are already familiar with another programming language, you will find PL/SQL constructs similar to Pascal, C, or Visual Basic 6. It includes features of modern

179

languages such as

- Data encapsulation
- Error handling
- Information hiding
- Object-Oriented Programming (OOP)

PL/SQL also allows embedding of SQL statements and data manipulation in its blocks. SQL statements are used to retrieve data and PL/SQL control statements are used to manipulate or process data in a PL/SQL program. The data can be inserted, deleted, or updated through a PL/SQL block, which makes it an efficient transaction processing language.

The Oracle server has an engine to execute SQL statements. There is a separate engine for PL/SQL on the server. Oracle tools, such as Developer 2000, which consists of Oracle Forms, Oracle Reports, and Oracle Graphics, also have a separate engine to execute PL/SQL. The SQL statements are sent one at a time to the server for execution, which results in individual calls to the server for each SQL statement. It may also result in heavy network traffic. On the other hand, all SQL statements within a PL/SQL block are sent in a single call to the server, which reduces the overhead and improves performance.

A BRIEF HISTORY OF PL/SQL

PL/SQL version 1.0 was introduced with Oracle 6.0 in 1991. It had very limited capabilities. It was far from being called a full-fledged programming language. It was merely used for batch processing.

With versions 2.0, 2.1, and 2.2, the following new features were introduced:

- The transaction control statements SAVEPOINT, ROLLBACK, and COMMIT
- The DML statements INSERT, DELETE, and UPDATE
- The extended data types Boolean, BINARY_INTEGER, PL/SQL records, and PL/SQL tables
- Built-in functions—character, numeric, conversion, and date functions
- Built-in packages
- The control structures sequence, selection, and looping
- Database access through work areas called cursors
- Error handling
- Modular programming with procedures and functions
- Stored procedures, functions, and packages
- Programmer-defined subtypes
- DDL support through DBMS_SQL package

- The PL/SQL wrapper
- The DBMS_JOB job scheduler
- File I/O with the UTF_FILE package

PL/SQL version 8.0, also known as PL/SQL8, came with Oracle 8, the "object-relational" database software. It allows creation of objects that can be accessed with Java, C++, Object COBOL, and other languages. It allows objects and relational tables to coexist. The external procedures in Oracle 8 allow you to compile procedures and store them in the shared library of the operating system, for example a *.SO* file in UNIX or a *.DLL* (Dynamic Linked Library) file in Windows NT. Oracle's library is written in C language. Another support is for LOB (Large Object) data types.

FUNDAMENTALS OF PL/SQL

A PL/SQL program consists of statements. Uppercase and lowercase letters in a PL/SQL code are treated the same. In other words, PL/SQL is not case sensitive except for the character string values enclosed in single quotes. Like any other programming language, the PL/SQL statements consist of reserved words, user-defined words, punctuation marks, and literal values.

Reserved Words

The reserved words, or keywords, are words provided by the language, and they have specific use in the language. For example, BEGIN, END, IF, WHILE, EXCEPTION, and DECLARE are some of the reserved words.

User-Defined Words

The user-defined words are used to name variables, constants, procedures, functions, cursors, tables, records, and exceptions. A user must follow the following rules in naming these identifiers:

- The name can be 1 to 30 characters long.
- The name must start with a letter.
- Letters (A–Z, a–z), numbers, dollar sign ($), number sign (#) and underscore (_) are allowed.
- Spaces are not allowed.
- Other special characters are not allowed.
- Keywords cannot be used as user defined.
- Names must be unique within a block.
- Name should not be the same as the name of a table's column used in the block.

User-defined names
Rate_of_pay
Num
A1234567890
Dollars$_and_cents
SS#

Figure 8-1   Valid user-defined names.

Invalid user-defined names	Reason
2Number	Starts with a number
Employee-name	Special character hyphen
END	Reserved word
Department number	Spaces
Largest_yearly_salary_paid_to_employees	Too long
Taxrate%	Special character %

Figure 8-2   Invalid user-defined names.

It is a good practice to create small and meaningful names. Figure 8-1 shows a list of valid user-defined names, and Fig. 8-2 shows invalid user-defined names with reasons.

Literals

Literals are values not represented by user-defined names. Literals are of three types: number, character string, and Boolean.

Number	100, 3.14, –55, 5.25E7, or NULL
Character string	'A', 'this is a string', '0001', '25-MAY-00', ' ' or NULL
Boolean	TRUE, FALSE, or NULL

In this list of values '25-MAY-00' looks like a date value, but it is a character string. It can be converted to date format by using the TO_DATE function. Value ' ' (two single quotes with nothing within) is another way of entering the NULL value.

PL/SQL is case sensitive about character values within single quotation marks. The values 'ORACLE', 'Oracle', and 'oracle' are three different values for PL/SQL. To embed a single quote in a string value, two single quote symbols are entered, for example, 'New Year''s Day'.

Numeric values can be entered in scientific notation with the letter *E* or *e*. Boolean values are not enclosed in quotation marks.

PL/SQL BLOCK STRUCTURE

PL/SQL is a block-structured language. A program can be divided into logical blocks. The block structure gives modularity to a PL/SQL program, and each object within a block has "scope." Blocks are of two types:

1. An *anonymous block* is a block of code without a name. It can be used anywhere in a program and is sent to the server engine for execution at runtime.
2. The procedures and functions are named *blocks.* A *subprogram* can be called and can take arguments. A procedure is a subprogram that can perform an action, whereas a function is a subprogram that returns a calculated value. A package is formed from a group of procedures and functions.

Section	Use
Declarative	An optional section to declare variables, constants, cursors, and user-defined exceptions, which are referenced in executable and exception-handling sections.
Executable	A mandatory section that contains PL/SQL statements to manipulate data in the block and SQL statements to manipulate the database.
Exception handling	It specifies action statements to perform when an error condition exists in the executable section. It is also an optional section.

Figure 8-3 Sections in a PL/SQL block.

A PL/SQL block consists of three sections: a declarative section, an executable section, and an exception-handling section. Figure 8-3 shows the use of three sections in a PL/SQL block. Out of three sections in a PL/SQL block, only the executable section is mandatory. The declarative and exception-handling sections are optional. The general syntax of an anonymous block is

```
DECLARE
    Declaration of constants, variables, cursors, and exceptions
BEGIN
    PL/SQL and SQL statements
EXCEPTION
    Actions for error conditions
END;
```

The DECLARE and EXCEPTION keywords are optional, but the BEGIN and END keywords are mandatory. The declarations made within a block are local to the block. When the block ends, all objects declared within the block cease to exist. The block is the scope of objects declared in that block. When blocks are nested within each other, the declarations made in the outer block are global to the inner block. However, the object declarations made in the inner block are local to it and cannot be referenced by the outer block. There is a variety of PL/SQL constructs, in which basic PL/SQL block is used. The table in Fig. 8-4 shows all constructs available in the Oracle server environment.

Construct	Use
Anonymous block	An unnamed block, which is independent or embedded within an application.
Procedure/function	A named block that is stored in the Oracle server, can be called by its name, and can take arguments.
Package	A named PL/SQL module that is a group of functions, procedures, and identifiers.
Trigger	A block that is associated with a database table. It is executed when automatically fired by a DML statement.

Figure 8-4   Programming constructs.

COMMENTS

The comments are used to document programs. They are written as a part of the program, but are not executed. In fact, comments are ignored by the executor. It is a good programming practice to add comments to a program. It helps in readability and debugging of the program. There are two ways to write comments in PL/SQL.

To write a single-line comment, two dashes (- -) are entered at the beginning of a new line. For example,

- -This is a single-line comment.

To write a multiline comment, comment text is placed between /* and */.

**/* This is a
multiline comment
that ends here.   */**

A programmer can insert a comment anywhere in the program.

DATA TYPES

Each constant and variable used in the program needs a data type. The data type decides the type of value that can be stored in a variable. PL/SQL has two data types:

- Scalar
- Composite

A scalar data type is not made up of a group of elements. It is atomic in nature. The composite data types are made up of elements or components. PL/SQL supports two composite data types, *records* and *tables,* which are discussed in a later chapter. There are four major categories of scalar data types: character, number, Boolean, and date.

Character

The variables with a character data type can store text. The text may include letters, numbers, and special characters. The text in character-type variables can be manipulated with built-in character functions. There are various character data types:

CHAR. The CHAR data type is used for fixed-length string values. The allowable string length is between 1 and 32,767. If you remember, the allowable length in the Oracle database is only 2000. If you do not specify a length for the variable, the default length is 1. Get into the habit of specifying length along with the data type to avoid any errors.

If you are going to declare a variable of the CHAR type in PL/SQL code and that value is to be inserted into a table's column, the limitation on database size is only 2000 characters. You will have to find the substring of that character value to avoid an error message for inserting a character string longer than the length of the column.

If you specify a length of 10 and the assigned value is only 5 characters long, the value is padded with trailing spaces due to the fixed-length nature of this data type. The CHAR type is not storage efficient, but it is performance efficient.

VARCHAR2. The VARCHAR2 type is used for variable-length string values. The allowable length is between 1 and 32,767. Again, a column in an Oracle database with a VARCHAR2 type can only take 4000 characters, which is smaller than the allowable length for the variable.

Suppose you have two variables with data type of CHAR (20) and VARCHAR2 (20), and both are assigned the same value, Oracle8 PL/SQL. The string value is only 14 characters long. The first variable, with CHAR (20), is assigned a value padded with 6 spaces; the one with VARCHAR2 (20) does not get a string value padded with spaces. If both variables' values are compared in a condition for equality, FALSE will be returned.

Other character data types are LONG (32,760 bytes, shorter than VARCHAR2), RAW (32,767 bytes), and LONG RAW (32,760 bytes, shorter than RAW). The RAW data values are neither interpreted nor converted by Oracle.

VARCHAR2 is the most recommended character data type.

Number

PL/SQL has a variety of numeric data types. Whole numbers or integer values can be handled by following data types:

BINARY_INTEGER (approximately $-2^{31} + 1$ to $2^{31} - 1$ or -2 billion to $+2$ billion)
INTEGER
INT
SMALLINT
POSITIVE (a subtype of BINARY_INTEGER—range 0 to 2^{31})
NATURAL (a subtype of BINARY_INTEGER— range 1 to 2^{31})

Similarly, there are various data types for decimal numbers:

NUMBER
DEC (fixed-point number)
DECIMAL (fixed-point number)
NUMERIC (fixed-point number)
FLOAT (floating-point number)
REAL (floating-point number)
DOUBLE PRECISION (floating-point number)

You are familiar with the NUMBER type from Oracle table's column type. The NUMBER type can be used for fixed-decimal-point or floating-decimal-point numbers. It provides accuracy of up to 38 decimal places. When using the NUMBER type, the precision and scale values are provided. The precision of a number is the total number of digits in that number, and the scale is the number of decimal places. The precision and scale values must be whole-number literals, for example,

NUMBER (p, s)

If the scale has a value that is negative, positive, or zero, it specifies rounding of number to the left of decimal place, to the right of decimal place, or to the nearest whole number respectively. If a scale value is not used, no rounding occurs.

Boolean

PL/SQL has a logical data type, Boolean, that is not available in SQL. It is used for Boolean data TRUE, FALSE, or NULL only. These values are not enclosed in single quotation marks like character and data values.

Date

The date type is a special data type that stores date and time information. The date values have specific format. A user can enter a date in many different formats with the TO_DATE function, but a date is always stored in standard 7 byte format. A date stores the following information:

Century

Year

Month

Day

Hour

Minute

Second

The valid date range is from January 1, 4712 B.C. to A.D. December 31, 9999. The time is stored as number of seconds past midnight. If the user leaves out the time portion of the data, it defaults to midnight (12:00:00 A.M.). Various DATE functions are available for date calculations. For example, the SYSDATE function is used to return the system's current date.

OTHER SCALAR DATA TYPES

NLS

The National Language Support (NLS) data type is for character sets where multiple bytes are used for character representation. NCHAR and NVARCHAR2 are examples of NLS data types.

LOB

Like Oracle 8, PL/SQL also supports Large Object (LOB) data types to store large values of character, raw, or binary data. They allow up to 4 gigabytes of data. LOB variables can be given one of the following data types:

The *BLOB* type contains a pointer to the large binary object inside the database.

The *CLOB* type contains a pointer to a large block of single-byte character data of fixed width.

The *NCLOB* type contains a pointer to a large block of multibyte character data of fixed width.

The *BFILE* type contains a pointer to large binary objects in an external operating system file. It would contain the directory name and the filename.

Oracle provides users with a built-in package, DBMS_LOB, to manipulate contents of LOBs.

VARIABLE DECLARATION

A scalar variable or a constant is declared with a data type and an initial value assignment. The declarations are done in the DECLARE section of the program block. The initial value assignment for a variable is optional unless it has a NOT NULL constraint. The constants and NOT NULL type variables must be initialized. The general syntax is

> *DECLARE*
> *IdentifierName [CONSTANT] DataType [NOT NULL] [:= / DEFAULT expression];*

where *identifiername* is the name of the variable or constant. A CONSTANT is an identifier that must be initialized and whose value cannot be changed in the program body. A NOT NULL constraint can be used for variables, and such variables must be initialized. The DEFAULT clause or : = can be used to initialize a constant or a variable to a value. An expression can be a literal, another variable, or an expression.

The identifiers are named based on rules given previously in this chapter. Different naming conventions can be used. You should declare one variable per line for good readability, for example,

```
DECLARE
   v_number         NUMBER (2);
   v_count          NUMBER (1) := 1;
   v_state          VARCHAR2 (2) DEFAULT 'NJ';
   c_pi             CONSTANT NUMBER := 3.14;
   v_invoicedate    DATE DEFAULT SYSDATE;
```

In this example, you see a naming convention that uses *prefix v_* for the variables and *prefix c_* for the constants.

ANCHORED DECLARATION

PL/SQL uses a %TYPE declaration attribute to anchor a variable's data type. Another variable or a column in a table can be used for anchoring. In anchoring, you tell PL/SQL to use a variable or a table's column's data type as a data type for another variable in the program. The general syntax is

> *VariableName TypeAttribute%TYPE [value assignment];*

Where TypeAttribute is another variable's name or table's column with a table qualifier (e.g., Tablename.ColumnName). It is very useful while retrieving a value of a column into a variable with a SELECT query in PL/SQL. For example,

```
DECLARE
  v_num1     NUMBER (3);
  v_num2     v_num1%TYPE;
```

In this example, *v_num1* is declared with a data type NUMBER (3). The next variable, *v_num2,* is declared using the anchoring method and the declaration attribute %TYPE. The variable *v_num2* gets the same data type as *v_num1*.

In the next example, two variables are declared and are assigned data types to match with the column's data type. The advantage is that you do not have to cross-reference the data type used in the table. Oracle does that for you.

```
DECLARE
  v_empsal      employee.Salary%TYPE;
  v_deptname    dept.DeptName%TYPE;
```

Suppose you do not use the anchoring method to declare variables, which are assigned values directly from table columns. You use the DESCRIBE command to list all the data types for columns. Then you declare variables in a program with the same types and lengths. It will work just fine. The problem will arise when the column lengths are increased to meet future demands. When you assign values from those columns to variables, VALUE_ERROR will occur. You will have to go back to all the programs to change the variable's data length! Anchoring definitely is an advantage in such situations.

The %TYPE anchors the data type of one variable based on another variable or column at the time of a PL/SQL block's compilation. If the source or original column's data type is changed, the PL/SQL block must be recompiled in order to re-anchor all anchored variables.

Nested Anchoring

%TYPE attribute's use can be nested. For example,

```
DECLARE
  - - source variable v_commission
   v_commission           NUMBER (7, 2);
  - - anchored variable v_total_commission
   v_total_commission     v_commission%TYPE;
  - - nested anchoring variable v_net_commission
   v_net_commission       v_total_commission%TYPE;
```

In this example, the original variable *v_commission* anchors *v_total_commission*, which in turn is used to anchor *v_net_commission*. There is no limit on the number of layers of nesting.

The source variable for a %TYPE declaration does not have to be in the same block. The variable could be a global variable, or it could be in the block that contains the current block.

NOT NULL Constraint for %TYPE Declarations

If the source variable is declared with a NOT NULL constraint, the %TYPE declaration inherits the NOT NULL constraint from the source declaration. The anchored variable must be initialized with a value in the %TYPE declaration.

If the source for a %TYPE declaration is a table's column, the NOT NULL constraint is not inherited by the anchored variable. There is no need to initialize the anchored variable, and it can be assigned a NULL value.

ASSIGNMENT OPERATION

The assignment operation is one of the ways to assign a value to a variable. You have already learned that a variable can be initialized at declaration time using the DEFAULT option or :=. The assignment operation is used in the executable section of the program block to assign a literal, another variable's value, or the result of an expression to a variable. The general syntax is

VariableName := Literal/VariableName/Expression;

For example,

```
v_num1 := 100;
v_num2 := v_num1;
v_sum   := v_num1 + v_num2;
```

In these examples, the assumption is made that three variables are already declared. The first example assigns 100 to the variable *v_num1*. The second example assigns the value of the variable *v_num1* to the variable *v_num2*. The third example assigns the result of an addition operation on *v_num1* and *v_num2* to the variable *v_sum*.

The following statements are examples of invalid assignment operations and the reasons for their lack of validity:

```
v_count = 10;            /* Wrong assignment operator, = sign */
v_count * 2 := v_double;  /* Expression cannot be on the left. */
v_num1 := v_num2 :=v_num3;  /* Cannot use two assignments in one statement. */
```

BIND VARIABLES

The bind variables are also known as host variables. These variables are declared in the host SQL*Plus environment and accessed by a PL/SQL block. Anonymous blocks do not take any arguments, but can access host variables with a colon prefix (:) with the host variable name. Host variables can be passed to procedures and functions as arguments. A host variable is declared at the SQL> prompt with SQL*Plus's VARIABLE statement. The syntax of a host variable declaration is

VARIABLE VariableName DataType

For example,

SQL> VARIABLE double NUMBER

A host variable's value can be printed in the SQL*Plus environment by using the PRINT command. Let us put everything together in a program. The program contains a script that includes SQL*Plus statements and a PL/SQL block.

In Fig. 8-5, two types of variables are used, a local variable *v_num* and a host variable *g_double*. The host variable *g_double* is declared in SQL*Plus with a VARIABLE statement, and the program block references it with a colon prefix (:). The local variable *v_num* is declared in the declarative section of the program block, and there is no need to use the colon prefix with it. Program assigns the value 5 to the local variable *v_num,* doubles it, and stores the result in the host variable *g_double*. Finally, the resulting variable is printed in the host environment with a PRINT statement.

```
VARIABLE g_double NUMBER
DECLARE
        v_num          NUMBER (2);
BEGIN
        v_num := 5;
        :g_double := v_num * 2;
END;
PRINT g_double
```

Figure 8-5   Using a host variable in a PL/SQL block.

Question: How does a PL/SQL block end?

Answer: It ends with an END and a semicolon on the same line or a slash (/) on the next line.

The use of host variables should be minimized in a program block, because they affect performance. Every time a host variable is accessed within the block, the PL/SQL engine has to stop to request the host environment for the value of the host variable. The variable's value can be assigned to a local variable in order to minimize calls to the host.

SUBSTITUTION VARIABLES IN PL/SQL

PL/SQL does not have any input capabilities. There are no explicit I/O statements, but substitution variables of SQL are also available in PL/SQL. Let us rewrite the program script of Fig. 8-5 with the one in Fig. 8-6. When the script of Fig. 8-6 is executed, a standard prompt for *p_num* appears on the screen for users to type in a value for it. As you see in the example, there is no need to declare substitution variables in the program block.

```
VARIABLE g_double NUMBER
DECLARE
        v_num           NUMBER (2);
BEGIN
        v_num := &p_num;
        :g_double := v_num * 2;
END
/
PRINT g_double
```

Figure 8-6   Local, host, and substitution variables.

PRINTING IN PL/SQL

There is no explicit output statement in PL/SQL. Oracle does have a built-in package called DBMS_OUTPUT with the procedure PUT_LINE to print. An environment variable named SERVEROUTPUT must be toggled ON to view output from it.

The DBMS_OUTPUT package is the most frequently used package due to its capabilities to get lines and put lines into the buffer. The PUT_LINE procedure puts information passed to the buffer and puts a new-line marker at the end. For example,

DBMS_OUTPUT.PUT_LINE ('This line will be displayed');

The maximum size of the buffer is 1 megabyte. The following command enables you to view information from the buffer by using the DBMS_OUTPUT package:

SET SERVEROUTPUT ON

The PL/SQL block in Fig. 8-7 shows the use of the DBMS_OUTPUT.PUT_LINE.

```
DECLARE
        v_num           NUMBER (2);
        v_double        NUMBER (3);
BEGIN
        v_num := 50;
        V_double := v_num * 2;
        DBMS_OUTPUT.PUT_LINE ('Number is ' || TO_CHAR (v_num));
        DBMS_OUTPUT.PUT_LINE ('Double is ' || TO_CHAR (v_double));
END;
```

```
Number is 50
Double is 100
```

Figure 8-7   DBMS_OUTPUT.PUT_LINE.

ARITHMETIC OPERATORS

All standard arithmetic operators are available in PL/SQL for calculations. If more than one operator exists in an arithmetic expression, the following order of precedence is used:

- Exponentiation is performed first, multiplication and division are performed next, and addition and subtraction are performed last.
- If more than one operator of the same priority is present, they are performed from left to right.
- Whatever is in parentheses is performed first.

Arithmetic Operator	Use
+	Addition
−	Subtraction and negation
*	Multiplication
/	Division
**	Exponentiation

Figure 8-8   Arithmetic operators.

The table in Fig. 8-8 shows arithmetic operators and their use.

Question: What is the answer from the following expression?

$$-2 + 3 * (10 - 2 * 3) / 6$$

Answer: 0

In this chapter, you learned the basics of PL/SQL. In the next chapter, you will learn about three programming control structures: sequence, selection, and looping. (You already know one of them. All the examples in this chapter were based on sequence structure). You will also learn to interface with the Oracle server by embedding SQL statements in PL/SQL program blocks.

IN A NUTSHELL . . .

- PL/SQL (Programming Language/Structured Query Language) is Oracle's proprietary language.
- PL/SQL contains features of modern languages such as data encapsulation, error handling, information hiding, and Object-Oriented Programming (OOP).
- PL/SQL is a block-structured language. A block is of two types: anonymous block and subprogram (procedures and functions).
- A program code contains reserved words, user-defined words, punctuation marks, and literals.
- A program block consists of three sections: declarative, executable, and exception-handling.
- A program uses variables and constants to hold values. A variable's value can be changed, but a constant's value remains the same throughout the execution of the program.

- A variable is declared in the declarative section with a scalar data type. The standard data types are number, character, Boolean, and date. PL/SQL also supports other LOB (Large Object) data types.
- A declaration attribute %TYPE is used to anchor a variable with another variable's data type or with a table's column's data type.
- A bind variable, or host variable, is global to a PL/SQL block. An anonymous block refers to it with a colon prefix (:). A bind variable is declared with the VARIABLE statement and is printed with the PRINT statement in the SQL*Plus environment.
- An assignment statement is used in an execution section to assign a literal, a variable's value, or the result of an expression to a variable. An assignment uses the := operator.
- PL/SQL does not have an input statement, but substitution variables are allowed in a block to assign a value to variable.
- A built-in Oracle package and its procedure DBMS_OUTPUT.PUT_LINE are used to output information. An environment variable SETVEROUTPUT must be set to ON before using it.
- Arithmetic operators (+, −, *, /, and **) are used in mathematical expressions. The operations follow rules of precedence for evaluating expressions with more than one operator.

EXERCISE QUESTIONS

True/False:

1. PL/SQL is a nonprocedural language developed by Oracle Corporation.
2. The SQL language has built-in error checking and error handling.
3. Three types of variables used in a PL/SQL program are local, host, and substitution.
4. A variable with a NOT NULL constraint and a constant must be initialized with a value at the declaration time.
5. An assignment statement is used in the executable section to assign a value to a variable or a constant.
6. In a declaration with %TYPE attribute, the source is either a variable or a column in a table.
7. If the source variable is declared with a NOT NULL constraint, the anchored variable inherits the same constraint.
8. If the source column in a table has a NOT NULL constraint, the anchored variable also contains the NOT NULL constraint.
9. Exponentiation is performed before addition in an expression without any parentheses.
10. The declarative and executable sections are mandatory in a PL/SQL block.

Answer the following questions.

1. State the differences between SQL and PL/SQL.
2. What are the two types of blocks in PL/SQL? What are the differences between them?
3. Name four standard scalar data types used in PL/SQL. When is each type used for variables?
4. Name three types of variables used in PL/SQL. Where are they declared? Give a sample declaration of each.
5. Give the differences and similarities between := and DEFAULT.
6. What are the advantages of %TYPE attribute in variable declaration?
7. State the rules of precedence used in arithmetic operations.

LAB ACTIVITY

1. Create a program script that uses a PL/SQL anonymous block to perform the following: Use a host variable AREA to store the result. Declare a local variable RADIUS with numeric data type. Declare a constant PI with value 3.14. Assign a value to the variable RADIUS by using a substitution variable. Calculate the area of a circle using the formula

AREA = PI * RADIUS * RADIUS

   Then print the result in SQL*Plus.
2. Write a PL/SQL block to find the square, cube, and double of a number, and print the results using built-in package DBMS_OUTPUT.
3. Write a PL/SQL block to swap the values of two variables. Print the variables before and after the swap.
4. Write a PL/SQL program to enter hours and rate. Find gross pay and net pay. The tax rate is 28%. Print your results.
5. Write a PL/SQL program with two variables for the first name and the last name. Print the full name with last name and first name separated by comma and a space.

9

SQL and Control Structures in PL/SQL

IN THIS CHAPTER . . .

- You will learn about various programming control structures in PL/SQL.
- Different decision-making statements based on various options are covered.
- Looping statements are introduced to perform a set of statements repetitively.
- SQL statements are embedded within a PL/SQL block to interact with the Oracle server.

In the previous chapter, you learned about the basics of the PL/SQL programming language. You are now able to write simple programs using local, host, and substitution variables, you can perform simple calculations by using assignment statements, and you know how to use Oracle's built-in package DBMS_OUTPUT. PUT_LINE in program blocks to display results from the buffer. The sample programs and lab exercises have a series of statements that are executed from the beginning to the end in a linear fashion. In this chapter, you will see the use of different control structures employed in a high-level programming language. In the beginning, this book teaches you PL/SQL language constructs to write any programs independent of database. Then the actual use of PL/SQL to interact with the Oracle server is introduced. A PL/SQL program block "talks" to the Oracle server by embedding SQL statements in its executable section.

CONTROL STRUCTURES

In a procedural language like PL/SQL, there are three basic programming control structures:

1. In a *sequential structure,* a series of instructions are performed from the beginning to the end in a linear order. None of the instructions is skipped, and none of the instructions is repeated.
2. The *selection structure* is also known as a *decision structure* or an *IF-structure.* It involves conditions with a TRUE or FALSE outcome. Based on the outcome, one of the options is performed and the other option is skipped. Selection statements are also available for multiple options.
3. In a *looping structure,* a series of instructions are performed repeatedly. There are different looping statements appropriate for a variety of situations. A programmer writes a loop correctly to perform a loop a certain number of times.

We have already covered sequential statements in the previous chapter. In this chapter, we will talk about the selection and the looping structure. In actuality, a program may utilize one or a combination of all control structures.

Selection Structure

There are three selection or conditional statements in PL/SQL. Relational operators, logical operators, and other special operators are used to create Boolean conditions. The tables in Fig. 9-1, 9-2, and 9-3 are repeated here from Chapter 5 for reading convenience only. Figure 9-1 shows the use of relational operators. The relational operators constitute simple conditions. Figure 9-2 explains the use of logical operators in compound conditions. Figure 9-3 shows a truth table for the AND, OR, and NOT operators. The AND and OR operators are binary operators because they work on two conditions. The NOT operator is a unary operator that works on a single condition.

Relational Operator	Meaning
=	Equal to
<>	Not equal to
>	Greater than
>=	Greater than or equal to
<	Less than
<=	Less than or equal to

Figure 9-1 Relational operators.

Logical Operator	Meaning
AND	Returns TRUE only if both conditions are true.
OR	Returns TRUE if one or both conditions are true.
NOT	Returns TRUE if the condition is false.

Figure 9-2 Logical operators.

AND	OR	NOT
TRUE AND TRUE = TRUE	TRUE OR TRUE = TRUE	NOT TRUE = FALSE
TRUE AND FALSE = FALSE	TRUE OR FALSE = TRUE	NOT FALSE = TRUE
FALSE AND TRUE = FALSE	FALSE OR TRUE = TRUE	NOT NULL = NULL
FALSE AND FALSE = FALSE	FALSE OR FALSE = FALSE	
NULL AND TRUE = NULL	NULL OR TRUE = TRUE	
NULL AND FALSE = FALSE	NULL OR FALSE = NULL	
NULL AND NULL = NULL	NULL OR NULL = NULL	

Figure 9-3 AND, OR, and NOT.

Other special operators (IS NULL, IN, LIKE, and BETWEEN...AND) discussed in SQL are also available in PL/SQL. PL/SQL has three conditional or selection statements available for decision making:

- IF-THEN-END IF
- IF-THEN-ELSE-END IF
- IF-THEN-ELSIF-END IF

IF-THEN-END IF. The IF-THEN-END IF statement is also known as a simple IF statement. The simple IF statement performs action statements if the result of the condition is TRUE. If the condition is FALSE, there is no action to perform and the program continues with the next statement in the block. The general syntax is

IF condition THEN
    Action statements
END IF

For example, Fig. 9-4 shows a simple IF statement with two assignment statements, which will be performed if the name is 'Dev'. If the condition is false, the statements are skipped. In this example, notice the use of the relational operator equals (=) in a Boolean condition and use of the assignment operator (:=) in the action assignment statements.

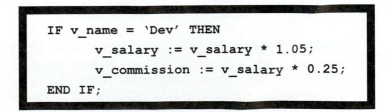

```
IF v_name = 'Dev' THEN
      v_salary := v_salary * 1.05;
      v_commission := v_salary * 0.25;
END IF;
```

Figure 9-4 Simple IF statement.

You must have noticed the ***indentation*** in program code. All program statements can start in the first column. In fact, you can write more than one statement on one line with the appropriate punctuation mark (;) separating them. However, such programming practice can make your program difficult to read. It is a good practice to indent statements within a block or a compound statement because it makes your program more readable. A program will work just the same without indenting statements or without adding a ***comment*** to it, but good programming practices make everybody's life easier.

IF-THEN-ELSE-END IF. The IF-THEN-ELSE-END IF statement is an extension of simple IF statement. This statement provides action statements for the TRUE outcome as well as the FALSE outcome. The general syntax is

```
IF condition THEN
    Action statements 1
ELSE
    Action statements 2
END IF
```

If the condition's outcome is TRUE, action statements 1 are performed. If the outcome is FALSE, action statements 2 are performed. One set of statements is skipped in any case. For example, see Fig. 9-5.

```
IF v_score >= 60 THEN
     v_grade := 'P';
     DBMS_OUTPUT.PUT_LINE ('Grade is ' || v_grade);
ELSE
     v_grade := 'F';
     DBMS_OUTPUT.PUT_LINE ('Grade is ' || v_grade);
END IF;
```

Figure 9-5 IF-ELSE-END IF statement.

IF-THEN-ELSIF-END IF. The IF-THEN-ELSIF-END IF statement is an extension to the previous statement. When you have many alternatives/options, you can use previously explained statements, but the ELSIF alternative is more efficient than the other two. The DECODE function discussed in SQL is not allowed in PL/SQL. The CASE structure is available in many other programming languages. The ELSIF statement is the PL/SQL version of such a function or statement. The general syntax is

IF condition1 THEN
  Action statements 1
ELSIF condition2 THEN
  Action statements 2
. . .
ELSIF conditionN THEN
  Action statement N
[ELSE
  Else Action statements]
END IF

Notice the word ELSIF, which does not have the last *E* in ELSE. ELSIF is a single word, but END IF uses two words. For example, let us revisit the DECODE function example of Chapter 5 (see Fig. 9-6). We will rewrite it using an ELSIF statement. Let us see the ELSIF equivalent of the DECODE function in Fig. 9-7.

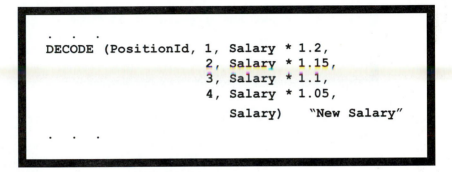

```
    .    .    .
DECODE (PositionId, 1, Salary * 1.2,
                    2, Salary * 1.15,
                    3, Salary * 1.1,
                    4, Salary * 1.05,

                    Salary)    "New Salary"

    .    .    .
```

Figure 9-6 DECODE function.

```
IF v_positionid = 1 THEN
    v_salary := v_salary * 1.2;
ELSIF v_positionid = 2 THEN
    v_salary := v_salary * 1.15;
ELSIF v_positionid = 3 THEN
    v_salary := v_salary * 1.1;
ELSIF v_positionid = 4 THEN
    v_salary := v_salary * 1.05;
ELSE
    v_salary := v_salary;
END IF;
```

Figure 9-7 ELSIF statement.

```
    IF v_score >=90 AND v_score <= 100 THEN
        v_grade := 'A';
END IF;
IF v_score >=80 AND v_score <= 89 THEN
        v_grade := 'B';
END IF;
IF v_score >=70 AND v_score <= 79 THEN
        v_grade := 'C';
END IF;
IF v_score >=60 AND v_score <= 69 THEN
        v_grade := 'D';
END IF;
IF v_score >=0 AND v_score <= 59 THEN
        v_grade := 'F';
END IF;
```

Figure 9-8 Simple IF with multiple conditions.

The same statement can be written with a simple IF statement, which is less efficient. You will need five simple IF statements to accomplish the same task as that performed by a single compound ELSIF statement. Let us take another example with compound conditions. First we will use a simple IF statement (Fig. 9-8), and then we will rewrite it by using ELSIF (Fig. 9-9).

The example here assigns a grade of A, B, C, D, or F based on *v_score*. We are assuming that the score is within the range of 0 to 100. You will need 5 simple IF statements with total of 10 conditions, 2 per each statement. Now, suppose the value of *v_score* is 95. The first statement's condition is TRUE, so *v_grade* will be assigned A. As all simple IF statements are independent statements, the execution will continue with the next IF, and so on. There is no other TRUE condition for *v_score* equal to 95, so *v_grade* will be A after execution of all 5 IF statements. This slows down your program's execution. The ELSIF, on the other hand, is one compound statement, and it stops as soon as a match is found. Let us see how the ELSIF looks.

The ELSIF statement reduces the number of conditions from 10 to 5 and the number of statements from 5 to 1. Now, let us consider the same value 95. The condition is TRUE in the first IF clause and *v_grade* is assigned value A. The statement will not continue down anymore because it will not enter the ELSIF part. The rest of the statement is ignored, thus making ELSIF more efficient than its counterpart (see Fig. 9-9).

```
IF v_score >=90 AND v_score <= 100 THEN
        v_grade := 'A';
ELSIF v_score >= 80 THEN
        v_grade := 'B';
ELSIF v_score >= 70 THEN
        v_grade := 'C';
ELSIF v_score >= 60 THEN
        v_grade := 'D';
ELSE
        v_grade := 'F';
END IF;
```

Figure 9-9 ELSIF statement.

Nested IF statement.   The nested IF statement contains an IF statement within another IF statement. If the condition in the outer IF statement is TRUE, then the inner IF statement is performed. Any IF statement with a compound condition can be written as a nested IF statement. For example, the program segment in Fig. 9-10 assigns an insurance surcharge based on an individual's gender and age.

```
IF (v_gender = 'M') AND (v_age >= 25) THEN
      v_insu_surcharge := 0.05;
END IF;
IF (v_gender = 'M') AND (v_age < 25) THEN
      v_insu_surcharge := 0.10;
END IF;
IF (v_gender = 'F') AND (v_age >= 25) THEN
      v_insu_surcharge := 0.03;
END IF;
IF (v_gender = 'F') AND (v_age < 25) THEN
      v_insu_surcharge := 0.06;
END IF;
```

Figure 9-10 Simple IF with multiple conditions.

```
IF (v_gender = 'M') THEN
     IF (v_age >= 25) THEN
          v_insu_surcharge := 0.05;
     ELSE                              /* ELSE for inner IF */
          v_insu_surcharge := 0.10;
     END IF;
ELSE                                   /* ELSE for outer IF */
     IF (v_age >= 25) THEN
          v_insu_surcharge := 0.03;
     ELSE                              /* ELSE for inner IF */
          v_insu_surcharge := 0.06;
     END IF;
END IF;
```

Figure 9-11   Nested IF statement.

There are four categories: male 25 or over, male under 25, female 25 or over, and female under 25.

Now we will rewrite the code done with a simple IF in Fig. 9-10 by using nested IF statements (see Fig. 9-11). Once again, remember that the nested IF statement will make the code more efficient than the simple IF version. The THEN portion of the outer IF calculates the insurance surcharge for male individuals and the ELSE portion calculates the same for the female individuals. The inner IF statements in each portion check for the age.

Looping Structure

Looping means iterations. A loop repeats a statement or a series of statements a certain number of times as defined by the programmer. You would use a loop to repeat the procedure many times rather than typing the same procedure many times. In PL/SQL, there are three types of looping statements available:

- Basic loop
- WHILE loop
- FOR loop

Each loop has a different syntax, and their working is a little different from each other.

Basic loop. A basic loop is a loop that is performed repeatedly. Once a loop is entered, all statements in the loop are performed. When the bottom of the loop is reached, control shifts back to the top of the loop. The loop will continue infinitely. An infinite loop or "never-ending loop" is a logical error in programming. The only way to terminate a basic loop is by adding an EXIT statement inside the loop. The general syntax is

```
LOOP
    Looping statement1;
    . . .
    EXIT [WHEN condition];
END LOOP;
```

The EXIT statement in the loop could be an independent statement, or it could be part of an IF statement. You can also add a condition with the optional WHEN clause that will end the loop when the condition becomes true. The condition is not checked at the top of the loop, but it is checked inside the body of the loop. The basic loop is performed at least once due to the post-testing.

The example shown in Fig. 9-12 uses a *counter* to control the number of loop executions. There are three necessary statements in a counter-controlled loop. The

```
SET SERVEROUTPUT ON
DECLARE
    v_count      NUMBER (2);
    v_sum        NUMBER (2) := 0;
    v_average    NUMBER (3,1);
BEGIN
    v_count := 1;                      /* counter initialized */
    LOOP
        v_sum := v_sum + v_count;
        v_count := v_count + 1;        /* counter incremented */
        EXIT WHEN v_count > 10;        /* condition */
    END LOOP;
    v_average := v_sum / 10;
    DBMS_OUTPUT.PUT_LINE
        ('Avg of 1 to 10 is ' || TO_CHAR (v_average));
END
/
```

Figure 9-12 Counter-controlled basic loop.

counter must be initialized, the value of the counter must change within the loop (increment or decrement), and a proper condition must exist in the loop. If value of the counter is not changed inside the loop, it will result in an infinite loop. The initial value, the increment/decrement, and the condition control the total number of loop executions.

> **Question:** In a basic loop, if the counter is initialized to 1 and is incremented within the loop by 2, and if the condition is EXIT WHEN counter <10, how many times the loop is performed?
>
> **Answer:** One time (the loop is performed once and then condition is true, so the loop ends).

> **Question:** In a basic loop, the counter is initialized to 0 and is incremented within the loop by 1. How many times will the loop be performed, if the condition is EXIT WHEN counter = 5?
>
> **Answer:** Five times (for counter values equal to 0, 1, 2, 3, and 4).

> **Question:** In a basic loop, the counter is initialized to 10 and is incremented within the loop by 1. How many times will the loop be performed, if the condition is EXIT WHEN counter = 10?
>
> **Answer:** The loop is infinite (the condition will never become true).

WHILE loop.   The WHILE loop is an alternative to the basic loop. The WHILE loop is performed as long as the condition is true. It terminates when the condition becomes false. If the condition is false at the beginning of the loop, the loop is not performed at all. The WHILE loop does not need an EXIT statement to terminate. The general syntax is

```
WHILE condition LOOP
    Looping statement 1;
    Looping statement 2;
    . . .
    Looping statement n;
END LOOP;
```

In Fig. 9-13, you see the same average program of Fig. 9-12 rewritten with a WHILE loop. There are obvious differences between the basic loop and the WHILE loop. The table in Fig. 9-14 explains the differences between the loops.

FOR loop.   The FOR loop is the simplest loop you can write. Unlike the other two loops, you do not have to initialize, test, and increment/decrement the counter separately. You do it in the loop's header. There is no need to use an EXIT statement, and the counter need not be declared. The counter used in the loop is implicitly declared as an integer, and it is destroyed on the loop's termination.

```
SET SERVEROUTPUT ON
DECLARE
    v_count       NUMBER (2);
    v_sum         NUMBER (2) := 0;
    v_average     NUMBER (3,1);
BEGIN
    v_count := 1;                          /* counter initialized */
    WHILE v_count <=10 LOOP                /* condition */
          v_sum := v_sum + v_count;
          v_count := v_count + 1;          /* counter incremented */
    END LOOP;
    v_average := v_sum / 10;
    DBMS_OUTPUT.PUT_LINE
          ('Avg of 1 to 10 is ' || TO_CHAR (v_average));
END
/
```

Figure 9-13   Counter-controlled WHILE loop.

Basic Loop	WHILE Loop
It is performed as long as the condition is false.	It is performed as long as the condition is true.
It tests the condition inside the loop (post-test loop).	It checks the condition before entering the loop (Pretest loop).
It is performed at least one time.	It is performed 0 or more times.
It needs EXIT statement to terminate.	There is no need for an EXIT statement.

Figure 9-14   Differences between a basic loop and a WHILE loop.

The general syntax is

> **FOR counter IN [REVERSE] lower..upper LOOP**
>   **Looping statement 1**
>   **Looping statement 2**
>   **. . .**
>   **Looping statement n**
> **END LOOP;**

The counter varies from the lower value to the upper value, incrementing by 1 with every loop execution. The loop can be used with the counter starting at a higher value and decrementing by 1 with every loop execution. The keyword REVERSE is used for varying the counter in the reverse order.

```
SET SERVEROUTPUT ON
DECLARE
    v_sum        NUMBER (2) := 0;
    v_average    NUMBER (3,1);
BEGIN
    FOR v_count IN 1..10 LOOP
        v_sum := v_sum + v_count;

    END LOOP;
    v_average := v_sum / 10;
    DBMS_OUTPUT.PUT_LINE
        ('Avg of 1 to 10 is ' || TO_CHAR (v_average));
END
/
```

Figure 9-15   FOR loop.

The program in Fig. 9-15 does not declare *v_count,* and there is no condition or explicit statement to change the counter's value. The same program with the counter's value in reverse order will only change one line. The FOR statement will look like

FOR v_count IN REVERSE 1..10 LOOP

Nested loops.   You can use a loop within another loop. The nesting of loops can be to many levels. When the inner loop ends, it does not automatically end the outer loop enclosing it. You can end an outer loop from within the inner loop by labeling each loop and then using the EXIT statement. The loop labels use the same naming rules used for identifiers. The loops are labeled before the keyword LOOP on the same line or on a separate line. The loop label is enclosed within two pairs of angle brackets (<<and>>). For example,

```
<<out_loop>>
LOOP
  . . .
    EXIT WHEN condition;
    <<in_loop>>
    LOOP
      . . .
        EXIT out_loop WHEN condition;     /* exits out loop */
        EXIT WHEN condition;              /*exits both loops */
      . . .
    END LOOP in_loop;                     /* label optional here */
  . . .
END LOOP out_loop;                        /*label optional here */
```

NESTED BLOCKS

The PL/SQL blocks can be nested also. The execution starts with the outer block and continues with the inner block. The variables declared in the outer block are global to the inner block, and they are accessible in the inner block. The variables declared in the inner block are not accessible in the outer block. For example,

```
DECLARE            /* Outer block starts here.*/
    Var1 NUMBER;   /* known to outer and inner*/
BEGIN
  . . .
  DECLARE          /*Inner block starts here.*/
    Var2 NUMBER;   /* known to inner block */
  BEGIN
  . . .
  END;             /* Inner block ends here.*/
  . . .
END;               /* Outer block ends here.*/
```

SQL IN PL/SQL

The PL/SQL statements have control structures for calculations, decision making, and iterations. You need to use SQL to interface with the Oracle server. When changes are necessary in the database, SQL can retrieve information from the database. PL/SQL supports all the Data Manipulation Language (DML) statements such as INSERT, UPDATE, and DELETE. It also supports the Transaction Control Language statements ROLLBACK, COMMIT, and SAVEPOINT. You can retrieve data using the Data Retrieval statement SELECT. A row of data can be used to assign values to variables. More than one row can be retrieved and processed using cursors (covered in the next chapter). PL/SQL statements can use single-row functions, but group functions are not available for PL/SQL statements. SQL statements in PL/SQL can still utilize those group functions.

PL/SQL does not support Data Definition Language (DDL) statements such as CREATE, ALTER, and DROP. The Data Control Language (DCL) statements GRANT and REVOKE are not available in PL/SQL either.

SELECT Statement in PL/SQL

The SELECT statement retrieves data from Oracle tables. The syntax of SELECT is different in PL/SQL because it is used to retrieve values from a row into a list of variables. The general syntax is

```
SELECT ColumnNames
INTO VariableNames / RecordName
FROM TableName
WHERE condition;
```

Where ColumnNames must contain at least one column and may include arithmetic or string expressions, single-row functions, and group functions. VariableNames contains a list of local or host variables to hold values retrieved by the SELECT clause. RecordName is a PL/SQL record covered in the next chapter. All the features of SELECT in SQL are available with an added mandatory INTO clause.

The INTO clause must contain one variable for each value retrieved from the table. The order and data type of columns and variables must correspond. The SELECT-INTO statement must return one and only one row. It is your responsibility to code a statement that returns one row of data. If no rows are returned, the standard exception (error condition) NO_DATA_FOUND occurs. If more than one row is retrieved, the TOO_MANY_ROWS exception occurs.

In Fig. 9-16, a few columns from a row of the EMPLOYEE table are retrieved into a series of variables. The variables can be declared with data types, but more appropriately declaration attribute %TYPE is used to avoid any data type mismatches.

The SQL statement in PL/SQL ends with a semicolon. The INTO clause is mandatory in SELECT statement, when used in a PL/SQL block. Let us look at another example, in Fig. 9-17, that uses a substitution variable and a group function in the SELECT-INTO statement.

```
DECLARE
        v_last        employee.Lname%TYPE;
        v_first       employee.Fname%TYPE;
        v_sal         employee.Salary%TYPE;
BEGIN
        SELECT Lname, Fname, Salary
               INTO v_last, v_first, v_sal
               FROM employee
               WHERE EmployeeId = 200;

        .   .   .

END;
```

Figure 9-16   SELECT-INTO in PL/SQL.

DATA MANIPULATION IN PL/SQL

You can use all DML statements in PL/SQL with the same syntax you used in SQL. The three DML statements to manipulate data are

- The INSERT statement to add a new row into the table.

- The DELETE statement to remove a row or rows.
- The UPDATE statement to change values in a row or rows.

INSERT Statement

We will use an INSERT statement to add a new employee in the table. The statement will use sequences created earlier. For simplicity, only a few columns are used in the statement in Fig. 9-18. NEXTVAL uses the next value from the sequence as the new EmployeeId, and CURRVAL uses the current value of the department from that sequence. If you decide to also insert today's date as the hire date, you could use SYSDATE function for the value.

DELETE Statement

You will see the use of DELETE statement in the PL/SQL block to remove some rows. Suppose the NamanNavan Corporation decides to remove the Marketing

```
DECLARE
      v_max          employee.Salary%TYPE;
BEGIN
      SELECT MAX (Salary)
            INTO v_max
            FROM employee
            WHERE DeptId = &dept_num;
      .  .  .
END;
```

Figure 9-17 Group function and substitution variable.

```
BEGIN
  INSERT INTO employee (EmployeeId, Lname, Fname, Salary, DeptId)
        VALUES (employee_EmployeeId_seq.NEXTVAL, 'Roshan',
                  'Hrithik', 90000, dept_DeptId_seq.CURRVAL);
  COMMIT;
END;
```

Figure 9-18 INSERT in PL/SQL.

```
DECLARE
        v_deptid        dept.DeptId%TYPE;
BEGIN
        SELECT DeptID
                INTO v_deptid
                FROM dept
                WHERE UPPER (DeptName) = 'MARKETING';
        DELETE FROM employee
                WHERE DeptId = v_deptid;
        COMMIT;
END;
```

Figure 9-19   DELETE in PL/SQL.

department. All the employees belonging to that department must be removed from the employee table. Figure 9-19 shows the DELETE statement in PL/SQL.

UPDATE Statement

The UPDATE statement can be used in a PL/SQL block for modification of data. The company decides to give a bonus commission to all the employees who are entitled to commission. The bonus is 10% of the commission received. Figure 9-20 shows an example of an UPDATE statement in PL/SQL block to modify commission.

```
DECLARE
        v_bonus        NUMBER (3,2) := 0.10;
BEGIN
        UPDATE employee
          SET commission = commission + (commission * v_bonus)
          WHERE commission IS NOT NULL;
        COMMIT;
END;
```

Figure 9-20   UPDATE in PL/SQL.

TRANSACTION CONTROL STATEMENTS

You know what a transaction is. You also know the transaction control capabilities in Oracle. In Figs. 9-18, 9-19, and 9-20, after performing a DML statement, the sample blocks have used a COMMIT statement. You do not have to commit within a PL/SQL block. If you decide to use it, your data manipulation would be written to the disk right away and the locks from those rows would be lifted. All transaction control statements are allowed in PL/SQL, and they are as follows:

- The COMMIT statement to commit the current transaction.
- The SAVEPOINT statement to mark a point in your transaction.
- The ROLLBACK [TO SAVEPOINT n] statement to discard all or part of the transaction.

IN A NUTSHELL . . .

- The three control structures in PL/SQL are sequence, selection, and looping.
- In a sequence structure, the instructions are performed in linear order.
- The selection structure involves decision making based on the outcome from a Boolean expression.
- The looping structure contains a series of instructions that are performed repeatedly.
- Three selection structure statements in PL/SQL are IF-THEN-END IF, IF-THEN-ELSE-END IF, and IF-THEN-ELSIF-END IF.
- Boolean expressions or conditions use relational operators (=, <>, >, >=, <, <=), logical operators (AND, OR, NOT) and other operators (BETWEEN..AND, IS NULL, LIKE).
- It is a good practice to add comments to a program and to indent statements within a programming block.
- The three types of loops in PL/SQL are basic loop, WHILE loop, and FOR loop.
- The basic loop is performed at least one time, and it is performed as long as the condition is false. It is known as a post-test loop. The basic loop needs the EXIT statement to terminate.
- The WHILE loop is performed 0 or more times. It is performed as long as the condition is true. It is a pretest loop. The WHILE loop does not need the EXIT statement to terminate.
- The FOR loop is the simplest loop to write. It declares a loop-control variable implicitly, and it does not need the EXIT statement to end.

- The nested loop has a loop within a loop. Termination of the inner loop does not automatically terminate the outer loop. The loops can be labeled and can be terminated with the EXIT statement.
- The PL/SQL programming blocks can also be nested. The variables declared in the outer block are available in the inner block, but variables declared in the inner loop are not accessible to the outer block.
- PL/SQL does not interact directly with the Oracle server. SQL is embedded in a PL/SQL block to work with tables.
- DML, data retrieval, and transaction control SQL statements are allowed in PL/SQL. DDL and DCL statements are not allowed in PL/SQL.
- The group functions are not supported in PL/SQL statements, but they can be used in SQL statements within a PL/SQL block.
- The SELECT-INTO statement retrieves data from a table into a set of variables. It must retrieve only one row at a time.
- The INSERT, DELETE, and UPDATE statements in a PL/SQL block are used to manipulate data in underlying tables.

EXERCISE QUESTIONS

True/False:
1. IF statements are used to repeat a series of instructions.
2. The WHILE loop is always performed at least one time.
3. A basic loop is performed as long as a condition is false.
4. The WHILE loop is performed as long as a condition is true.
5. The FOR loop exits when the EXIT statement is encountered.
6. The counter used in a FOR loop need not be declared explicitly.
7. The SELECT statement must have a mandatory INTO clause when used in a PL/SQL block.
8. The group functions are not supported in PL/SQL statements, but the single-row functions are.
9. The GRANT statement is allowed in PL/SQL.
10. When two PL/SQL blocks are nested, the variables declared in the outer block are accessible in the inner block.

Answer the following questions.
1. Name and explain the control structures used in PL/SQL programming.
2. What is the difference between IF-THEN-ELSE-END IF and IF-THEN-ELSIF-END IF statements?
3. Give four differences between the basic loop and the WHILE loop.
4. List the SQL statements allowed and not allowed in a PL/SQL block.
5. What is the purpose of a SELECT statement in the PL/SQL block? Explain it with an example.

Fill in the following table for a counter-controlled WHILE loop.

Initial Value of Counter	Condition	Increment/Decrement	Number of Loop Executions
1	< 10	1	
0	<= 100	5	
10	<= 5	−1	
1	>= 7	1	
0	<= 10	2	

LAB ACTIVITY

1. Write a PL/SQL block to find out if a number is odd or even. (*Hint:* The function MOD (n, d) divides *n* by *d* and returns the integer remainder from the operation)
2. Write a PL/SQL block to print all odd numbers between 1 and 10 using a basic loop.
3. Using a FOR loop, print the values 10 to 1 in reverse order.
4. Create a table called ITEM with one attribute ItemNum with NUMBER type. Write a PL/SQL program to insert values of 1 to 5 for ItemNum.
5. Input a number with a substitution variable and then print its multiplication table using a WHILE loop.
6. Use a PL/SQL block to delete item number 4 from the ITEM table created in Lab Activity 4.

10

Cursors and Exceptions

IN THIS CHAPTER . . .

- You will learn about a private work area for a SQL statement and its active set, called a cursor.
- You will be introduced to implicit and explicit cursor types.
- You will perform open, fetch, and close actions on explicit cursors.
- Cursor FOR loops are explained.
- Cursors as parameters and variable cursors are introduced.
- PL/SQL errors, known as exceptions, are explained.
- The process of declaring, raising, and handling different types of exceptions is covered.

In previous chapters, you learned about different control structures: sequence, selection, and looping. All structured programming languages support these structures. Other statements are also available in most of the languages. One of the statements is the GOTO statement. The GOTO statement allows you to branch unconditionally. All you have to code is GOTO <<LabelName>>, and the control shifts to the statement after the label. The GOTO statement, though available, is not preferred due to its nonstructured nature. You also know how to use a SQL statement within a PL/SQL block for data retrieval, data manipulation, and transaction control. In this chapter, you will learn about some advanced features of PL/SQL such as retrieving more than one row from a database into a work area called Cursor. One of the strongest benefits of PL/SQL is its error-handling capabilities. The error conditions, known as exceptions in PL/SQL, are also covered in this chapter.

CURSORS

When you execute an SQL statement from a PL/SQL block, Oracle assigns a private work area for that statement. The work area stores the statement and the results returned by execution of that statement. A cursor is either created automatically or is created by you explicitly.

TYPES OF CURSORS

The cursor in PL/SQL is of two types:

- The contents of a *static cursor* are known at compile time. The cursor object for such an SQL statement is always based on one SQL statement.
- In a *dynamic cursor*, a cursor variable is used that can change its value. The variable can refer to different SQL statements at different times.

This chapter covers static cursors in detail and also introduces you to the new concept of dynamic cursors using a cursor variable. The static cursors are of two types:

- You do not declare an *implicit cursor*. PL/SQL declares, manages, and closes it for every Data Manipulation Language statement such as INSERT, UPDATE, or DELETE.
- You declare an *explicit cursor* when you have an SQL statement in a PL/SQL block that returns more than one row from an underlying table. The rows retrieved by such a statement into an explicit cursor make up the "active set." The cursor points to one row in the active set. You can work with one row at a time from the active set. The cursor returns the current row it is pointing to.

IMPLICIT CURSORS

PL/SQL creates an implicit cursor when an SQL statement is executed from within the program block. The implicit cursor is created only if an explicit cursor is not attached to that SQL statement. Oracle opens an implicit cursor, and the pointer is set to the first (and the only row) in the cursor. Then the SQL statement is fetched and executed by SQL engine on the Oracle server. The PL/SQL engine closes the implicit cursor automatically. A programmer cannot perform all these operations on an implicit cursor with commands. PL/SQL creates an implicit cursor for each DML statement in PL/SQL code. You cannot use an explicit cursor for DML statements. You can choose to declare an explicit cursor for a SELECT statement that returns only one row of data. If you don't declare an explicit cursor for a SELECT statement returning one row of data, an implicit cursor is created for it.

You have no control over an implicit cursor. The implied queries perform operations on implicit cursors. PL/SQL actually tries to fetch twice to make sure that a TOO_MANY_ROWS exception does not exist. The explicit cursor is more efficient because it does not try that extra fetch. It is advisable to use an explicit cursor for a SELECT statement that returns just one row because you have control over it.

EXPLICIT CURSORS

An explicit cursor is declared as a SELECT statement in the PL/SQL block. It is given a name, and you can use commands to work with it. You have total control of when to open the cursor, when to fetch a row from it, and when to close that cursor. There are cursor attributes in PL/SQL to get the status information on explicit cursors. Remember that an explicit cursor can be declared for a SELECT statement that returns one or more rows, but you cannot use an explicit cursor for a DML statement.

Four actions can be performed on an explicit cursor:

- Declare it.
- Open it.
- Fetch row(s) from it.
- Close it.

Declaring an Explicit Cursor

A cursor is declared as a SELECT statement. The SELECT statement must not have an INTO clause in a cursor's declaration. If you want to retrieve rows in a specific order into a cursor, an ORDER BY clause can be used in the SELECT statement. The general syntax is

CURSOR CursorName IS
SELECT statement;

where CursorName is the name of the cursor that follows identifier's naming rules. The SELECT statement is any valid data retrieval statement. The cursor declaration

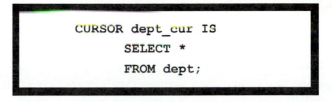

```
        CURSOR dept_cur IS
            SELECT *
            FROM dept;
```

Figure 10-1   Explicit cursor.

```
CURSOR employee_cur IS
        SELECT EmployeeId, Salary
        FROM employee
        WHERE DeptId = 20;
```

Figure 10-2   Explicit cursor.

is done in the DECLARE section of the PL/SQL block, but a cursor cannot be used in programming statements or expressions like other variables. For example, Figs. 10-1 and 10-2 show declarations of two cursors.

A cursor is based on a SELECT statement, so it is linked to at least one table from the database. The list that follows can contain names of columns, local variables, constants, functions, and bind variables. It is possible for a variable to have the same name as a column in a table. If you try to use them both together in a SELECT statement, the column gets higher precedence. It is advisable not to use the same name for a variable that exists in a column retrieved by the SELECT statement.

In the next section, we will talk about the actions performed on an explicit cursor.

Actions on Explicit Cursors

Actions are performed on cursors declared in the DECLARE section of the block. Before rows can be retrieved from a cursor, you must first open the cursor.

Opening a cursor.   When a cursor is opened, its SELECT query is executed. The active set is created using all tables in the query and restricting rows that meet the criteria. The data retrieved by the SELECT query is brought into the cursor or the work area. The cursor points to the first row in the active set. PL/SQL uses an OPEN statement to open a cursor. The general syntax is

OPEN CursorName;

For example,

OPEN employee_cur;

If the SELECT query does not return any rows, PL/SQL does not raise an exception. You should open a cursor that is never opened in the program block or is closed. If you try to open a cursor that is already open, it results in the following Oracle server error:

ORA-06511: PL/SQL: cursor already open

You will see later how this can be avoided using the cursor attribute %ISOPEN.

Fetching data from a cursor.   The SELECT statement creates an active set based on tables in the FROM clause, column names in the SELECT clause, and rows based on conditions in the WHERE clause. The cursor is a virtual table that you can work with. You can retrieve a row that the cursor is pointing to. The values from a row are retrieved into variables to perform processing. After reading values from a row into variables, the cursor pointer moves to the next row in the active set. The number of variables must match the number of columns in the row. In PL/SQL, a FETCH statement is used for this action. The general syntax is

FETCH CursorName INTO VariableList / RecordName;

where VariableList may include a local variable, a table, or a bind variable. RecordName is the name of the record structure. For example,

FETCH employee_cur INTO v_empnum, v_sal;

or

FETCH employee_cur INTO emp_rec;

where *emp_rec* is declared with %ROWTYPE declaration attribute:

emp_rec employee_cur%ROWTYPE;

In the first example, two columns, EmployeeID and Salary, are retrieved into *v_empnum* and *v_sal* respectively. The number of items matches the number of variables in the SELECT statement. The order of items and variables must also match. The variables should be declared with a %TYPE declaration variable to ensure the correct data type. If the number of items in SELECT does not match the number of variables, it results in the following compiler error:

PLS-00394: wrong number of values in the INTO list of a FETCH statement

The second example of FETCH uses a record. A composite data type of record can be used instead of the CursorName%ROWTYPE declaration. You will learn about the record data type in the next chapter.

Suppose you opened a cursor in a PL/SQL block to retrieve data from a table and inserts, deletes, and updates are performed on that table after the OPEN statement is executed. Oracle shows **read consistency,** and the data manipulation statements are ignored. You will have the same data from the point of execution of OPEN to the point of execution of CLOSE statements.

Closing a cursor.   When you are done with a cursor, you should close it. A closed cursor can be reopened again. If you terminate your PL/SQL program without closing an open cursor, it will not result in an exception. In fact, the local cursor declared in a PL/SQL block is closed automatically when the block terminates. It is a good habit to close an open cursor before terminating the block. There is a limit to the number of cursors a user may open simultaneously. The default value is in a parameter called OPEN_CURSORS, which has default value of 50. A user releases memory by closing a cursor. PL/SQL uses the CLOSE statement to close a cursor. The general syntax is

CLOSE CursorName;

For example,

CLOSE employee_cur;

EXPLICIT CURSOR ATTRIBUTES

Actions can be performed on cursors with OPEN, FETCH, and CLOSE statements. You can get information about the current status of a cursor or result of the last fetch by using cursor attributes. The four explicit cursor attributes are

%ISOPEN	it returns a TRUE if the cursor is open, otherwise it returns FALSE.
%FOUND	it returns a TRUE if the last fetch returned a row, otherwise it returns a FALSE.
%NOTFOUND	it returns a TRUE if the last fetch did not return a row, otherwise it returns a FALSE.
%ROWCOUNT	it returns the total number of rows returned.

%ISOPEN

The %ISOPEN attribute is useful in making sure that you do not open a cursor that is already open. It is also appropriate to make sure that a cursor is open

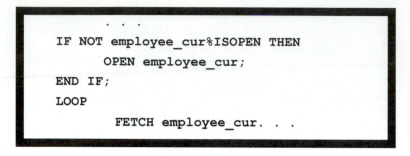

```
        . . .
    IF NOT employee_cur%ISOPEN THEN
            OPEN employee_cur;
    END IF;
    LOOP
            FETCH employee_cur. . .
```

Figure 10-3   %ISOPEN.

before trying to fetch from it. For example, Fig. 10-3 tests to see if a cursor is open. If it is not open, then it opens it. Then execution continues with a loop and a fetch in it.

%FOUND

The %FOUND attribute returns a TRUE if the last FETCH returned a row, otherwise it returns a FALSE. For example, Fig. 10-4 shows a block segment that exits the loop if a row is not found. The loop continues as long as a row is fetched.

```
OPEN employee_cur;
LOOP
        FETCH employee_cur INTO v_empnum, v_sal;
        EXIT WHEN NOT employee_cur%FOUND;
        UPDATE employee
            SET Salary = Salary * 1.10
        WHERE Salary > 75000;
END LOOP;
CLOSE employee_cur;
```

Figure 10-4   %FOUND.

%NOTFOUND

The %NOTFOUND attribute returns a TRUE if the last FETCH did not return a row, otherwise it returns a FALSE. It is the opposite of the %FOUND attribute. The statement

EXIT WHEN NOT employee_cur%FOUND;

can be written as

EXIT WHEN employee_cur%NOTFOUND;

%ROWCOUNT

When a cursor is opened and no fetch is done from it, %ROWCOUNT is equal to zero. With every fetch, %ROWCOUNT is incremented by 1. The cursor must be open before using %ROWCOUNT on it. For example, the code in Fig. 10-5 goes through the loop as long as a row is fetched. A count of the number of rows fetched is kept by the PL/SQL engine. In the code, we are printing the total number of rows fetched by the cursor.

```
OPEN employee_cur;
LOOP
      FETCH employee_cur INTO v_empnum, v_sal;
      EXIT WHEN employee_cur%NOTFOUND;
      .   .   .
END LOOP;
DBMS_OUTPUT.PUT_LINE (TO_CHAR (employee_cur%ROWCOUNT));
CLOSE employee_cur;
```

Figure 10-5   %ROWCOUNT.

IMPLICIT CURSOR ATTRIBUTES

An implicit cursor cannot be opened, fetched from, or closed with a statement. You do not name implicit cursors. The cursor attributes are available for an implicit cursor with the name SQL as a prefix. The attributes for a implicit cursor are:

    SQL%ISOPEN
    SQL%ROWCOUNT
    SQL%NOTFOUND
    SQL%FOUND

If an implicit cursor is not open, SQL%ROWCOUNT will return a NULL. Similarly, the other three attributes will return a FALSE. You will never get an

INVALID_CURSOR error for an implicit cursor. The %ISOPEN attribute will always return a FALSE because it is open within the statement itself. It is opened and closed implicitly. When a SELECT statement returns no rows or more than one row, NO_DATA_FOUND or TOO_MANY_ROWS exceptions respectively are raised. The cursor attribute SQL applies to the last SQL statement executed in the block.

CURSOR FOR LOOPS

The cursor FOR loop is the easiest way to write a loop for explicit cursors. The cursor is opened implicitly when the loop starts, a row is fetched into the record from the cursor with every pass of the loop, the cursor is closed automatically when the loop ends, and the loop ends when there is no more row. The cursor FOR loop automates all the cursor actions. The general syntax is

```
FOR RecordName IN CursorName LOOP
    Loop statements;
    . . .
END LOOP;
```

where RecordName is the name of the record that is declared implicitly in the loop and is destroyed when the loop ends. During the loop execution, implicit fetch retrieves a row into the record for processing. CursorName is the name of declared explicit cursor. For example, Fig. 10-6 uses a Cursor FOR loop with a record. The open, fetch, and close statements are missing because these operations are performed implicitly.

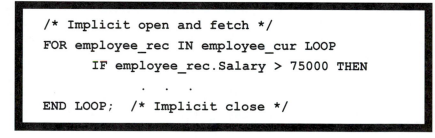

```
/* Implicit open and fetch */
FOR employee_rec IN employee_cur LOOP
        IF employee_rec.Salary > 75000 THEN

                .   .   .
END LOOP;   /* Implicit close */
```

Figure 10-6 Cursor FOR loop.

Cursor FOR Loop Using a Sub-Query

The use of a sub-query in the cursor FOR loop eliminates declaration of an explicit cursor. The cursor is created by a sub-query in the FOR loop statement itself. In

```
BEGIN
/* Implicit open and fetch */
FOR employee_rec IN (SELECT EmployeeId, Salary
                     FROM employee
                     WHERE DeptId = 20) LOOP
      IF employee_rec.Salary > 75000 THEN
               .   .   .
END LOOP;
/* Implicit close */
```

Figure 10-7   Cursor FOR loop with a sub-query.

Fig. 10-7, an explicit cursor is used with implicit actions. One thing that is missing is the cursor name. The cursor declaration is not necessary because it is created through the sub-query.

SELECT . . . FOR UPDATE CURSOR

When you type a SELECT query, the result is returned to you without locking any rows in the table. The row locking is kept at minimum. You can explicitly lock rows for update before changing them in the program. The FOR UPDATE clause is used with the SELECT for row locking. The locked rows are not available to other users until you release them with COMMIT or ROLLBACK commands. The rows locked for update do not have to be updated. The general syntax is

> CURSOR CursorName IS
> SELECT ColumnNames
> FROM TableName
> [WHERE condition]
> FOR UPDATE [OF ColumnNames] [NOWAIT];

The optional part of FOR UPDATE is OF ColumnNames, which enables you to specify columns to be updated. You can actually update any column in a locked row. The optional word NOWAIT tells you right away if another user has already locked the table and lets you continue with other tasks. If you do not use NOWAIT, you will have to wait till the lock is released.

WHERE CURRENT OF CLAUSE

In a cursor, data manipulation in the form of an UPDATE or DELETE is performed on rows fetched. The WHERE CURRENT OF clause allows you to perform data manipulation on a recently fetched row. The general syntax is

> *UPDATE TableName*
>   *SET clause*
> *WHERE CURRENT OF CursorName;*
> _____
> *DELETE FROM TableName*
> *WHERE CURRENT OF CursorName;*

You do not have to use a separate WHERE condition. The WHERE CURRENT OF clause references the cursor, and changes apply to only the current row fetched.

CURSOR WITH PARAMETERS

A cursor can be declared with parameters, which allow you to pass values to the cursor. The values are passed to the cursor when it is opened, and they are used in the query when it is executed. With the use of parameters you can open and close a cursor many times with different values. The cursor with different values will then return different active sets each time it is opened. When parameters are passed, you need not worry about the scope of variables. The general syntax is

> *CURSOR CursorName*
>   *[(Parameter1 DataType, Parameter2 DataType, . . .)]*
> *IS*
> *SELECT query;*

Where Parameter1, Parameter2, . . . are formal parameters passed to the cursor. The DataType is any scalar data type assigned to the parameter. The parameters are assigned only data types. Size is not assigned to them.

When a cursor is opened, values are passed to the cursor. Each value must match the positional order of parameters in a cursor's declaration. The values can be passed through literals, PL/SQL variables, or bind variables. The parameters in a cursor are passed in to the cursor, but you cannot pass any value out of the function through parameters.

For example, in the PL/SQL program in Fig. 10-8, the cursor *employee_cur* is declared with a parameter *dept_id,* which is also used in the cursor's SELECT statement's WHERE clause. The cursor is opened with a value of 10 for the parameter. The active set is created based on *dept_id,* = 10. Then the cursor loop prints all employees and their salary for department number 10. The parameter can be passed a value with a literal (as done in the figure), a bind variable, or an expression.

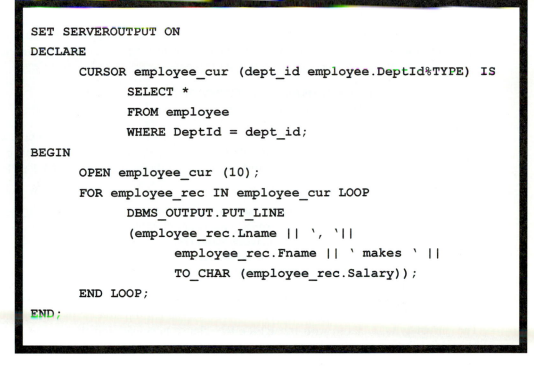

```
SET SERVEROUTPUT ON
DECLARE
      CURSOR employee_cur (dept_id employee.DeptId%TYPE) IS
            SELECT *
            FROM employee
            WHERE DeptId = dept_id;
BEGIN
      OPEN employee_cur (10);
      FOR employee_rec IN employee_cur LOOP
            DBMS_OUTPUT.PUT_LINE
            (employee_rec.Lname || ', '||
                  employee_rec.Fname || ' makes ' ||
                  TO_CHAR (employee_rec.Salary));
      END LOOP;
END;
```

Figure 10-8   Cursor with parameter.

When you declare a cursor with a parameter, you can initialize it to a default value as follows:

CURSOR employee_cur (dept_id employee.DeptId%TYPE := 99) IS

CURSOR VARIABLES: AN INTRODUCTION

An explicit cursor is the name of the work area for an active set. The cursor variable is a reference to the work area. A cursor is based on one specific query, whereas a cursor variable can be opened with different queries within a program. A static cursor is like a constant, and a cursor variable is like a pointer to that cursor. You can also use the action statements OPEN, FETCH, and CLOSE with cursor variables. The cursor attributes %ISOPEN, %FOUND, %NOTFOUND, and %ROW-COUNT are available for cursor variables. Cursor variables have many similarities with static cursors.

The cursor variable has other capabilities in addition to the features of a static cursor. It is a variable, so it can be used in an assignment statement. A cursor variable can be assigned to another cursor variable.

REF CURSOR Type

There are two steps involved in creating a cursor variable. First, you have to create a referenced cursor type. Second, you have to declare an actual cursor variable with referenced cursor type. The general syntax is

> TYPE CursorTypeName IS REF CURSOR [RETURN ReturnType];
> CursorVarName CursorTypeName;

where CursorTypeName is the name of the type of cursor. The RETURN clause is optional. The ReturnType is the RETURN data type. The ReturnType can be any valid data structure such as a record or structure defined with %ROWTYPE. For example,

> TYPE any_cursor_type IS REF CURSOR;
> TYPE employee_cursor_type IS REF CURSOR
>   RETURN employee%ROWTYPE;
> any_cursor_var any_cursor_type;
> employee_cursor_var employee_cursor_type;

The first cursor type, *any_cursor_type,* is called the **weak** type because its RETURN clause is missing. This type of cursor type can be used with any query. The cursor type declared with the RETURN clause is considered the **strong** type because it links a row type to the cursor type at the declaration time.

Opening a Cursor Variable

You assign a cursor to the cursor variable when you OPEN it. The general syntax is

> OPEN CursorName / CursorVarName FOR SELECT query;

If the cursor type is declared with the RETURN clause, the structure from the SELECT query must match the structure specified in the REF TYPE declaration. For example,

> OPEN employee_cursor_var FOR SELECT * FROM employee;

The structure returned by the SELECT query matches the RETURN type employee%ROWTYPE.

The other cursor type, *any_cursor_type,* is declared without the RETURN clause. It can be opened without any worry about matching the query's result with anything. The weak type is more flexible than the strong type, but there is no error checking. Let us look at some OPEN statements for the weak cursor variable:

> OPEN any_cursor_var FOR SELECT * FROM dept;
> OPEN any_cursor_var FOR SELECT * FROM employee;
> OPEN any_cursor_var FOR SELECT DeptId FROM dept;

It is possible to have all three statements in one program block. The cursor variable assumes different structures with each OPEN.

Fetching from a Cursor Variable

The fetching action is same as that of a cursor. The compiler checks the data structure type after the INTO clause to see if it matches the query linked to the cursor. The general syntax is

FETCH CursorVarName INTO RecordName / VariableList;

EXCEPTIONS

In PL/SQL, language errors are known as exceptions. An exception occurs during the execution of a program when an unwanted situation arises. The exceptions can occur due to a system error, a user error, or an application error. When the exception occurs, control of the current program block shifts to another section of the program known as the exception section to handle exceptions. If the exception handler part exists, it is performed. If an exception handler does not exist in the current block, control propagates to the outer blocks. If the not handler is in any blocks, PL/SQL returns an error.

A programmer writes a program to perform certain tasks keeping only the positive things in mind. Programming is not only writing statements to perform a task. It requires a lot more than that. A programmer must think of all the negative things that may happen while the program is executed: The system might run out of memory, the database might not be accessible, the user might type in the wrong value, or the user might press the wrong key. The programmer must put extra effort into program design to remove bugs and make the program error-proof with additional code to perform in case of exceptions. PL/SQL provides ways to trap and handle errors, and it is possible to create PL/SQL programs with full protection against errors. When an exception-handling code is written for an exception, the exception can occur anywhere in the block and the same handler can handle it.

The syntax of an anonymous block is given below. Control transfers from the execution section to the exception section. PL/SQL browses through the section to look for the handler. If the handler is present, it is executed. The execution section can have more than one exception handler in it, written like an ELSIF structure or other programming language's CASE structure.

```
DECLARE
    Declaration of constants, variables, cursors, and exceptions
BEGIN
    /* Exception is raised here.*/
EXCEPTION
    /* Exception is trapped here.*/
END;
```

The general syntax of an exception section is

```
EXCEPTION
    WHEN ExceptionName1 [OR ExceptionName2, . . .] THEN
        Executable statements
    [WHEN ExceptionName3 [OR ExceptionName4, . . .] THEN
        Executable statements]
    [WHEN OTHERS THEN
        Executable statements]
```

An exception is handled when the exception name matches the name of the raised exception. The exceptions are trapped by names. If an exception is raised but there is no handler for it, a WHEN OTHERS clause is performed if present. If there is no handler for an exception and there is no WHEN OTHERS clause, the error number and associated message are displayed to the user.

TYPES OF EXCEPTIONS

There are three types of exceptions in PL/SQL:

- *Predefined Oracle server exceptions* are exceptions that are named by PL/SQL and are raised implicitly when a PL/SQL or DBMS error occurs. There are about 20 such errors.

- *Nonpredefined Oracle server exceptions* are standard Oracle server errors that are not named by the system. They can be declared in the declarative section but are raised implicitly by the server.

- *User-defined exceptions* are exceptions that are declared in the declarative section and raised by the user explicitly. The user decides which abnormal condition is an exception.

Predefined Oracle Server Exceptions

The exceptions that are given names by PL/SQL are declared in a PL/SQL package called STANDARD. The exception handling routine is also defined. The user does not have to declare or raise predefined server exceptions. The table in Fig. 10-9 provides the exception name, the error code returned by the built-in function SQLCODE, and a brief description of the exception.

Suppose a program block generates an error message for exception error number ORA-01403 that is not handled by the exception section. The error has occurred due to a SELECT statement that did not return any data. You can write an exception handler as shown here:

```
EXCEPTION
    WHEN NO_DATA_FOUND THEN
        DBMS_OUTPUT.PUT_LINE ('No row returned');
END;
```

Exception Name	Oracle Error	Brief Description
NO_DATA_FOUND	ORA-01403	Single-row SELECT returned no data.
TOO_MANY_ROWS	ORA-01422	Single-row SELECT returned more than one row.
ZERO_DIVIDE	ORA-01476	Attempted to divide by zero.
VALUE_ERROR	ORA-06502	Arithmetic, conversion, truncation, or size constraint error occurred.
STORAGE_ERROR	ORA-06500	PL/SQL ran out of memory, or memory is corrupted.
LOGIN_DENIED	ORA-01017	Logging on to Oracle with an invalid username or password.
NOT_LOGGED_ON	ORA-01012	PL/SQL program issues a database call without being connected to Oracle.
PROGRAM_ERROR	ORA-06501	PL/SQL has an internal problem.
ACCESS_INTO_NULL	ORA-06530	Attempted to assign values to the attributes of an uninitialized object.
CURSOR_ALREADY_OPEN	ORA-06511	Attempted to open already open cursor.
DUP_VAL_ON_INDEX	ORA-00001	Attempted to insert a duplicate value.
INVALID_CURSOR	ORA-01001	Illegal cursor operation occurred.
INVALID_NUMBER	ORA-01722	Conversion of a character string to number failed.
ROWTYPE_MISMATCH	ORA-06504	Host cursor variable and PL/SQL cursor variable involved in an assignment have incompatible return types.
TIMEOUT_ON_RESOURCE	ORA-00051	Time-out occurred while Oracle is waiting for a resource.

Figure 10-9   Predefined/named system exceptions.

Nonpredefined Oracle Server Exceptions

A nonpredefined Oracle server exception has an Oracle error code attached to it, but it is not named by Oracle. You can trap such exceptions with a WHEN OTHERS clause or by declaring them with names in the DECLARE section. The declared exception is raised implicitly by Oracle, or you can raise it explicitly. You can write exception handler code for it.

PRAGMA_EXCEPTION_INIT.   PRAGMA is a compiler directive that associates an exception name to an internal Oracle error code. The PRAGMA directive is not processed with the execution of a PL/SQL block, but it directs the PL/SQL compiler to associate a name to the error code. You can use more than one PRAGMA_EXCEPTION_INIT directive in your DECLARE section and assign more than one name to the same error number. Naming an internal error code makes your program more readable.

Naming and associating are two separate statements in the declaration section. First, an exception name is declared as an EXCEPTION. Second, the declared name is associated with an internal error code returned by SQLCODE with the PRAGMA directive. The general syntax is

> *ExceptionName EXCEPTION;*
> *PRAGMA_EXCEPTION_INIT (ExceptionName, ErrorNumber);*

where ExceptionName is user supplied and ErrorNumber is Oracle's internal error code. The error code is a numeric literal with a negative sign.

Suppose you tried to remove a department from the DEPT table but the child rows still exist in the EMPLOYEE table because there are employees with that DeptId. You will get an Oracle error ORA-02292. You can declare an exception and associate it with the server error code number 2292. Fig. 10-10 shows a PL/SQL

```
DECLARE
      emp_remain   EXCEPTION;
      PRAGMA_EXCEPTION_INIT (emp_remain, -2292);
      v_deptid     dept.DeptId%TYPE := &p_deptnum;
BEGIN
      DELETE FROM dept
            WHERE DeptId = v_deptid;
      COMMIT;
EXCEPTION
      WHEN emp_remain THEN
         DBMS_OUTPUT.PUT_LINE ('Department ' ||
            TO_CHAR (v_deptid) ||' cannot be removed. ');
         DBMS_OUTPUT.PUT_LINE ('Employees in department');
END;
```

Figure 10-10 Nonpredefined Oracle server exception.

block with a declaration, an implicit raise, and exception trapping of a nonpredefined Oracle exception.

Exception trapping functions.   When an exception occurs in your program, you can find the error code for the error and its associated message. Once
you know the error code and the message, you can modify your program to take
action based on the error. The two functions to identify the error code and error
message are

- **SQLCODE.** The SQLCODE function returns the number of the error code.
  The number can be assigned to a variable of NUMBER type.
- **SQLERRM.** The SQLERRM function returns the error message associated with the error code. It can be assigned to a VARCHAR2 type
  variable.

Figure 10-11 shows the use of the functions SQLCODE and SQLERRM to
identify the error code and message for further modifications of the exception section of the program based on information displayed.

```
DECLARE
        v_code          NUMBER;
        v_message       VARCHAR2 (255);
BEGIN
        . . .
EXCEPTION
        WHEN OTHERS THEN
                v_code := SQLCODE;
                v_message := SQLERRM;
                DBMS_OUTPUT.PUT_LINE
                        ('Error Code: ' || TO_CHAR (v_code));
                DBMS_OUTPUT.PUT_LINE
                        ('Error Message: ' || v_message);
                ROLLBACK;
END;
```

Figure 10-11   SQLCODE and SQLERRM.

User-Defined Exceptions

The standard errors covered under the previous two types are in the STAN-
DARD package with error code and accompanying message. Often you will
encounter situations that are specific to the program. For example, a birth date
falls in the future, a quantity in the invoice is negative, a department does not
exist, and so on.

You are allowed to define exceptions in PL/SQL. You must perform three
steps for exceptions you want to define:

- You must declare the exception in the DECLARE section. There is no need
  to use a PRAGMA directive because there is no standard error number to
  associate.
- You must raise the exception in the execution section of the program with
  an explicit RAISE statement.
- You must write the handler for the exception.

```
DECLARE
      invalid_deptid EXCEPTION;
BEGIN
      UPDATE employee
      SET Salary := Salary * 1.10
      WHERE DeptId = &dept_num;
      IF SQL%NOTFOUND THEN
            RAISE invalid_deptid;
      END IF;
EXCEPTION
      WHEN invalid_deptid THEN
            DBMS_OUTPUT.PUT_LINE
                  ('Invalid Department ID');
END;
```

Figure 10-12   User-defined exception.

Figure 10-12 is an example of a user-defined exception *invalid_deptid*. If you are
trying to modify rows in an EMPLOYEE table based on a department and the supplied DeptId does not exist, no rows will be updated.

RAISE_APPLICATION_ERROR procedure. The RAISE APPLICA-
TION_ERROR procedure allows you to display nonstandard error codes and user-
defined error messages from a stored subprogram. The general syntax is

RAISE_APPLICATION_ERROR (error_code, error_message [, TRUE/FALSE];

where the error_code is a user-specified number between $-20,000$ and $-20,999$.
Here error_message is a user-supplied message that can be up to 2048 bytes long.
The third Boolean parameter, TRUE/FALSE, is optional. The TRUE value means
"place the error on stack of other errors." The FALSE value is default value, and
it replaces all previous errors. For example,

```
                    EXCEPTION
                 WHEN NO_DATA_FOUND THEN
                 RAISE_APPLICATION_ERROR
                 (–20001, 'Department does not exist');
```

You can use a RAISE_APPLICATION_ERROR procedure in the execution and
exception sections of the program. It is very useful in communicating errors between the client and the server.

In a PL/SQL program with an anonymous block that has nested blocks and
procedures and functions, the outermost block nests other blocks and calls the procedures and functions. Each block can have its own exception-handling section, and
some blocks may not have an exception section. An exception declared in the inner block cannot be raised in the enclosing outer block. If an exception is declared
in the outer block, it can be raised in the block itself or in its subblock. When the
exception is raised implicitly or explicitly in the inner block without the exception
section, control shifts to the adjacent outer block and propagates outward until its
handler is found and handled or it ends up being an unhandled exception. The
RAISE statement is very much like the GOTO statement. They both branch to another part of the program. The difference is that the RAISE statement branches
to the exception section, whereas the GOTO statement branches to another statement in an executable block.

SAMPLE PROGRAMS

In this section, you will see the PL/SQL blocks based on the topics covered in this
chapter such as an explicit cursor, a cursor FOR loop, a cursor with parameters,
and exception handling. The code in Fig. 10-13 uses an explicit cursor
employee_cur. The active set contains the employee's last name, salary, and
commission. The WHILE loop is used to work with one row at a time. Within
the loop, an employee's salary and commission are added together to find total
income. Also, note the use of a single-row function NVL in case the commission

```
SQL> SET SERVEROUTPUT ON
  2   /* The program uses a cursor to get employee information.
  3      Then it prints employee's total pay if the total pay is
  4      below $50,000. */
  5   DECLARE
  6     CURSOR employee_cur IS
  7     SELECT Lname, Salary, Commission FROM employee;
  8     v_last            employee.Lname%TYPE;
  9     v_sal             employee.Salary%TYPE;
 10     v_commi           employee.Commission%TYPE;
 11     v_total_sal       employee.Salary%TYPE;
 12   BEGIN
 13     OPEN employee_cur;
 14     FETCH employee_cur INTO v_last, v_sal, v_commi;
 15     WHILE employee_cur%FOUND LOOP
 16       v_total_sal := v_sal + NVL (v_commi, 0);
 17       IF v_total_sal < 50000 THEN
 18         DBMS_OUTPUT.PUT_LINE (v_last || ' makes $ ' ||
 19               TO_CHAR (v_total_sal));
 20       END IF;
 21       FETCH employee_cur INTO v_last, v_sal, v_commi;
 22     END LOOP;
 23     CLOSE employee_cur;
 24   END
 25   /
Shaw makes $ 27500
Chen makes $ 35000


PL/SQL procedure successfully completed.
```

Figure 10-13 Sample program—explicit cursor.

value is NULL. The employee information is printed if the total income for the employee is below $50,000.

When the program in Fig. 10-14 is executed, you will be prompted to enter the date for the substitution variable *p_date*. When the cursor is opened with *v_date* as a parameter, it will retrieve rows that have HireDate on or after the entered date. The information for those employees will be printed.

The program in Fig. 10-15 selects employees with PositionId equal to 2 who are managers. It locks those rows for future update. Using a cursor FOR loop, each

```
SQL> SET SERVEROUTPUT ON
  2  /* The program uses a cursor with a date type parameter.
  3     It retrieves information based on user input for
  4     the parameter.  Then it prints the information.*/
  5  DECLARE
  6    CURSOR empl_cur (start_date DATE) IS
  7    SELECT Lname, Fname, HireDate, DeptId FROM employee
  8      WHERE HireDate >= start_date;
  9    v_last            employee.Lname%TYPE;
 10    v_first           employee.Fname%TYPE;
 11    v_hiredate        employee.HireDate%TYPE;
 12    v_dept            employee.DeptId%TYPE;
 13    v_date            employee.HireDate%TYPE := '&p_date';
 14  BEGIN
 15    OPEN empl_cur (v_date);
 16    FETCH empl_cur INTO v_last, v_first, v_hiredate, v_dept;
 17    WHILE empl_cur%FOUND LOOP
 18      DBMS_OUTPUT.PUT_LINE (v_last || ', ' || v_first ||
 19        TO_CHAR (v_hiredate) || TO_CHAR (v_dept));
 20      FETCH empl_cur INTO v_last, v_first, v_hiredate, v_dept;
 21    END LOOP;
 22    CLOSE empl_cur;
 23  END;
```

Figure 10-14 Sample program—cursor with parameter.

```
SQL> SET SERVEROUTPUT ON
  2  /* The program uses a cursor to update salary of employees,
  3     who are Managers.   It locks rows with FOR UPDATE clause.
  4     It updates row fetched with WHERE CURRENT OF clause */
  5  DECLARE
  6    CURSOR mgr_cur IS
  7    SELECT Lname, Salary FROM employee
  8      WHERE PositionId = 2
  9      FOR UPDATE;
 10  BEGIN
 11    FOR mgr_rec IN mgr_cur LOOP
 12      UPDATE employee
 13        SET Salary = Salary * 1.07
 14      WHERE CURRENT OF mgr_cur;
 15    END LOOP;
 16    COMMIT;
 17  END
 18  /
```

Figure 10-15   Sample program—cursor FOR loop.

manager's salary is modified to give a 7% raise. The WHERE CURRENT OF clause is used to modify the current row fetched. The rows are released with the COMMIT command.

The program in Fig. 10-16 displays two customized prompts for an employee's ID and the percentage increment. The UPDATE statement changes the salary if the ID is correct. If the employee ID does not exist, a standard exception is raised implicitly. The exception is handled by adding a comment or message into Oracle's MESSAGE table.

IN A NUTSHELL . . .

- A cursor is a private work area to store a statement and its active set.
- A static cursor's contents are known at compile time, and a dynamic cursor uses a cursor variable, which can refer to different SQL statements at different times.

```
SQL> SET SERVEROUTPUT ON
  2  /* The program uses a substitution variable for
  3     employee's id and percentage of salary increase.   If
  4     employee is not found, an exception is raised*/
  5  ACCEPT p_empid PROMPT 'Enter employee Id: '
  6  ACCEPT p_raise PROMPT 'Enter raise in decimal (0.05 for 5%): '
  7  DECLARE
  8    v_empid              employee.EmployeeId%TYPE := &p_empid;
  9    v_sal                employee.Salary%TYPE;
 10    v_raise              NUMBER (3,2) := &p_raise;
 11  BEGIN
 12    UPDATE employee
 13      SET Salary = Salary + Salary * v_raise
 14    WHERE EmployeeId = v_empid;
 15    DBMS_OUTPUT.PUT_LINE ('Salary Updated');
 16  EXCEPTION
 17    WHEN NO_DATA_FOUND THEN
 18      INSERT INTO MESSAGES VALUES ('EmployeeId not found');
 19  END
 19  /

PL/SQL procedure successfully completed.
```

Figure 10-16   Sample program—exception handling.

- An implicit cursor is declared, managed, and closed by PL/SQL.
- The user declares an explicit cursor for a PL/SQL block that returns more than one row from the table.
- Four actions are performed on explicit cursors: declare, open, fetch, and close.
- The cursor attributes %ISOPEN, %FOUND, %NOTFOUND, and %ROWCOUNT give the status of the cursor.
- The cursor attributes are used with an implicit cursor with SQL as a qualifier or a prefix, for example SQL%ISOPEN.
- A cursor FOR loop implicitly opens, fetches, and closes a cursor.
- An explicit cursor does not need to be declared if the cursor FOR loop uses a sub-query to create a cursor.

- The SELECT...FOR UPDATE statement is used with a cursor to lock rows for future updates. These rows are released with COMMIT or ROLLBACK statements.
- The WHERE CURRENT OF clause allows you to perform data manipulation on a recently fetched row.
- A cursor with parameters enables you to pass values to a cursor.
- A cursor variable can be opened with different queries within the same program. All action statements and cursor attributes can be used with a cursor variable.
- PL/SQL errors are called exceptions. The exceptions are handled in the exception section of the PL/SQL block.
- The three types of exceptions are predefined Oracle server exceptions, non-predefined Oracle server exceptions, and user-defined exceptions.
- Predefined Oracle server exceptions are declared in the Oracle package called STANDARD. There are approximately 20 such exceptions.
- Non-predefined Oracle server exceptions are declared with a PRAGMA_EXCEPTION_INIT directive to associate an exception name with the standard error code.
- User-defined exceptions are declared, raised, and handled explicitly.
- The exception-trapping functions SQLCODE and SQLERRM return an error code and the associated error message respectively.

EXERCISE QUESTIONS

True/False:
1. A cursor variable is a dynamic cursor that can refer to different SQL statements at different times.
2. An implicit cursor is used when an SQL statement in the PL/SQL block returns more than one row from the table.
3. The ORDER BY clause is not allowed in the SELECT statement of an explicit cursor's declaration.
4. If a cursor FOR loop uses a sub-query with an IN clause, there is no need to declare that cursor.
5. A nonpredefined Oracle server error is declared with a PRAGMA_EXCEPTION_INIT directive.
6. A user-defined exception is declared with a PRAGMA_EXCEPTION_INIT directive.
7. The RAISE statement is used to raise a predefined Oracle server exception.

State the differences between the following terms.
1. Static cursor and dynamic cursor
2. Implicit cursor and explicit cursor
3. Predefined Oracle server exception and user-defined exception

Answer the following questions.

1. What actions can be performed on an explicit cursor? Give an example of each statement used.
2. What are the four cursor attributes? State their use.
3. Can you use cursor attributes with implicit cursors? If yes, how?
4. What is a cursor FOR loop? What are its benefits?
5. What are exceptions? Where are they handled?
6. Name three error-trapping functions. How are they useful?
7. How are the three types of exceptions declared, raised, and handled?

LAB ACTIVITY

1. Create a PL/SQL block to declare a cursor to select last name, first name, salary, and hire date from the EMPLOYEE table. Retrieve each row from the cursor and print the employee's information if the employee's salary is greater than $50,000 and the hire date is after 31-DEC-1995 (explicit cursor problem).
2. Create a PL/SQL block that declares a cursor. Pass a parameter to the cursor of the type that is the same as the Salary column in EMPLOYEE table to the cursor. Open the cursor with a value for the parameter. Retrieve information into the cursor for a salary higher than the parameter value. Use a loop to print each employee's information from the cursor (cursor with parameter problem).
3. Create a PL/SQL block to increase the salary of employees in department 10. The salary increase is 15% for the employees making less than $100,000 and 10% for the employees making $100,000 or more. Use a cursor with a FOR UPDATE clause. Update the salary with a WHERE CURRENT OF clause in a cursor FOR loop (cursor FOR loop problem).
4. Write a PL/SQL block to retrieve employees from the EMPLOYEE table based on a department number. If the department number returns more than one row, handle the exception with the appropriate handler and print the message 'More than one employee in the department'. If the department returns no employee, handle the exception with the appropriate handler and display the message 'No employees in the department'. If the department returns one employee, then print that employee's name and salary (predefined server exception problem).
5. Write a PL/SQL block with an exception handler that displays a message 'Department does not exist' in the DEPT table when you execute the block with a department ID of 99 (user-defined exception problem).

11

Composite Data Types:
Records and Tables

IN THIS CHAPTER . . .

- You will learn about composite data types in PL/SQL.
- The basics of a PL/SQL record structure and its declaration, assignment of a value, and use in a program are covered.
- The PL/SQL composite data type of table is discussed, together with its declaration, referencing, and types of assignments.
- Built-in methods to obtain table information are outlined.
- A complex structure, a table of records, is also introduced.

COMPOSITE DATA TYPES

Composite data types are data types like scalar data types. Scalar data types are atomic because they do not consist of a group. Composite data types, on the other hand, are groups, or "collections." The examples of composite data types are RECORD, TABLE, nested TABLE, and VARRAY. In this chapter, we will talk about the RECORD and TABLE types. The other two are not covered in this book.

242

PL/SQL RECORDS

PL/SQL records are similar in structure to a row in a database table. A record consists of components of any scalar, PL/SQL record, or PL/SQL table type. These components are known as "fields," and they have their own values. The PL/SQL records are similar in structure to "structures" in C language. The record does not have a value as a whole. A record enables you to access these components as a group. It makes your life easier by transferring the entire row into a record, rather than transferring each column into a variable separately.

You already have learned about a cursor-based record in the previous chapter:

```
CURSOR CursorName IS
   SELECT Query;
RecordName CursorName%ROWTYPE;
```

A record is also based on another composite data type called TABLE. We will examine user-defined records in this next section.

Creating a PL/SQL Record

In this section, you will learn to create a user-defined record. You create a RECORD type first and then declare a record with that RECORD type. The general syntax is

```
TYPE RecordTypeName IS RECORD
   (FieldName1 DataType / Variable%TYPE / table.column%TYPE /
   table%ROWTYPE [[NOT NULL] := / DEFAULT Expression]
   [, FieldName2...
   , FieldName3...);
RecordName RecordTypeName;
```

For example,

```
TYPE employee_rectype IS RECORD
   (e_last     VARCHAR2 (15),
    e_first    VARCHAR2 (15),
    e_sal      NUMBER (8,2));
employee_rec  employee_rectype;
```

In this declaration, *employee_rectype* is the user-defined RECORD type. There are three fields included in the structure. The record *employee_rec* is a record declared with user-defined record type *employee_rectype*. Each field declaration is like a scalar variable declaration.

Now, you will look at another declaration with the %TYPE attribute.

For example,

```
TYPE employee_rectype IS RECORD
      (e_id        NUMBER (3) NOT NULL := 111,
      e_last       employee.Lname%TYPE,
      e_first      employee.Fname%TYPE,
      e_sal        employee.Salary%TYPE);
employee_rec    employee_rectype;
```

The NOT NULL constraint can be used for any field to prevent NULL values, but that field must be initialized with a value.

Referencing Fields in a Record

A field in a record has a name given in the RECORD type definition. You cannot reference a field by its name only, you must use the record name as a qualifier:

RecordName.FieldName

The record name and field name are joined by a dot (.). For example, you can reference the *e_sal* field from the previous declaration as

```
employee_rec.e_sal
```

You can use a field in an assignment statement to assign value to it, for example,

```
employee_rec.e_sal := 100000;
employee_rec.e_last := 'Spreewell';
```

Working with Records

A record is known in the block it is declared in. When the block ends, the record does not exist anymore. You can assign values to a record from columns in a table's row by using the SELECT statement or the FETCH statement. The order of fields in the record must match the order of columns in the table's row. A record can be assigned to another record if they have the same structure.

A record can be set to NULL and all fields will be set to NULL, but do not try to assign a NULL to a record that has fields with NOT NULL constraints. For example,

```
Employee_rec := NULL;
```

In the previous chapter, you saw the use of %ROWTYPE attribute. The record declared with %ROWTYPE has the same structure as the table's row. For example,

```
emp_rec       employee%ROWTYPE;
```

Here *emp_rec* assumes the structure of the EMPLOYEE table. The fields in
emp_rec take column names and their data types from the table. It is advantageous
to use %ROWTYPE because it does not require you to know the column names
and their data types in the underlying table. If you change the data type and/or the
size of a column, the record is created at execution time and will be defined with
the updated structure. The fields in the record declared with %ROWTYPE are referenced with the qualified name RecordName.Fieldname.

Nested Records

You can create a nested record by including a record into another record as a field.
The record that contains another record as a field is called the **enclosing record.**
For example,

```
DECLARE
   TYPE address_rectype IS RECORD
      (first   VARCHAR2 (15),
       last    VARCHAR2 (15),
       street  VARCHAR2 (25),
       city    VARCHAR2 (15),
       state   CHAR (2),
       zip     CHAR (5));
   TYPE all_address_rectype IS RECORD
      (home_address       address_rectype,
       bus_address        address_rectype,
       vacation_address   address_rectype);
   address_rec   all_address_rectype;
```

In the example, *all_address_rectype* nests *address_rectype* as its field type. If
you decide to use an unnested simple record, the record becomes cumbersome.
There are six fields in *address_rectype*. You will have to use six fields each for each
of the three fields *home_address, bus_address,* and *vacation_address,* which will result
in 18 fields.

Nesting records makes code more readable and easy to maintain. You can
nest records to multiple levels. Dot notation is also used to reference fields in nested
situation. For example, *address_rec.home_address.city* references a field called *city*
in the nested record *home_address,* which is enclosed by the record *address_rec.*

PL/SQL TABLES

A table, like a record, is composite data structure in PL/SQL. A PL/SQL table is
a single-dimensional structure with a collection of elements that store the same type
of value. In other words, it is like an array in other programming languages. If you
know COBOL, arrays are called tables in COBOL terminology, although there are

dissimilarities between a traditional array and a PL/SQL table. A table is a dynamic structure that is not constrained.

Declaring a PL/SQL Table

A PL/SQL table declaration is done in two steps, like a record declaration:

- Declare a PL/SQL Table type with a TYPE statement. The structure could use any of the scalar data types.
- Declare an actual table based on the type declared in the previous step.

The general syntax is

```
TYPE TableTypeName IS TABLE OF
    DataType / VariableName%TYPE / TableName.ColumnName%TYPE
    [NOT NULL] INDEX BY BINARY_INTEGER;
```

For example,

```
TYPE deptname_table_type IS TABLE OF dept.DeptName%TYPE
    INDEX BY BINARY_INTEGER;
TYPE major_table_type IS TABLE OF VARCHAR2 (50)
    INDEX BY BINARY_INTEGER;
```

You can declare a table type with a scalar data type (VARCHAR2, DATE, BOOLEAN, or POSITIVE) or with the declaration attribute %TYPE. You can optionally use NOT NULL in a declaration, which means that none of the elements in the table may have a NULL value. You must add an INDEX BY BINARY_IN-TEGER clause to the declaration. This is the only available clause for indexing a table at present. The indexing speeds up the search process from the table. The primary key is stored internally in the table along with the data column. The table consists of two columns, the index/primary key column and the data column.

You define the actual table based on the table type declared earlier. The general syntax is

```
TableName TableTypeName;
```

For example,

```
deptname_table deptname_table_type;
major_table major_table_type;
```

Figure 11-1 illustrates a table's structure. It contains a primary key (pk) column and a data column. You cannot name these columns. The primary key has the type BINARY_INTEGER, and the data column is of any valid type. There is

PK	Data Column
...	...
1	Sales
2	Marketing
3	Information Systems
4	Finance
5	Production
...	...

Figure 11-1 PL/SQL table structure.

no limit on the number of elements. You cannot initialize elements of a table at declaration time.

Referencing Table Elements/Rows

The row of a table is referenced the same way as an element in an array is referenced. You cannot reference a table by its name only. You have to use the primary key value in a pair of parentheses as its subscript or index:

TableName (PrimaryKeyValue)

The following are valid assignments for the table's rows:

```
deptname_table (5) := 'Human Resources';
major_table (100) := v_major;
```

You can use an expression or a value other than a BINARY_INTEGER value, and PL/SQL will convert it. For example,

```
/* 25.7 is rounded to 26. */
deptname_table (25.7) := 'Training';
/* '5' || '00' is converted to 500. */
deptname_table ('5' || '00') := 'Research';
/* v_num + 7 is evaluated. */
deptname_table (v_num + 7) := 'Development';
```

In other programming languages, such as C or Visual Basic 6, when you declare an array, you specify the number of elements in it. The memory locations are reserved for the elements in an array at the declaration time. In a PL/SQL table, the primary key values are not set aside. The row is created when you assign a value to it. If a row does not exist and you try to access it, the PL/SQL predefined server exception NO_DATA_FOUND is raised. You can keep track of rows' primary key values if you use them in a sequence and keep track of the minimum and the maximum value.

Assigning Values to Rows in a PL/SQL Table

You can assign values to the rows in a table in three different ways:

- Direct assignment
- Assignment in a loop
- Aggregate assignment

Direct assignment.   You can assign a value to a row with an assignment statement as you already have learned in the previous topic. This is preferable if only a few assignments are to be done. If an entire database table's values are to be assigned to a table, a looping method is preferable.

Assignment in a loop.   You can use any of the three PL/SQL loops to assign values to the rows in a table. The program block in Fig. 11-2 assigns all Sunday dates for the year 2000 to a table. The primary key index value will vary from 1 to 52. The table column will contain dates for 52 Sundays. If are innovative, you can create great applications with loops and tables.

```
DECLARE
      TYPE date_table_type IS TABLE OF DATE
            INDEX BY BINARY_INTEGER;
      sunday_table date_table_type;
      v_day BINARY_INTEGER := 1;
      v_date DATE;
BEGIN
      v_date := TO_DATE ('01/01/2000', 'MM/DD/YYYY');
      WHILE v_day <= 52 LOOP
            IF TO_CHAR (v_date, 'DAY') = ('SUNDAY') THEN
                  Sunday_table (v_day):= v_date;
                  DBMS_OUTPUT.PUT_LINE (v_date);
                  v_day := v_day + 1;
            END IF;
            v_date := v_date + 1;
      END LOOP;
END;
```

Figure 11-2   Table row assignments in a loop.

Aggregate assignment. You can assign a table's values to another table. The data types of both tables must be compatible. When you assign a table's values to another table, the table receiving values loses all its previous primary key values as well as its data column values. If you assign an empty table with no rows to another table with rows, the recipient table is cleared. It loses all its rows. Both tables must have the same type for such an assignment.

Built-In Table Methods

The built-in table methods are procedures or functions that provide information about a PL/SQL table. The table in Fig. 11-3 lists the built-in table methods and their use. The general syntax to use built-in methods is

TableName.MethodName [(index1 [, index2])]

where MethodName is one of the methods described in Fig. 11-3. For example,

```
total_rows := deptname_table.COUNT;
deptname_table.DELETE (5);
deptname_table.DELETE (7, 10);
deptname_table.DELETE;
next_row := deptname_table.NEXT (25);
previous_row := deptname_table.PRIOR (20);
first_row := deptname_table.FIRST;
last_row := deptname_table.LAST;
IF deptname_table.EXISTS (11) THEN ...
```

Built-in Method	Use
FIRST	Returns the smallest index number in a PL/SQL table.
LAST	Returns the largest index number in a PL/SQL table.
COUNT	Returns the total number of elements in a PL/SQL table.
PRIOR (n)	Returns the index number that is before index number n.
NEXT (n)	Returns the index number that is after index number n.
EXISTS (n)	Returns TRUE if index n exists in the table.
TRIM	TRIM removes one element from the end of the table.
	TRIM (n) Removes n elements from the end of the table.
DELETE	DELETE removes all elements from a PL/SQL table.
	DELETE (n) removes the nth element from the table.
	DELETE (m, n) removes all elements in the range $m \ldots n$ from a table.
EXTEND (n, x)	Increases the size of a table.
	EXTEND appends a null element to a table.
	EXTEND (n) appends n null elements to a table.
	EXTEND (n, x) appends n copies of the xth element to a table.

Figure 11-3 PL/SQL built-in table methods.

Table of Records

The PL/SQL table type is declared with a data type. You may use a record type as a table's data type. The %ROWTYPE declaration attribute can be used to define the record type. When a table is based on a record, the record must consist of fields with scalar data types. The record must not have a nested record in it. The following examples show different ways to declare table types based on records:

> *A PL/SQL table type based on a programmer-defined record:*
> TYPE student_record_type IS
>   RECORD (stu_id NUMBER (3), stu_name VARCHAR2 (30));
> TYPE student_table_type IS TABLE OF student_record_type
>   INDEX BY BINARY_INTEGER;
> Student_table student_table_type;
> *A PL/SQL table type based on a database table:*
> TYPE employee_table_type IS TABLE OF employee%ROWTYPE
>   INDEX BY BINARY_INTEGER;
> Employee_table employee_table_type;
> *A PL/SQL table type based on a row returned by a cursor:*
> CURSOR employee_cur IS SELECT * FROM employee;
> TYPE employee_cur_table_type IS employee_cur%ROWTYPE
>   INDEX BY BINARY_INTEGER;
> Employee_cur_table employee_cur_table_type;

The %ROWTYPE attribute is not used when the table is based on a user-defined record. You use the %ROWTYPE attribute when the table is based on a database table or a cursor.

The fields of a PL/SQL table based on a record are referenced with the following syntax:

> *TableName (index).FieldName*

For example,

> Student_table (10).stu_name := 'Ephrem';
> Employee_table (13).Salary := 50000;

There are two other types of collections in PL/SQL:

- *Nested tables* are single-dimensional unbounded collections of elements with the same data type. A nested table can be used in PL/SQL as well as a database table. You can use a column that has a table type as its data type in a database table.
- *VARRAYs* are single-dimensional bounded collections of elements with same data type. They retain their ordering and subscripts when stored in and retrieved from a database table.

SAMPLE PROGRAMS

In Fig. 11-4, the program declares two table types. The two tables based on these table types are parallel tables. The corresponding values in the two tables are related. The program populates these two tables using a cursor FOR loop. Then another simple FOR loop is used to print information from the two tables.

The program in Fig. 11-5 declares a record with the %ROWTYPE attribute. The SELECT query retrieves a row into the record based on the department number entered at the prompt. The fields in the record are printed using RecordName.FieldName notation.

```
SQL> SET SERVEROUTPUT ON
  2    DECLARE
  3      TYPE lname_tabtype IS TABLE OF employee.Lname%TYPE
  4        INDEX BY BINARY_INTEGER;
  5      TYPE salary_tabtype IS TABLE OF employee.Salary%TYPE
  6        INDEX BY BINARY_INTEGER;
  7      v_last_tab          lname_tabtype;
  8      v_salary_tab        salary_tabtype;
  9      c                   BINARY_INTEGER := 0;
 10      Cursor c_lastSal IS SELECT Lname, Salary FROM employee;
 11      v_totemp            NUMBER (2);
 12    BEGIN
 13      SELECT COUNT (*) INTO v_totemp FROM employee;
 14      FOR lastsal_rec IN c_lastSal LOOP
 15        c := c +1;
 16        v_last_tab (c) := lastsal_rec.Lname;
 17        v_salary_tab (c) := lastsal_rec.Salary;
 18      END LOOP;
 19      FOR c IN 1..v_totemp LOOP
 20        DBMS_OUTPUT.PUT_LINE (v_last_tab (c) || ' makes ' ||
 21              TO_CHAR (v_salary_tab (c)));
 22      END LOOP;
 23    END
 24    /
```

Figure 11-4   PL/SQL table.

```
SQL> SET SERVEROUTPUT ON
2    ACCEPT dept_num PROMPT 'Please enter a department number:
3    DECLARE
4      dept_rec              dept%ROWTYPE;
5 BEGIN
6    SELECT *
7      INTO dept_rec
8      FROM dept
9    WHERE DeptId = &dept_num;
10   DBMS_OUTPUT.PUT_LINE ('Dept# ' || TO_CHAR (dept_rec.DeptId));
11   DBMS_OUTPUT.PUT_LINE ('Name: ' || dept_rec.DeptName);
12   DBMS_OUTPUT.PUT_LINE ('Location: ' || dept_rec.Location);
13   DBMS_OUTPUT.PUT_LINE ('Manager# ' ||
14                        TO_CHAR (dept_rec.EmployeeId));
15 END
16 /
```

Figure 11-5 PL/SQL record.

IN A NUTSHELL . . .

- PL/SQL has composite data types, which are data types like scalar data types. The composite data types consist of groups or collections.
- The PL/SQL composite data types include records, tables, nested tables, and VARRAYs.
- PL/SQL records are similar in structure to rows in the database table. They consist of components of any scalar type, PL/SQL record type, or PL/SQL table type.
- The components in a PL/SQL record are called fields.
- A record declaration is performed in two steps: First a record type is declared, and then a record is declared with declared record type.
- The fields in a record are referenced with the record name as a qualifier, for example, RecordName.ColumnName.
- A record's fields can be assigned values using a simple assignment statement with the SELECT statement or with the FETCH statement.

- A nested record is a record used as a field in another record. A record containing another record is called the enclosing record.
- A PL/SQL table is another composite data type. It is a single dimensional structure with a collection of elements that store the same type of values.
- A table is like an array but is unbounded.
- A table declaration is in two steps: First a table is declared, and then a table is declared with that table type.
- A table consists of two columns, a primary key column and a data column. The primary key is of type BINARY_INTEGER.
- A table element is referenced by the table name with its index number within the parentheses.
- There are three ways to assign values to a table's elements: direct assignment, assignment in a loop, and aggregate assignment.
- The table's information is obtained with built-in methods, which are PL/SQL functions and procedures. The methods are used with a table name as a qualifier, for example, TableName.Method.
- A table of records is declared with a record type as the table's data type. It can be declared with a record type as its type, with a database table and %ROWTYPE, or with a row returned by a cursor.
- The fields in a table of records are referenced with TableName(index). FieldName.
- The nested tables use a column that has a table type as its data type. They are single-dimensional unbounded collections of elements.
- The VARRAYs are single-dimensional bounded collections of elements. They retain their ordering and subscripts when stored and retrieved from a database table.

EXERCISE QUESTIONS

True/False:

1. A database table is an example of a PL/SQL composite data type.
2. A PL/SQL record can be set to a NULL value with an assignment, in which case all its fields are set to NULL.
3. A record that contains another record as a field is called the enclosing record.
4. A PL/SQL table has a specified number of rows, which cannot be changed, at declaration time.
5. A PL/SQL table has two columns, a primary key column and a data column.
6. A PL/SQL table's row is referenced by the table name and a numeric index.
7. When a PL/SQL table is assigned to another PL/SQL table of the same type, the recipient table loses its previous rows and indexes.

Answer the following questions.

1. How do you declare a PL/SQL record? Explain with an example.
2. Give examples of assignment of values to the fields in a PL/SQL record.
3. What is a PL/SQL table? What are its similarities and differences when compared to an array?
4. How do you declare a PL/SQL table? Explain it with an example.
5. Give three methods used in assigning values to the rows in a PL/SQL table.
6. What is a table of records?

LAB ACTIVITY

1. Create a PL/SQL block to retrieve last name, first name, and salary from the EMPLOYEE table into a cursor. Populate three tables with the values retrieved into the cursor: one to store last names, one to store first names, and one to store salaries. Use a loop to retrieve this information from the three tables and print it to the screen, using the package DBMS_OUTPUT.PUT_LINE.

2. Declare a PL/SQL record based on the structure of the DEPT table. Use a substitution variable to retrieve information about a specific department and store it in the PL/SQL record. Print the record information using DBMS_OUTPUT.PUT_LINE.

3. Use a PL/SQL table of records to retrieve all information from the DEPT table and print information to the screen. You will declare a table to store the names and locations of the departments. Remember that the department number is a multiple of 10. Retrieve all department information from the DEPT table to the PL/SQL table using a loop, and then use another loop to print the information.

12

Procedures, Functions, and Packages

IN THIS CHAPTER . . .

- You will learn about PL/SQL Modules.
- The basics of a named module-called procedure (its call, its body, and its parameter types) are explained.
- The PL/SQL module called *function* is covered, together with its call, body, and RETURN types.
- The structure, specification, and body of a package and its benefits are discussed.
- The triggers and their functioning are introduced.

In the previous chapters dealing with PL/SQL, an anonymous block is used for all programming examples. The anonymous block does not have a name. It cannot be called by another block in the program. It cannot take arguments from another block, either. An anonymous block can call other types of PL/SQL blocks called *procedures* and *functions*. The procedures and functions are named blocks, and they can be called with parameters. An anonymous block can be nested within a procedure, function, or another anonymous block. The purpose of a procedure or function call is to modularize a PL/SQL program.

PROCEDURES

A procedure is a named PL/SQL program block that can perform one or more tasks. A procedure is the building block of modular programming. The general block structure of a procedure is

```
CREATE [OR REPLACE] PROCEDURE ProcedureName
    [ (parameter1 [, parameter2...]) ]
IS
    [ Constant/Variable declarations ]
BEGIN
    Executable statements
[ EXCEPTION
    exception handling statements ]
END [ ProcedureName ];
```

where ProcedureName is a user-supplied name that follows the rules used in naming identifiers. The parameter list has the names of parameters passed to the procedure by the calling program as well as the information passed out of the procedure to the calling program. The local constants and variables are declared after the reserved word IS. If there are no local identifiers to declare, there is nothing between the reserved words IS and BEGIN. The executable statements are written after BEGIN and before EXCEPTION or END. There must be at least one executable statement in the body. The reserved word EXCEPTION and the exception-handling statements are optional.

Calling a Procedure

A call to the procedure is made through an executable PL/SQL statement. The procedure is called by mentioning its name, along with the list of parameters (if any) in parentheses. The call statement ends with a semicolon. The general syntax is

```
ProcedureName [ (parameter1, ...) ];
```

For example,

```
monthly_salary (v_salary);
calculate_net (v_monthly_salary, 0.28);
display_messages;
```

In these examples of procedure calls, the parameters are enclosed in parentheses. You can use a variable, constant, expression, or literal value as a parameter. If you are not passing any parameters to a procedure, there is no need to use parentheses.

Procedure Header

The procedure definition that comes before the IS reserved word is called the procedure header. The procedure header contains the name of the procedure and the parameter list, if any. For example,

```
CREATE OR REPLACE PROCEDURE monthly_salary
    (v_salary_in IN employee.Salary%TYPE)
CREATE OR REPLACE PROCEDURE calculate_net
    (v_monthly_salary_in IN employee.Salary%TYPE,
     v_taxrate_in IN NUMBER)
CREATE OR REPLACE PROCEDURE display_messages
```

The procedure headers in the examples are based on the procedure calls in the previous section. The parameter list in the header contains the name of a parameter with its type. The parameter names used in the procedure do not have to be the same as the names used in the call. The number of parameters in the call and in the header must match, and the parameters must be in the same order.

Procedure Body

The procedure body contains the declarative, executive, and exception-handling sections. The declarative and exception-handling sections are optional. The executive section contains action statements, and it must contain at least one action statement.

The procedure body starts after the IS reserved word. If there is no local declaration, the IS reserved word is followed by the reserved word BEGIN. The body ends with the reserved word END. There can be more than one END statement in the program, so it is a good idea to use the procedure name as the optional label after the END reserved word.

Parameters

Parameters are used to pass values back and forth from the calling environment to the Oracle server. The values passed are processed and/or returned with procedure execution. There are three types of parameters: IN, OUT, and IN OUT. Figure 12-1 shows the uses of the three types of parameters.

Parameter Type	Use
IN	Passes a value into the program. Read-only type of value. It cannot be changed. Constants, literal, and expressions. Default type.
OUT	Passes a value back from the program. Write-only type of value. Cannot assign default value. Variable. If a program is successful, value is assigned.
IN OUT	Passes value in and returns value back. Value is read and then written. Variable.

Figure 12-1 Types of parameters.

Actual and Formal Parameters

The parameters passed in a call statement are called the actual parameters. The parameter names in the header of a module are called the formal parameters. The actual parameters and their matching formal parameters must have the same data types. In the procedure call, the parameters are passed without data types. The procedure header contains formal parameters with data types, but the size of the data type is not required. In Fig. 12-2, the relationship between actual and formal parameters is explained.

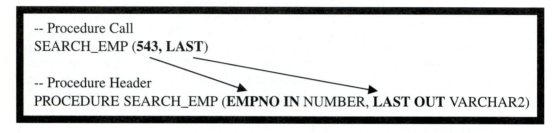

-- Procedure Call
SEARCH_EMP (**543, LAST**)

-- Procedure Header
PROCEDURE SEARCH_EMP (**EMPNO IN** NUMBER, **LAST OUT** VARCHAR2)

Figure 12-2   Actual and formal parameters.

Matching Actual and Formal Parameters

There are two different ways in PL/SQL to link formal parameters and actual parameters:

> In *Positional notation* the formal parameter is linked with an actual parameter implicitly by position (Fig. 12-2).
>
> In *Named notation* the formal parameter is linked with an actual parameter explicitly by name. The formal parameter and actual parameters (the values of the parameters) are linked in the call statement with the symbol =>.

The general syntax is

FormalParameterName => ArgumentValue

For example,

EMPNO => 543

In Fig. 12-3, a procedure script is shown. If a procedure with same name already exists, it is replaced. You can type it in any editor such as Notepad. When you run it, a "Procedure created" message is displayed. The procedure named *total_salary* is compiled into p-code and stored in the database for future execution.

```
CREATE OR REPLACE PROCEDURE total_salary
IS
/* The procedure uses a cursor to get employee information.
   Then it prints employee's total pay if the total pay is
   below $50,000 */
   CURSOR employee_cur IS
     SELECT Lname, Salary, Commission FROM employee;
   v_last                employee.Lname%TYPE;
   v_sal                 employee.Salary%TYPE;
   v_commi               employee.Commission%TYPE;
   v_total_sal           employee.Salary%TYPE;
BEGIN
   OPEN employee_cur;
   FETCH employee_cur INTO v_last, v_sal, v_commi;
   WHILE employee_cur%FOUND LOOP
     v_total_sal := v_sal + NVL (v_commi, 0);
     IF v_total_sal < 50000 THEN
        DBMS_OUTPUT.PUT_LINE (v_last || ` makes $ ` ||
             TO_CHAR (v_total_sal));
     END IF;
     FETCH employee_cur INTO v_last, v_sal, v_commi;
   END LOOP;
   CLOSE employee_cur;
END;
```

Figure 12-3 Procedure without parameters.

You can execute this procedure from SQL*Plus environment (SQL> prompt) with the EXECUTE command. For example,

```
SQL> EXECUTE total_salary
Shaw makes $ 27500
Chen makes $ 35000
PL/SQL procedure successfully completed.
```

If you receive an error, then use the command

```
SHOW ERROR
```

The procedure becomes invalid if the table it is based on is deleted or altered. You can recompile that procedure with the following command:

ALTER PROCEDURE ProcedureName COMPILE;

In Fig. 12-4, the procedure *search_emp* receives three parameters—*i_empid*, *o_lname,* and *o_fname*— as IN, OUT, and OUT types respectively. In Fig. 12-5,

```
CREATE OR REPLACE PROCEDURE search_emp
        (i_empid IN NUMBER,
        o_lname OUT VARCHAR2,
        o_fname OUT VARCHAR2)
IS
BEGIN
        SELECT Lname, Fname
                INTO o_lname, o_fname
                FROM employee
                WHERE EmployeeId = i_empid;
        EXCEPTION
                WHEN OTHERS THEN
                        DBMS_OUTPUT.PUT_LINE
                        (TO_CHAR (i_empid) || ' not found');
END search_emp;
```

Figure 12-4   Procedure with parameters.

```
DECLARE
        v_lname        employee.Lname%TYPE;
        v_fname        employee.Fname%TYPE;
BEGIN
        search_emp (543, v_lname, v_fname);
        DBMS_OUTPUT.PUT_LINE ('Employee: 543');
        DBMS_OUTPUT.PUT_LINE ('Name: '||v_fname||' '||v_lname);
END;
```

Figure 12-5   Anonymous block with procedure call.

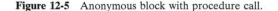

you will see an anonymous block that calls the procedure in Fig. 12-4 with three parameters. The procedure searches for the employee's name based on the ID passed. If the employee is not found, the exception is handled in the procedure. If the employee exists, the procedure sends out the last name and first name of the employee to the calling anonymous block. The anonymous block prints the employee's information.

FUNCTIONS

A function, like a procedure, is a named PL/SQL block. Like a procedure, it is also a stored code. The main difference between a function and a procedure is that a function always returns a value back to the calling block. A function is characterized as follows:

- A function can be passed one, more, or no parameters.
- A function must have an explicit RETURN statement in the executable section to return a value.
- The data type of the return value must be declared in the function's header.
- A function cannot be executed as a standalone program.

A function may have parameters of IN, OUT, and IN OUT types, but the primary use of a function is to return a value with an explicit RETURN statement. The use of OUT and IN OUT parameter types is rare and considered a bad practice. The general syntax is

```
CREATE [ OR REPLACE ] FUNCTION FunctionName
      [ (parameter1 [, parameter2...]) ]
      RETURN DataType
IS
   [ Constant / Variable declarations ]
BEGIN
   Executable statements
   RETURN ReturnValue
[ EXCEPTION
   exception handling statements
   RETURN ReturnValue ]
END [ FunctionName ];
```

The RETURN statement does not have to be the last statement in the body of the function. The body may contain more than one RETURN statement, but only one RETURN is executed with each function call. You would need one return for each exception.

Function Header

The function header comes before the reserved word IS. The header contains the name of the function, the list of parameters (if any), and the RETURN data type.

Function Body

A function's body must contain at least one executable statement. If there is no declaration, the reserved word BEGIN follows the reserved word IS. If there is no exception handler, you can omit the word EXCEPTION. The function name label next to END is optional. There can be more than one return statement, but only one RETURN is executed in a function call.

Return Data Types

A function can return a value of scalar data type such as VARCHAR2, NUMBER, BINARY_INTEGER, or BOOLEAN. It can also return a composite or complex data type such as a PL/SQL table, a PL/SQL record, a nested table, VARRAY, or LOB.

Calling a Function

A function call is similar to the procedure call. You call a function by mentioning its name along with its parameters, if any. The parameter list is enclosed within parentheses. A procedure does not have an explicit RETURN statement, so a procedure call can be an independent statement on a separate line. A function does return a value back, so the function call is made via an executable statement. For example,

```
v_salary := get_salary (&emp_id);
IF emp_exists (v_empid) ...
```

In the first example of a function call, the function *get_salary* is called from an assignment statement with the substitution variable *emp_id* as its actual parameter. The function returns the employee's salary, which is assigned to the variable *v_salary*. In the second example, the function call to the function *emp_exists* is made from an IF statement. The function searches for the employee and returns a Boolean TRUE or FALSE to the statement. An anonymous block calls a function *get_deptname* (see Fig. 12-6) in Fig. 12-7, with an employee's department number as a parameter. The function returns the department name back to the calling block. The calling block prints the employee's information along with the department name.

```
CREATE OR REPLACE FUNCTION get_deptname
      (i_deptid IN NUMBER)
      RETURN VARCHAR2
IS
v_deptname   VARCHAR2 (12);
BEGIN
      SELECT DeptName
            INTO v_deptname FROM dept
            WHERE DeptId = i_deptid;
      RETURN v_deptname;
END get_deptname;
```

Figure 12-6   Function with parameters.

```
SET SERVEROUTPUT ON
DECLARE
      v_deptid              employee.DeptId%TYPE;
      v_department_name VARCHAR2 (12);
      v_empid               employee.EmployeeId%TYPE := &emp_id;
BEGIN
      SELECT DeptId
            INTO v_deptid FROM employee
            WHERE EmployeeId = v_empid;
      v_department_name := get_deptname (v_deptid);
      DBMS_OUTPUT.PUT_LINE ('Employee# '||to_char(v_empid));
      DBMS_OUTPUT.PUT_LINE ('Department Name: '||
                               v_department_name);
      EXCEPTION
            WHEN OTHERS THEN
                  DBMS_OUTPUT.PUT_LINE
                  (TO_CHAR (v_empid) || ' not found');
END;
```

Figure 12-7   Function call from an anonymous block.

The script of the function *get_deptname* is executed in SQL*Plus, which returns a "Function created" message if there are no syntactical errors in the function code. Then the calling anonymous block is executed, which calls the compiled function *get_deptname* with the *v_deptid* parameter of NUMBER type. The function searches through DEPT table and retrieves corresponding department name and returns *v_deptname* back to *v_department_name* in the anonymous block.

The execution of the anonymous block of Fig. 12-7 after the function *get_deptname* is

Enter value for emp_id: 111
Employee# 111
Department Name: Finance
PL/SQL procedure successfully completed.

In the next example, reusability of a function is explained. When a function is compiled and stored, it can be called many times. You write it once and use it many times. Figure 12-8 has a WHILE loop in the anonymous block that

```
SET SERVEROUTPUT ON
DECLARE
      v_sal               employee.Salary%TYPE;
      v_com               employee.Commission%TYPE;
      v_tot_salcom        employee.Salary%TYPE;
      counter             NUMBER(2) := 10;
BEGIN
      WHILE counter <=40 LOOP
            SELECT SUM(Salary), SUM(NVL(Commission, 0))
                  INTO v_sal, v_com FROM employee
                  WHERE DeptId = counter;
            v_tot_salcom := do_total (v_sal, v_com);
            DBMS_OUTPUT.PUT_LINE ('Dept '||TO_CHAR (counter)||
               ' has total Payroll of '||TO_CHAR (v_tot_salcom));
            counter := counter + 10;
      END LOOP;
END;
```

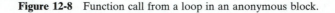

Figure 12-8   Function call from a loop in an anonymous block.

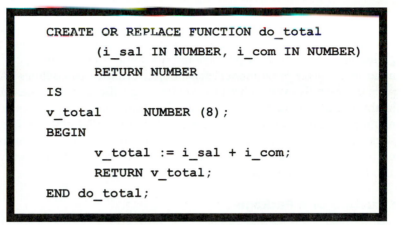

```
CREATE OR REPLACE FUNCTION do_total
        (i_sal IN NUMBER, i_com IN NUMBER)
        RETURN NUMBER
IS
v_total       NUMBER (8);
BEGIN
        v_total := i_sal + i_com;
        RETURN v_total;
END do_total;
```

Figure 12-9   Function called multiple times.

calls the function *do_total* in Fig. 12-9 four times, for values of the counter (or DeptId) equal to 10, 20, 30, and 40. Each time *do_total* adds salary and commission values and returns the total as *v_total*. The variable *v_tot_salcom* gets that value in the anonymous block. The block then prints the total payroll for each department.

PACKAGES

A package is a collection of PL/SQL objects. The objects in a package are grouped within BEGIN and END blocks. A package may contain objects from the following list:

- Cursors
- Scalar variables
- Composite variables
- Constants
- Exception names
- TYPE declarations for records and tables
- Procedures
- Functions

Packages are modular in nature. Oracle has many built-in packages. If you remember, DBMS_OUTPUT is a built-in package. You also know that a package called STANDARD contains definitions of many operators used in Oracle. There are many benefits of a package.

The objects in a package can be declared as public objects, which can be referenced from outside, or private objects, which are known only to the package. You can restrict access to a package to its specification only and hide the actual programming aspect of it. A package follows some rules of object-oriented programming, and it gives programmers some object-oriented capabilities. A package compiles successfully even without a body, if the specification compiles. When an object in the package is referenced for the first time, the entire package is loaded into memory. All package elements are available from that point on because the entire package stays in memory. This one-time loading improves performance. It is very useful when functions and procedures in it are accessed frequently. The package also follows top-down design.

Structure of a Package

A package provides an extra layer to a module. A module has a header and a body, whereas a package has specification and a body. A module's header specifies the name and the parameters, which tell us how to call that module. Similarly, the package specification tells us how to call different modules within a package.

Package Specification

A package specification does not contain any code, but it contains information about the elements of the package. It contains definitions of functions and procedures, declarations of global or public variables, and anything else that can be declared in a PL/SQL block's declaration section. The objects in the specification section of a package are called public objects. The general syntax is

```
CREATE [OR REPLACE] PACKAGE PackageName
IS
   [ constant, variable and type declarations ]
   [ exception declarations ]
   [ cursor specifications ]
   [ function specifications ]
   [ procedure specifications ]
END [ PackageName ];
```

For example,

```
PACKAGE bb_team
IS   total_players CONSTANT INTEGER := 12;
     player_on_dl EXCEPTION;
FUNCTION team_average (points IN NUMBER, players IN NUMBER)
                                        RETURN NUMBER;
END bb_team;
```

Package Body

A package body contains actual programming code for the modules described in the specification section. It also contains code for the modules not described in the specification section. The module code in the body without its description in the specification is called a private or hidden module, and it is not visible outside the body of the package. The general syntax is

```
PACKAGE BODY PackageName
IS   [ variable and type declarations ]
     [ cursor specifications and SELECT queries ]
     [ specification and body of functions ]
     [ specification and body of procedures ]
[ BEGIN
     executable statements ]
[ EXCEPTION
     exception handlers ]
END [ PackageName ];
```

As a column is to the table, so is an object to the package. When you reference an object in a package, you must qualify it with the name of the package with dot notation. If you do not use dot notation to reference an object, the compilation will fail. Within the body of a package, you do not have to use dot notation for that package's objects, but you definitely have to use it to reference an object from another package. For example,

```
IF bb_team.total_players < 10 THEN
   EXCEPTION
      WHEN bb_team.player_on_dl THEN
```

There is a set of rules that you must follow in writing a package's body:

- The variables, constants, exceptions, and so on declared in the specification must not be declared again in the package body.
- The number of cursor and module definitions in the specification must match the number of cursor and module headers in the body.
- Any element declared in the specification can be referenced in the body.

In Fig. 12-10 and Fig. 12-11, package specification and body for course_info package are shown respectively. The calls to a procedure and a function in package course_info are shown in Fig. 12-12 and Fig. 12-13.

```
-- Package specification
  CREATE OR REPLACE PACKAGE course_info
  AS
        PROCEDURE find_title
                (i_courseid IN course.CourseId%TYPE,
                 o_title OUT course.title%TYPE);

        FUNCTION is_it_open
                (i_courseid IN crssection.CourseId%TYPE,
                 i_section IN crssection.Section%TYPE,
                 i_termid IN crssection.TermId%TYPE)
                RETURN BOOLEAN;
  END course_info;
```

Figure 12-10 Package specification.

Triggers

A database trigger, known simply as a trigger, is a PL/SQL block. It is stored in the database and is called implicitly when a triggering event occurs. A user does not call a trigger explicitly. The triggering event is based on a Data Manipulation Language statement such as INSERT, UPDATE, or DELETE. A trigger can be created to fire before or after the triggering event. For example, if you design a trigger to execute after you INSERT a new employee in the EMPLOYEE table, the trigger executes after the INSERT statement. The execution of a trigger is also known as **firing the trigger.** The general syntax is

```
CREATE [ OR REPLACE ] TRIGGER TriggerName
BEFORE / AFTER TriggeringEvent ON TableName
[ FOR EACH ROW ]
[ WHEN condition ]
DECLARE
   Declaration statements
BEGIN
   Executable statements
EXCEPTION
   Exception handling statements
END;
```

```
-- Package Body
CREATE OR REPLACE PACKAGE BODY course_info
IS
      PROCEDURE find_title
            (i_courseid IN course.CourseId%TYPE,
             o_title OUT course.title%TYPE)
      IS
      BEGIN
            SELECT Title
                  INTO o_title
                  FROM course
                  WHERE CourseId = i_courseid;
      EXCEPTION
            WHEN OTHERS THEN
                  DBMS_OUTPUT.PUT_LINE
                  (TO_CHAR(i_courseid)||' not found');
      END find_title;

      /*********************************************/
      FUNCTION is_it_open
            (i_courseid IN crssection.CourseId%TYPE,
             i_section IN crssection.Section%TYPE,
             i_termid IN crssection.TermId%TYPE)
             RETURN BOOLEAN
      IS
            v_count NUMBER;
      BEGIN
            SELECT COUNT (*)
                  INTO v_count
                  WHERE CourseId = i_courseid
                  AND Section = i_section
                  AND TermId = i_termid
                  AND ActualCount < MaxCount;
            IF v_count = 1 THEN
                  RETURN TRUE;
            ELSE
                  RETURN FALSE;
      EXCEPTION
            WHEN OTHERS THEN
                  RETURN FALSE;
      END is_it_open;
END course_info;
```

Figure 12-11 Package body.

```
/* Anonymous block calling a module in a package -
   Procedure find_title in package course_info */
SET SERVEROUTPUT ON
DECLARE
     v_courseid   course.CourseId%TYPE := &p_courseid;
     v_title      course.Title%TYPE;
BEGIN
     Course_info.find_title (v_courseid, v_title);
     DBMS_OUTPUT.PUT_LINE (v_courseid || ' : ' || v_title);
END;
```

Figure 12-12   Call to a procedure in the package of Fig. 12-11.

```
/* Anonymous block calling a module in a package -
   Function is_it_open in package course_info */
DECLARE
     v_flag       Boolean;
BEGIN
     v_flag := Course_info.is_it_open
                    (&&v_courseid, &&v_section, &&v_termid);
     DBMS_OUTPUT.PUT_LINE ('CourseId: ' || &v_courseid);
     DBMS_OUTPUT.PUT_LINE ('Section: ' || &v_section);
     DBMS_OUTPUT.PUT_LINE ('Term: ' || &v_termid);
     IF v_flag = TRUE THEN
          DBMS_OUTPUT.PUT_LINE ('Status: OPEN');
     ELSE
          DBMS_OUTPUT.PUT_LINE ('Status: CLOSED');
     END IF;
END;
```

Figure 12-13   Call to a function in the package of Fig. 12-11.

where CREATE means you are creating a new trigger and REPLACE means you are replacing an existing trigger. The keyword REPLACE is optional, and you should only use it to modify a trigger. If you use REPLACE and a procedure, function, or package exists with the same name, the trigger replaces it. If you create a trigger for a table and then decide to modify it and associate it with another table, you will get an error. If a trigger already exists in one table, you cannot replace it and associate it with another table.

A trigger is very useful in generating values for derived columns, for keeping track of table access, for preventing invalid entries, for performing validity checks, or for maintaining security. There are some restrictions involving creation of a trigger:

- A trigger cannot use a Transaction Control Language statement such as COMMIT, ROLLBACK, or SAVEPOINT. All operations performed by a trigger become part of the transaction. The trigger operations get committed or rolled back with the transaction.
- A procedure or function called by a trigger cannot perform Transaction Control Language statements.
- A variable in a trigger cannot be declared with LONG or LONG RAW data types.

BEFORE Triggers

The BEFORE trigger is fired before execution of a DML statement. The BEFORE trigger is useful when you want to plug in some values in a new row, to insert a calculated column into a new row, or to validate a value in the INSERT query with a lookup in another table.

Figure 12-14 is an example of a trigger that fires before a new row is inserted into a table. If a new employee is being added to the EMPLOYEE table, you can use a trigger to get the next employee number from sequence, use SYSDATE as employee's hire date, and so on. The trigger in Fig. 12-14 fires before the INSERT statement. The naming convention used in the example uses the table name the trigger is for, followed by *bi* for "before insert," and then the word *trigger*. A trigger uses a pseudo-record called :NEW, which allows you to access the currently processed row. The type of record :NEW is TableName%TYPE. In this example the type of :NEW is employee%TYPE. The columns in this :NEW record are referenced with dot notation, for example, :NEW.EmployeeId.

The trigger *employee_bi_trigger* provides values of EmployeeId and HireDate, so you need not include those values in your INSERT statement. If you have many columns that can be assigned values via a trigger, your INSERT statement will be shortened considerably.

```
CREATE OR REPLACE TRIGGER employee_bi_trigger
BEFORE INSERT ON employee
FOR EACH ROW
DECLARE
      v_employee_id      employee.EmployeeId%TYPE;
      v_hiredate         employee.HireDate%TYPE;
BEGIN
      SELECT empoyeeid_seq.NEXTVAL
            INTO v_employee_id
            FROM DUAL;
      :NEW.EmployeeId := v_employee_id;
      :NEW.HireDate := SYSDATE;
END;
```

Figure 12-14   BEFORE trigger.

AFTER Triggers

An AFTER trigger fires after a DML statement is executed. It utilizes the built-in Boolean functions INSERTING, UPDATING, and DELETING. If the triggering event is one of the three DML statements, the function related to the DML statement returns a TRUE and the other two return FALSE. For example, if the current DML statement is INSERT, then INSERTING returns TRUE, but DELETING and UPDATING return FALSE.

The example in Fig. 12-15 uses a table named TRANSHISTORY, which keeps track of transactions performed on a table. It keeps track of the last update and delete, the user who performs it, and the date it is performed. The trigger is named *employee_adu_trigger,* where *adu* stands for "after delete or update." The trigger uses the transaction_type_based on the last DML statement. It also plugs in the user name and today's date. If such a transaction record does not exist in the TRANSHISTORY table, it is inserted into it.

In our example in Fig. 12-14, we used FOR EACH ROW; such a trigger is known as a **row trigger.** If it is based on INSERT, the trigger fires once for every new row inserted. If it is based on UPDATE statement and the UPDATE affects five rows, the trigger is fired five times, once for each affected row. In Fig. 12-15, we did not use a FOR EACH ROW clause. Such a trigger is known as a **statement trigger.** A statement trigger is fired only once for the statement, irrespective of the number of rows affected.

```
CREATE OR REPLACE TRIGGER employee_adu_trigger
AFTER DELETE OR UPDATE ON employee
DECLARE
     v_trans_type        VARCHAR2 (6);
BEGIN
     IF DELETING THEN
          v_tran_type := 'DELETE';
     ELSIF UPDATING THEN
          v_tran_type := 'UPDATE';
     END IF;
     UPDATE transhistory
          SET    transaction_user := USER,
                 transaction_date := SYSDATE;
     WHERE table_name = 'EMPLOYEE' AND
          transaction_name := v_tran_type;
     IF NOT SQL%FOUND THEN
          INSERT INTO transhistory
          VALUES ('EMPLOYEE', v_tran_type, USER, SYSDATE);
     END IF;
END;
```

Figure 12-15   AFTER trigger.

IN A NUTSHELL . . .

- A procedure is a named PL/SQL module that can perform one or more tasks.
- A procedure call contains the name of the procedure along with the list of parameters enclosed within parentheses.
- A procedure body, like an anonymous block, consists of declarative, executive, and exception sections.
- There are three types of parameters: the IN type passes a value into the program; the OUT type passes a value back to the calling program; and the IN OUT type passes a value into a program and returns a value back.
- The formal parameters in a module's header must match the actual parameters in the call to the module.
- A function is a PL/SQL named module that always returns a value back to the calling program.

- A function can return a scalar data type, such as VARCHAR2, NUMBER, BINARY_INTEGER, and BOOLEAN, or complex or composite data type such as a table, a record, a nested table, VARRAY, or LOB.
- A function call is made via an executable PL/SQL statement such as an assignment or an IF statement.
- A function or a procedure is stored in memory by executing it first. It is then called by another module.
- A package is a collection of PL/SQL objects, which are public (can be called by an outside module) or private (known only to the package).
- The structure of a package includes specification and body. The members in a package are referenced with the package name as a qualifier and dot notation.
- A database trigger, or simply a trigger, is stored in the database and called implicitly when a triggering event occurs.
- A trigger is based on a DML statement such as INSERT, DELETE, or UPDATE.
- A BEFORE trigger is fired before execution of a DML statement, and an AFTER trigger is fired after execution of a DML statement.
- A row trigger is fired once for each affected row, whereas a statement trigger is fired only once irrespective of the number of rows affected by the DML statement.

EXERCISE QUESTIONS

True/False:

1. A parameter of type IN passes a read-only value to a module.
2. A parameter of type OUT is assigned a value only if the called module is performed successfully.
3. If a procedure has an IN parameter, it also has an OUT parameter.
4. A function always has an OUT parameter to return a value back.
5. V_EMPNAME IN VARCHAR2 (25) is a valid parameter definition in the header of a module.
6. A procedure does not require a RETURN type, but a function does.
7. Control of execution shifts from a function to the calling program with the RETURN statement.
8. All procedures and functions in a package body must be declared in the package specification.
9. A trigger is fired before or after a triggering event.
10. A trigger based on a SELECT statement fires automatically after the statement's execution.

Answer the following questions.

1. Name three types of PL/SQL modules. Describe each module with one characteristic specific to the module.
2. What are the differences between a procedure and a function?
3. Name three types of parameters. List characteristics of each type.
4. How are actual parameters and formal parameters associated? Explain with an example.
5. What are the benefits of a package? Describe two parts of a package and their contents.
6. What is a trigger? Explain the working of each type of trigger.

LAB ACTIVITY

1. Write a procedure that is passed a student's identification number and returns back the student's full name and phone number from the STUDENT table to the calling program. Also write an anonymous block with the procedure call.
2. Write a function and pass a department number to it. If the DEPT table does not contain that department number, return a FALSE value, otherwise return a TRUE value. Print the appropriate message in the calling program based on the result.
3. Write a package that contains a procedure and a function. The procedure is passed a room number. If the room number exists, the procedure gets the capacity of the room and the building name from the LOCATION table. If the room number does not exist, the procedure performs the appropriate exception-handling routine. The function is passed a *csid* and returns the number of seats available in the course section, if there are any, from the CRSSECTION table. If enrollment has reached the maximum, a zero is returned.
4. Write a trigger that is fired before the DML statement's execution on the EMPLOYEE table. The trigger checks the day based on SYSDATE. If the day is Sunday, the trigger does not allow the DML statement's execution and raises an exception. Write the appropriate message in the exception-handling section.
5. Write a trigger that is fired after an INSERT statement is executed for the STUDENT table. The trigger writes the new student's ID, user's name, and system's date in a table called TRACKING.

13

Oracle Database Administration

IN THIS CHAPTER . . .

- You will learn about Oracle Database Administration.
- Different aspects of Oracle's architecture are explained.
- Oracle installation and networking are discussed.
- Oracle security, users, roles, and system privileges are covered.
- Various SQL*Plus commands and their uses are explained.

An Oracle database is a very complex product, and its capabilities are increasing with every new release of the software. The Database Administrator (DBA) is the most critical position in the database environment. The successful implementation of a database depends on the DBA.

DATABASE ADMINISTRATOR (DBA)

A DBA is responsible for installing the Oracle database, managing the day-to-day needs of the complex database, and running the system at peak performance. A DBA performs software maintenance, resource management, data administration, database tuning, and troubleshooting, data security, and backup and recovery. Some of the duties performed by the DBA are

- Install and upgrade Oracle and its tools
- Configure the Oracle instance and SQL*Net
- Create a database
- Create, alter, and remove database users and roles
- Grant and restrict access rights
- Allocate and manage physical and logical storage structures
- Develop security strategies
- Develop backup and recovery procedures
- Monitor system performance
- Analyze database performance and implement solutions to problems
- Communicate with Oracle support service personnel
- Troubleshoot locking problems

In short, the DBA is the most trusted user in the database environment. The DBA must possess a thorough knowledge of the operating system Oracle works on top of, the hardware specifications needed for the server and the clients, the memory structures and Oracle processes, PL/SQL modules and their behavior in the system, client-server architecture, and networking-related issues.

ORACLE ARCHITECTURE: AN OVERVIEW

The Oracle **database** is the data stored on disk under an operating system's directory structure. The Oracle **instance** is the System Global Area (SGA) memory and the background processes. The Oracle Enterprise Manager (OEM) starts the instance. The database is mounted on the instance and then opened. The users connect to the instance to access the database. The database is mounted on a single instance in most cases, except for the Oracle Parallel Server (OPS) environment, where a database can be mounted on many instances.

The **background processes** run simultaneously and independently of each other. These processes work on databases, and there can be a number of such processes depending upon the configuration of the Oracle initialization file (INIT.ORA).

The **System Global Area** (SGA) memory area is used for instance to store information that is shared by database and user processes. The SGA consists of a database buffer cache, a shared pool, and redo log buffers. The database buffer cache contains actual data from the database. The user transactions are first stored in the buffer and then written to the disk. The shared pool contains the executed SQL and PL/SQL statements for reuse of the information. The redo log buffers store the redo entries for the online redo logs before writing them to the disk.

The instance contains four types of files. The **parameter file** INIT.ORA is read when an instance is opened. The **control files** are read when the database is mounted. The **data files** are read when the database is opened. The changes to a database are logged in the **redo log files.**

Oracle uses many different logical database structures. A **tablespace** is the basic storage allocation to a database. During Oracle's installation many tablespaces are created with minimal capacity. Every database has a SYSTEM tablespace, and it also has other tablespaces like TEMPORARY. The tablespaces are operating system files with the .ORA extension. The DBA creates tablespaces for databases according to the need.

A user account or a username is called **schema.** Each object is stored under its owner's schema. An Oracle database is created with two schemas: SYS to store the data dictionary, and SYSTEM to store more data dictionary information and tables for Oracle tools.

Each object is stored as one or more **segments.** A segment resides in only one tablespace. Every time a user updates a table, the old value is written to the **rollback segment** for read consistency. This also allows a user to rollback updates without committing them. Oracle uses **temporary segments** during table creation and joins.

Other database structures are **tables** to store user data and a data dictionary, and an **index** for fast search operation from the table.

The Oracle relational database management system (RDBMS) is sold as a base product in two versions, Enterprise and Server. It also comes with other options, data cartridges, development tools, and enterprise applications. The available licensing options are concurrent user license, named user license, and site license.

The **version** number uses four numbers (see Fig. 3-4), for example, 8.0.4.2. The first number is the major release number, the second number is the minor release number, the third number is the code release number, and the fourth number is the patch number for the code number.

The **performance** can be measured in terms of time taken in execution of a complex query, number of users on-line concurrently, or time taken by a batch job. The performance depends on the amount of memory, disk space, CPU, bus speed, and network speed. All database packages are I/O bound. The speed of I/O affects the performance of such a system. The available resources must be configured properly for optimum performance.

The database must be readily available to the users at all times. There are safety measures considered at the planning phase, configuration phase, and implementation phase for the availability issue. The three configurations are replication, hot standby database, and parallel server. The **Replication** method uses separate databases by duplicating the entire implementation of the database on multiple computer systems, where all updates are performed on all database implementations. The operations can still continue if one of the databases crashes. The **hot standby database** method uses only one database at a time. The other standby copy is in recover mode at all times. The redo log files are used to recover the standby copy. If the primary copy fails, the standby copy is recovered completely and is brought up as the primary database. In an Oracle **parallel server** configuration, multiple computer systems are used with parallel processing capability to share a common database. In the event of a computer system failure, the operations still continue as long as the shared database is available.

Even with an implementation with redundant hardware and redundant database, you still need a good backup mechanism. Oracle has utilities to perform the logical backup or physical backup at the data level. The logical backup utility **export,** or **EXP,** copies all SQL statements to re-create all database objects and insert data as well. The export can be at the database, schema, or table level. The backed up data with EXP can be recovered on different platforms with different operating systems and different versions of Oracle. The backup format with EXP is proprietary to Oracle. The import or IMP utility copies the logical backup of data back to the database. A **cold backup** is performed on database, when it is down, or "cold." When a database is running in archive log mode, Oracle saves the redo log into **archive log files.** These files can be used to reconstruct transactions after the last backup. The database can be backed up while it is running, or "hot"; such a backup is called the **hot backup.** The archive log files can be used with cold as well as hot backups. The recovery manager (RMAN) manages cold backup, hot backup, and the archive log files. The RMAN also enables you to perform incremental hot backups but does not support export. There are many third-party tools available for backup and recovery of a database.

INSTALLATION

The Oracle installer software is called **orainst.** The installer looks different based on the platform it is bought for. The installer is available for character mode, Windows mode, or Motif mode. In spite of the different look, the installer performs the same task on all platforms. It performs the following steps:

- Installs Oracle software components
- Creates a starter database
- Executes operating system functions to run Oracle

You have to select the components to install based on your installation's needs and licenses bought from Oracle Corporation. If an installer installs a component you don't need, you can remove it with the installer. If you select a component that is dependent on another component, the installer automatically selects it. Many decisions are made before the installation process. You decide to create or not to create a starter database; select a "home" location for the Oracle software; plan the directory structure for the Oracle data files; define the database block size; specify the number, size, and location of log files; and specify the maximum number of data files allowed.

If the installer creates a starter database, the SYSTEM and USERS table spaces are not allocated enough space, and the block size is very small. The block size for a database cannot be changed. You should find out the block size used by the operating system and the hardware, and select a block size that is a multiple of it. The block size should not be larger than the amount of data your operating system can transfer in a single operation. You should select a small block size for a transaction-based system, which has queries involving single rows. For a large system with bulk data retrievals and transfers, you should select a large block size. The block size is specified in the INIT.ORA file with the DB_BLOCK_SIZE parameter.

Figure 13-1 illustrates use of Oracle Storage Manager in creating a new table space, CIS253_DATA, for students in a course, and its actual location on the Oracle Server. The default tablespaces are allocated inadequate space. The tablespace created in this figure was allocated 500 MB.

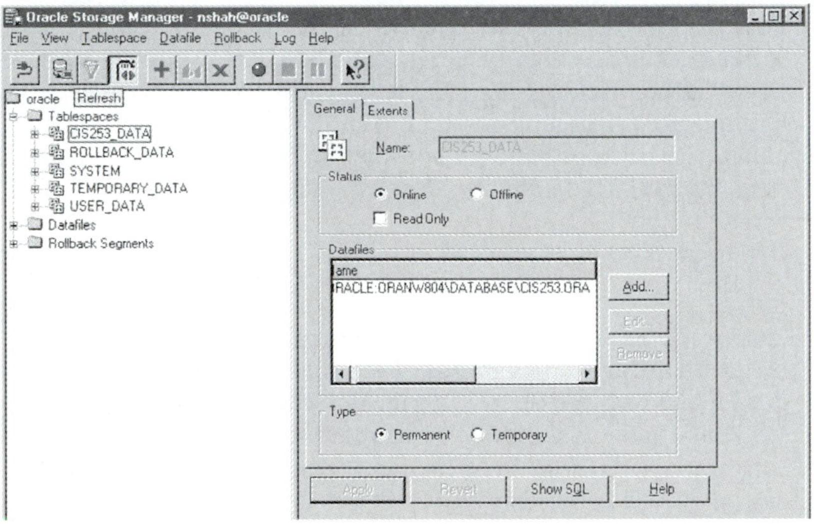

Figure 13-1   Storage manager and creation of a tablespace.

You can create a tablespace and specify the operating system file that makes up the tablespace with a CREATE TABLESPACE statement at the command prompt:

CREATE TABLESPACE TablespaceName
DATAFILE 'filespecs' SIZE size;

You also must select the database name and its instance name. The initialization file has a name that has INIT as a prefix to the instance name with extension

ORA. For example, if the instance name is ORCL, then the initialization file is INITORCL.ORA. The database name is specified in the INIT.ORA file in the DB_NAME parameter. The INIT.ORA file is in the DBS directory of the ORACLE_HOME.

NETWORKING

Oracle networking is about connecting clients to the database and connecting a database to another database. Oracle runs on any network using any available protocol. Oracle hides the complexity of connections through a product called Net8, which was formerly known as SQL*Net. Net8 utilizes a protocol adapter on both sides of the connection to conform to the network protocol already in use. The following protocol adapters are available to support various network protocols:

- **SPX/IPX**—a protocol developed by Novell for the Netware operating system that is supported by many other operating systems.
- **TCP/IP**—the most popular protocol from the UNIX environment, one that is supported by many other operating systems.
- **LU6.2**—a protocol developed by IBM and used in its System Network Architecture (SNA).

The connections to Oracle databases are through **services,** which are processes on an Oracle server or host. The service name is also known as a database alias, which refers to an instance on a host. The relation between a service and an instance is stored in a file called **TNSNAMES.ORA,** which is in the \orant\net80\admin folder in the Windows NT environment. If there is a change to TNSNAMES.ORA, the change has to be enterprise wide. The changes to TNSNAMES.ORA are a problem during the implementation. Oracle solves this problem with an **Oracle Names server,** which performs name resolution without using TNSNAMES.ORA. An Oracle Names server can integrate with other name-resolution services such as the Novell Netware Directory service (NDS).

Oracle can connect to databases created under different vendors' software, ranging from Microsoft's PC-database Access to Microsoft's SQL-Server. Microsoft's **Open Database Connectivity** (ODBC) driver running on a client enables the client to connect to a server running SQL*Net or Net8. The client need not run SQL*Net because the ODBC driver emulates it. Oracle also utilizes **Gateway** products to connect to non-Oracle database hosts. The gateway translates Oracle SQL queries to a non-Oracle host's native SQL and returns data to the Oracle server. Oracle gateway is available from the server with a database link, but it is not available from a client.

SECURITY

The security of data is a very important issue for a DBA. Figure 13-2 shows the login screen to log into different modules in the Enterprise Manager, such as Security Manager, Storage Manager, and so on.

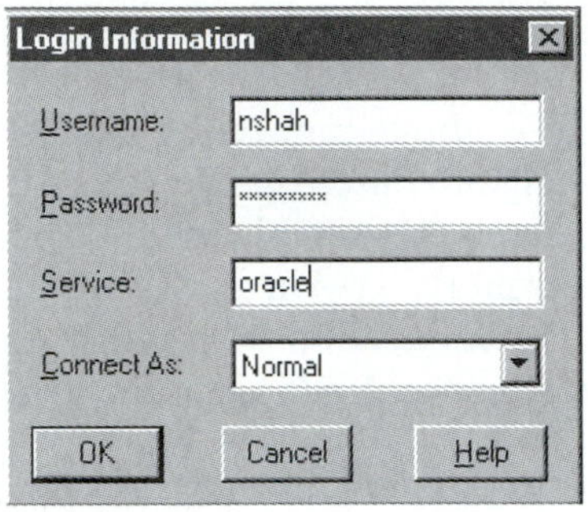

Figure 13-2   Login to Enterprise Manager.

The DBA assigns a unique userid to each authorized user. The general syntax to create a **user** is

```
CREATE USER UserName IDENTIFIED BY PasswordName
   [DEFAULT TABLESPACE Default TableSpaceName]
   [TEMPORARY TABLESPACE Temporary TableSpaceName]
   [QUOTA StorageSpace ON DefaultTableSpaceName]
   [PROFILE ProfileName];
```

The DBA or anyone with the CREATE USER system privilege can log into the Security Manager to create a user. If the default tablespace is not specified, DEFAULT TABLESPACE is used. You must define the quota to enable user to create tables and indexes. If a profile is not specified, the DEFAULT profile is used.

You can create a user with Graphical User Interface (GUI) tool called Security Manager using the following series of steps:

Start → **Programs** → **Oracle Enterprise Manager** → **Security Manager**

Then you select "Create" from the User menu in Security Manager as shown in Fig. 13-3.

The user creation involves Name, Profile, Authentication, Password, Confirm Password, Default Tablespace, and Temporary Tablespace entries. You can lock a user's account and expire the user's password from the same screen.

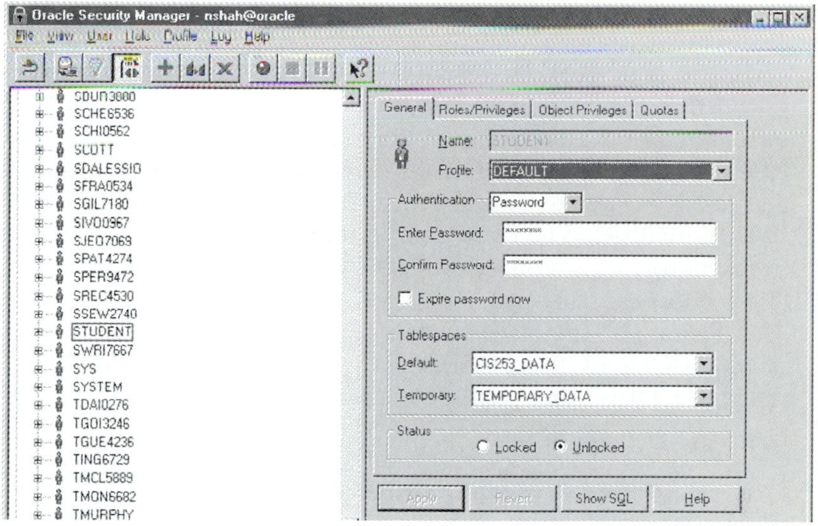

Figure 13-3   User created in Security Manager.

Once a user is created, you can use that user as a template and create another user based on it. You need to supply the new username and password only because the new user inherits the profile, tablespaces, and system privileges from the template user. Figure 13-4 shows the process of creating a user based on another user.

System privileges enable users to perform actions within the database. There are 90 system privileges that can be assigned to a user. Object privileges allow users

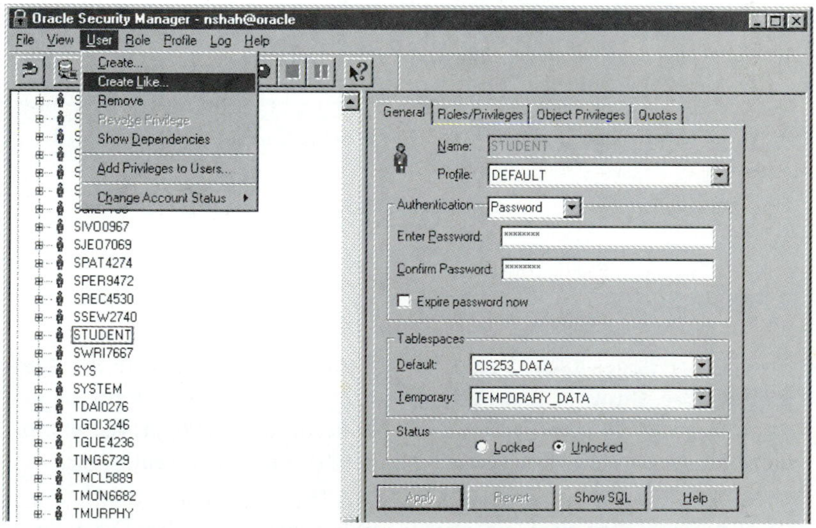

Figure 13-4   Creating a user based on another user.

to access and manipulate objects in the database. The owner of an object has all object privileges on it. You already have learned about granting privileges on your objects to other users.

Roles are the same as groups in Novell Netware. Oracle uses roles to grant system and object privileges to the users. A DBA or anyone with the CREATE ROLE privilege can create a role. The role is granted system and object privileges. The role is granted to a user by the DBA or anyone with the GRANT ANY ROLE system privilege. When you grant a role to a user, the user inherits all privileges from the role. A user needs CONNECT and RESOURCE roles to create a table in the allocated tablespace.

Figure 13-5 shows the creation of a role called STUDENT_ROLE with two basic roles CONNECT and RESOURCE. You can grant STUDENT_ROLE to a user called STUDENT, and the user will get the same system privileges from the role.

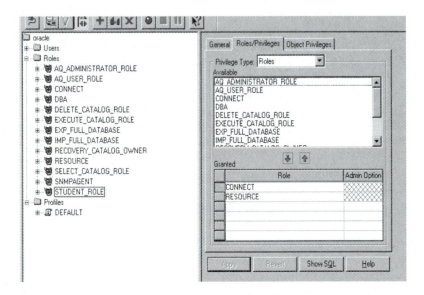

Figure 13-5 Creating a role.

SYSTEM PRIVILEGES

System privileges allow a user to take certain actions within the database. The table in Fig. 13-6 shows a few system prvileges needed for types of actions within the database. As you know, there are 90 defined system privileges in Oracle 8. They can be categorized into three types based on their effect:

- **Privileges that affect the entire database.** The DBA or the user who is granted the DBA role has such privileges. These privileges allow the DBA

System Privilege	Type of Action
CREATE	Create an object in a user's own schema
CREATE ANY	Create an object in another user's schema
CREATE SESSION	Connect to database
DROP	Drop an object in a user's own schema
DROP ANY	Drop an object in another user's schema
ALTER SYSTEM	Manipulate an instance
ALTER DATABASE	Manipulate database
ALTER USER	Change a user's role or password
ALTER/CREATE/DROP/ MANAGE TABLESPACE	Manipulate a tablespace

Figure 13-6   System privileges and actions.

to alter the database, create users, create roles, grant roles, manage tablespace, remove users, and so on.

- **Privileges that allow a user to create objects in the user's own schema.** These privileges allow the user to create tables, views, sequences, synonyms, procedures, triggers, and so on. These privileges are granted to CONNECT and RESOURCE roles. These roles are then granted to a user rather than granting individual privileges.
- **Privileges that allow a user to manipulate objects in any schema.** These privileges allow you to manipulate objects in other users' schemas. The DBA and users with the DBA role are granted these privileges, for example, CREATE ANY, DROP ANY, ALTER ANY, SELECT ANY, INSERT ANY, EXECUTE ANY, and so on.

ROLES

There are some default roles in the database that also allow the user to take certain actions. When a new database is created with the CREATE DATABASE command, six default roles are automatically created. The DBA can run different scripts and create nine more roles. The six default roles are

- **CONNECT.** A user with this role can connect to the database and create any object other than a segment.
- **RESOURCE.** This role is an extension to the CONNECT role. A user with this role can create types, procedures, triggers, and snapshots.
- **DBA.** This role has all system privileges except for UNLIMITED TABLESPACE, because that is not granted to a role.
- **DELETE_CATALOG_ROLE.** This role, which allows deletion of any object owned by SYS, is granted to the DBA and the SYS schema explicitly.

- **EXECUTE_CATALOG_ROLE.** This role, which allows execution of any object owned by SYS, is granted to the DBA, SYS schema, EXP_FULL_DATABASE role, and IMP_FULL_DATABASE role.
- **SELECT_CATALOG_ROLE.** This role, which allows selection from any object owned by SYS, is granted to the DBA, SYS schema, EXP_FULL_DATABASE role, and IMP_FULL_DATABASE role.

USERS

The Oracle database and initialization files of various components create the initial users. These users have different levels of privileges and are granted different roles. Some of the initial users are

- **SYS.** This user is granted the DBA role and owns the data dictionary. The SYS user is granted all roles.
- **SYSTEM.** This user can manage the database and can also manage the packages and tables for additional features within the database. The SYSTEM user is also granted the DBA role.
- **SCOTT.** This user has only the CONNECT and RESOURCE roles. The SCOTT user is a user with the basic end-user privileges.

The other initial users are RMAN, CTXSYS, ORDSYS, MDSYS, and DBSNMP. The SYS and SYSTEM users are granted the DBA roles, so they inherit all system privileges through the DBA role. The users CTXSYS and MDSYS are also granted all system privileges, but not through the DBA role.

ORACLE TOOLS

Oracle provides users with a powerful set of tools in addition to the means to configure and administer databases and create applications. These Oracle tools are

- **SQL*Plus.** The SQL*Plus environment is used to create and modify database objects; to insert, delete, and update data; to execute SQL statements; and to generate formatted reports.
- **SQL*Loader.** This tool loads data into a database.
- **Export.** The EXP utility copies part or all of a database.
- **Import.** This utility reloads data from a previous export.
- **Net8 Assistant.** This tool configures Net8.
- **Server or Enterprise Manager.** This tool is used to perform DBA tasks, to administer Oracle databases, and to create and modify database objects.

SQL*PLUS

SQL*Plus is the environment through which you can interface with the database. You can execute SQL and PL/SQL from SQL*Plus's default prompt SQL>. You can login to SQL*Plus by running *c:\orant\bin\plus80w.exe* in the Windows NT environment or by using the following command at the command-line prompt:

SQLPLUS [UserName[/Password]] [@HostName] [@script][parameter list]

where HostName is the database name to connect to, which is in the Oracle Names or in the TNSNAMES.ORA file. The script is the name of the script to execute on connection to the database. The parameters are the substitution variables passed to the SQL*Plus script.

SQL*Plus has its own commands, which do not need a semicolon as a terminator. SQL*Plus commands can be abbreviated and are not stored in the buffer. The file-related commands and editing commands are covered in Chapter 3 (Figs. 3-6 and 3-7). Other variable-related commands are covered with SQL and PL/SQL, for example, ACCEPT, DEFINE, UNDEFINE, VARIABLE, and PRINT. Following are some **formatting commands** in SQL*Plus (the allowable command abbreviations are underlined):

BREAK. The BREAK Command specifies action based on a change of a value of a column or an expression, or when a row is returned. The general syntax is

BREAK [ON column / expression / ROW / REPORT [action list]]...

The actions are SKIP n lines, SKIP PAGE, NODUPLICATES or DUPLICATES.

BTITLE. The BTITLE command specifies the format of the title at the bottom of each page. The general syntax is

BTITLE [ON / OFF] [printspec [text/variable]...]

where ON/OFF turns the title on or off. The printspecs are COL n, SKIP n, LEFT, CENTER, RIGHT, and BOLD. The text is a character string to be printed, and the variable is a user-defined or system variable.

COMPUTE. The COMPUTE command calculates using standard mathematical functions and displays the summary lines. The general syntax is

COMPUTE [function ... OF column/alias/expression ...
ON column/alias/expression/REPORT/ROW]

where the functions are SUM, AVG, COUNT, MAXIMUM, MINIMUM, NUMBER, STD, and VARIANCE. The ON clause must match the BREAK statement.

TTITLE.   The TTITLE command specifies the title's format, which is displayed at the top of each page. The general syntax is

TTITLE [ON/OFF] [printspec [text/variable] ...]

CONNECT.   The CONNECT command connects a user to a database. The general syntax is

CONNECT UserName [/Password [@HostName]]

DISCONNECT.   The DISCONNECT command commits the current transaction and disconnects a user from the database, but does not exit from SQL*Plus. The general syntax is

DISCONNECT

HELP.   The HELP command starts SQL*Plus help and displays help on specified topic, otherwise it displays a list of topics. The general syntax is

HELP [Topic]

HOST.   The HOST command executes an operating system command from SQL*Plus. If the command is not specified, the system prompt is displayed. You can return back to SQL*Plus by typing EXIT. The general syntax is

HOST [Command]

PAUSE.   The PAUSE command displays a blank line followed by a line with specified text, then waits for the user to press the Enter key. The general syntax is

PAUSE [text]

REMARK.   The characters followed by the REMARK keyword on the same line are treated as a comment that is ignored by SQL*Plus. The general syntax is

REMARK [text]

The SQL*Plus system variables are used in SET commands and SHOW commands.

ARRAYSIZE.   The ARRAYSIZE command sets the number of rows fetched from the database. The valid values are 1 to 5000. The general syntax is

ARRAYSIZE n

COLSEP.   The COLSEP command sets the text printed between columns retrieved by a SELECT statement. The default text is a single space. The general syntax is

COLSEP text

DEFINE   The DEFINE command sets the character used as a prefix for sub-stitution variables. The default character is &. The general syntax is

DEFINE c / OFF / ON

ECHO.   The ECHO command controls the display of a command as it is executed. ON lists it, OFF suppresses the display. The general syntax is

ECHO ON / OFF

FEEDBACK.   The FEEDBACK command displays the number of rows returned by a query when the query returns at least *n* rows. It can also suppress the display with the OFF switch. The default value for *n* is 6. The general syntax is

FEEDBACK n / OFF / ON

LINESIZE.   LINESIZE command is used to set the total number of characters displayed by SQL*Plus per each line before wrapping. The default line size is 80. The general syntax is

LINESIZE n

NUMWIDTH.   The NUMWIDTH command sets the width for displaying numbers. The default is 9. The general syntax is

NUMWIDTH n

PAGESIZE.   The PAGESIZE command sets the number of lines per each page. The default is 24. You can change it to 0 to suppress all titles, headings, and page breaks. The general syntax is

PAGESIZE n

SHOWMODE.   The SHOWMODE command controls the display of old and new settings when a variable setting is changed with SET. The general syntax is

SHOWMODE ON / OFF

SQLCASE.   The SQLCASE command converts the case of SQL statements, PL/SQL statements, and text including text in quotation marks. The general syntax is

SQLCASE UPPER / LOWER / MIXED

SQLPROMPT.   The SQLPROMPT command can be used to set the SQL*Plus prompt. The default prompt is SQL>. The general syntax is

SQLPROMPT text

WRAP.   The WRAP command controls the truncation of a row if it is longer than the line width. The general syntax is

WRAP ON / OFF

ORACLE DATA DICTIONARY

The data dictionary in Oracle consists of tables and related views. The data dictionary gives the structure and inside view of Oracle database. You can get information about various Oracle objects and users of the database. The data dictionary contains **static data dictionary views,** which are owned by SYS. The static data dictionary views are based on tables that are updated with Oracle DDL statements. The SYS tables, views, and synonyms are created by the CATALOG.SQL script file. There are additional views known as **dynamic performance data dictionary views,** or simply V$ views. The V$ views are based on internal memory structures, or virtual tables, which begin with X$ prefix. The V$ views and X$ tables have information about the instance. The information in the two data dictionary views is

- *Static data dictionary views.* These views are for information on database objects, database data files, and database users. The views begin with USER_(objects you own), ALL_(objects you have access to), or DBA_(all objects), for example, DBA_CONSTRAINTS, DBA_CONS_COLUMNS, DICTIONARY, DBA_INDEXES, USER_TABLES, ALL_TRIGGERS, DBA_ROLES, DBA_PROFILES, DBA_SYS_PRIVS, DBA_USERS, DBA_TABLESPACES, DBA_VIEWS, and so on.

- *Dynamic performance data dictionary views.* These views are for information on instance objects, archive log files, and currently connected users, for example, V$SESSION, V$PROCESS, V$TABLESPACE, and so on.

IN A NUTSHELL . . .

- The DBA is responsible for installing the Oracle database, managing daily operations, and running the database at peak performance.
- The Oracle database is the data stored on disk, and the Oracle instance is the System Global Area (SGA) memory and background processes.
- An instance contains four types of files: the parameter file INST.ORA, control files, data files, and redo log files.
- A tablespace is the basic storage allocation to a database.
- A user account or username is called a schema. An oracle database is created with two schemas, SYS and SYSTEM.
- Oracle uses three configurations for availability to users: replication, hot standby, and Oracle parallel server.

- Oracle provides good backup mechanisms in the forms of EXP/IMP, cold backup, archive log files, and hot backup.
- The installation process installs Oracle components, creates a starter database, and executes operating system functions to run Oracle.
- Oracle networking connects clients to a database and a database to another database. Connections in Oracle are through services. The TNSNAMES.ORA file contains relations between a service and an instance.
- Oracle can connect to other vendor-supplied databases by using ODBC drivers and Gateway products.
- Security is a very important issue for the DBA. The DBA creates users and grants them privileges and roles.
- System privileges are categorized into privileges that affect the entire database, privileges that allow users to create objects in their own schema, and privileges that allow users to manipulate objects in any schema.
- Oracle creates default roles and initial users at the installation time.
- Oracle provides a powerful set of tools such as SQL*Plus, SQL*Loader, EXP/IMP, Net8 Assistant, and Server/Enterprise Manager.
- SQL*Plus is the environment to interface with the database. It provides users with editing, file-related, variable-related, formatting, and environment variable commands.
- Oracle's data dictionary contains static and dynamic tables and views.

EXERCISE QUESTIONS

True/False:

1. The file TNSNAMES.ORA contains the names of default roles and initial users.
2. SQL*Plus environment variables are used in the SET and SHOW commands.
3. A user needs CONNECT and RESOURCE roles to create a table in the user's own schema.
4. The replication method uses separate databases by duplicating the entire implementation of a database on multiple computer systems.
5. The hot standby database method uses only one database at a time, and the other standby copy is in recover mode at all times.
6. The Oracle protocol adapter supports all networking protocols but TCP/IP.
7. A SYS user is granted the DBA role and owns the data dictionary.
8. An initial SCOTT user has all system privileges.
9. The SQL*Plus prompt can be changed with the SQLPROMPT command.
10. The DISCONNECT command disconnects a user from the database but does not exit SQL*Plus.

Answer the following questions.

1. What is the difference among users, roles, and system privileges?
2. What are the duties of a DBA?
3. How does Oracle make sure that the database is available to users at all times?
4. Explain the backup mechanisms used by Oracle.
5. Discuss three types of Oracle system privileges.
6. Name various Oracle tools.
7. What are the different types of SQL*Plus commands? Give an example of each type.

14

Oracle8i: An Overview and Web Tools

IN THIS CHAPTER . . .

- You will learn about utilities packaged with Oracle8i.
- The object-relational database concept is defined.
- The syntax of SQL data retrieval and data manipulation statements on objects is taught.
- The role of Oracle8i in Internet computing is discussed.
- Oracle's Internet tools and three-tier Internet architecture are briefly explained.
- Two web developing tools, WebDB and JDeveloper, are introduced.

In previous chapters, you have learned about Oracle 8, the relational database. Oracle8i is called an object-relational database. In other words Oracle8i possesses all the features of a relational database with additional features of an object-oriented database. A very few features of Oracle8i can be used with SQL. Oracle8i supports other programming languages such as PL/SQL, C++, and Java to use these additional features that use Oracle8i objects.

ORACLE 8i CORE PACKAGE

The Oracle 8i database engine and its core utilities make up the core package for the Oracle8i Enterprise version. The core package behaves the same on all platforms. Its ingredients are

293

- **Oracle8i database engine.**
- **Enterprise Manager.** The Enterprise Manager is an easy-to-use Database Administration utility that also contains a tool called SQL*Plus Worksheet to perform SQL queries and DBA duties.
- **SQL*Plus.**
- **Precompilers.** Based on the platform, COBOL, C, C++, Pascal, FORTRAN, and other compilers are packaged.
- **EXP/IMP.** The EXP/IMP is a utility to export and import data among PC, Unix, IBM mainframe, and other platforms.
- **Assistants.** Assistants contain wizards to migrate from Access to Oracle8i, translating a relational database structure to an object, creating web pages, and establishing network connections.
- **Net8.** Net8 helps you connect to a remote database on the network.
- **WebDB.** WebDB enables you to create and store web pages in the database as programs in order to publish data on the web. WebDB has converted Oracle8i to the Internet database. It uses Java-based web pages that are run from an Internet browser.

AN OBJECT

An object in Oracle8i is a reusable component that represents real-word things such as computer parts. An object is defined with a user-defined data type called an object type. Object types are used as data types to define columns (known as object column) in a table. Object types are also used in place of a list of columns for an object table. An object type can also be used as an element in another object type.

An object contains a name, attribute(s), and methods. An object contains data and information about what can be done with the data. An object may also contain another object. The methods are procedures and functions written in one of the Oracle8i supported languages. Each method has a name and the name of the object that contains that method. The method can be passed data through parameters from the calling program.

Oracle 8i is a relational database as well as an object-oriented database. It provides ways to connect relational tables and objects:

- *Object view.* An object view is like the relational view. It does not contain any data but is based on underlying tables. It allows users to view a relational table with object orientation. You can modify data in the underlying table with SQL statements, with object methods, or by using an object view.

- *Object table.* An object table is a table that is described by object type and not by attribute names. The elements in an object type define the data for the object table. The object table also can contain object methods as part of a table's definition. These methods are used to perform data manipulation on the object table. You can define a primary key for an object table and also create an index for it.

- *Relational table with object column.* A relational table may contain one or more columns with the object type as their data type. Such a table is also known as a hybrid table because it contains columns with scalar data types as well as object columns.

An object reference (keyword REF) is a special data type in a table that facilitates a foreign key in the table. It establishes a relationship between two objects, for example, an object table called SOFTWARE_COMPANY_OBJ with a primary key and a second object table, SOFTWARE_OBJ that has a foreign key column that connects software to the company that makes it. This foreign key column is defined with the data type REF and references the object named SOFTWARE_COMPANY_OBJ.

In Oracle8i, you use **Schema Manager** to create object types, table types, object tables, and hybrid tables. In the Windows XX environment,

Click Start → Programs → Oracle HomeX → DBA Manager Pack → Schema Manager

Let us take examples of object types, object tables, REF columns, and tables with the object type, and look at Object SQL statements on these objects (see Fig. 14-1).

Name	Item Type	Attribute Name	Data Type
NAME_TYPE	Object Type	LAST_NAME	VARCHAR2
		FIRST_NAME	VARCHAR2
FULLNAME_TYPE	Object Type	NAME_REF	REF to *NAME_TYPE*
		MID_INITIAL	VARCHAR2
NAME_TABLE	Object Table		Row of *FULLNAME_TYPE*
STUDENT_TABLE	Hybrid Table	STUDENT_ID	NUMBER
		FULL_NAME	*FULLNAME_TYPE*
		PHONE_NUM	VARCHAR2

Figure 14-1   Object types, REF column, object column, and hybrid table.

SQL QUERIES FOR OBJECTS

Retrieving Data from an Object Table

In Fig. 14-1, the object table NAME_TABLE contains rows with the object type FULLNAME_TYPE, which in turn has two attributes of type VARCHAR2. You can write a standard SQL query to display the contents of the object table NAME_TABLE. For example,

SELECT * FROM NAME_TABLE;

The retrieved rows are displayed with column headings as follows:

LAST_NAME FIRST_NAME MID_INITIAL
---------- ---------- ----------

You can use WHERE, ORDER BY, and GROUP BY clauses with the SELECT statement, just as in standard relational SQL.

Now, let us display the last name, first name, and phone number of students from STUDENT_TABLE. The attributes belonging to the object type are referenced using dot notation:

TableAlias.ObjectType.Attribute

For example,

SELECT S.FULL_NAME.LAST_NAME, S.FULL_NAME.FIRST_NAME,
PHONE_NUM FROM STUDENT_TABLE S;

When you use a column related to an object, you must use a table alias. If you do not use it, you get the following error:

ORA-00904: invalid column name

Inserting a Row into an Object Table

The value for an object is inserted by entering the name of the object and then enclosing all values for the object's attributes in parentheses. For example,

INSERT INTO STUDENT_TABLE VALUES
(543, FULL_NAME ('Spencer', 'Karen', 'A'), '732-555-6789');

where FULL_NAME ('Spencer', 'Karen', 'A') contains values for three attributes in the object FULL_NAME, which are LAST_NAME, FIRST_NAME, and MID_INITIAL.

Updating an Object

Suppose you want to change a student's last name. You use the UPDATE statement with an alias for the table name and qualify the attribute with the table name and the object name. For example,

```
UPDATE STUDENT_TABLE S
   SET S.FULL_NAME.LAST_NAME = 'Martinez'
WHERE STUDENT_ID = 543;
```

Deleting Rows from an Object Table

```
DELETE FROM NAME_TABLE N
   WHERE LAST_NAME = 'Smith';
```

INTERNET COMPUTING AND ORACLE8i

Oracle 8 employs client-server computing. The Oracle database's web solution strictly relates to Oracle8i. The Oracle Corporation has developed technology in which Oracle products operate as server, client, and web server in the middle. Oracle supports large enterprise servers and clients using various platforms. The new "Internet computing" does not take anything away from the existing capability of Oracle database. The Internet solution is an addition to it. You do not have to replace anything in the existing implementation. The elements of Internet computing platform are

- A **server** running Novell Netware, Unix, Linux, or Microsoft Windows NT operating system.
- A **web server** for receiving routing server requests to the server.
- A **network** running HTTP protocol on top of TCP/IP protocol.
- A **thin client** using any platform.

The thin client in an Internet computing environment needs a web browser capable of displaying HTML pages and Java Virtual Machine (JVM). The Thin Client also needs the ability to talk to the network. The resource requirement on a thin client is minimal. Compact devices such as palm pilots make perfect thin clients of the near future. The web server is software that can perform different tasks. It contains a piece of software known as **Listener,** that listens to the HTTP calls and sends HTML pages to the client.

Internet Terminology

- **HTTP.** The HyperText Transmission Protocol is a communication protocol between Internet server and clients. Listener receives HTTP requests.
- **HTML.** The HyperText Markup Language is the formatting language for web browsers. Oracle8i contains WebDB (briefly covered later in this chapter), which creates HTML clients that interact with Oracle8i.
- **URL.** A Uniform Resource Locator allows a call to any stored procedure.
- **CGI.** The Common Gateway Interface is used from a Web Server as a call-out to languages and environments. Oracle8i receives such CGI calls.
- **XML.** This is an open standard for describing data. Oracle8i will use XML as a way to define structure of all data types in future.
- **Java.** This is an object-oriented language that is associated with the Internet. The Virtual Java Machine (VJM) can run on any platforms, including thin clients. Oracle8i supports Java-based interfaces to Oracle data in SQLJ and JDBC. Oracle8i also allows execution of stored Java procedures and triggers in a Java Virtual Machine called **JServer.** Any JServer application can call PL/SQL procedures through an embedded SQLJ interface.

Oracle Internet Tools

Oracle is one of the top enterprise servers in the world. In fact, 96% of the Fortune 500 companies use Oracle for e-business. (Remember the commercial!) With its new added features, Oracle8i has become the core of Internet computing. Oracle8i has a product called WebDB, which includes a web listener. The listener listens to port numbers for requests for stored procedures over the HTTP protocol. Oracle uses a **Data Access Descriptor** (DAD), which defines as Oracle database, a username/password to access the database, and a routing mechanism to route calls to a PL/SQL procedure. The routing mechanism is transparent in WebDB but is called PL/SQL agent in Oracle Application Server (OAS). The OAS acts in the middle, with HTTP communications on one side and a Net8 interface on the other (see Fig. 14-2). The request comes to the Listener as a URL, which consists of the server name, port number, PL/SQL agent, and stored procedure name.

   Oracle8i employs its own Virtual Java Machine (VJM) called JServer. Java programs can be developed using standard Java and can be stored in the database or loaded at run time. JServer is part of the Oracle8i database, so it can directly access information and use the same authentication method. Oracle8i has a native Java code compiler called JServer Accelerator, which converts Java binaries to C programs and then compiles them to the native library. PL/SQL procedures can be called from JServer with an **SQLJ** interface. SQLJ

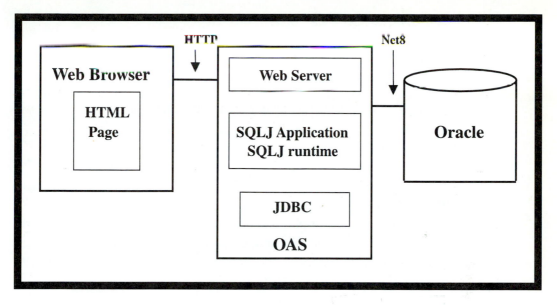

Figure 14-2 Browser-based HTML client and Java-based middle tier.

allows you to use SQL statements in Java applications. An SQLJ translator translates SQL database calls into **JDBC.** If your SQL statement has an error, JDBC cannot find those errors, but an SQLJ translator can. PL/SQL and Java will coexist in an Oracle database because they both can call each other. PL/SQL teams up with SQL to manipulate data, whereas Java performs object orientation to transform data in a client/server environment. Oracle8i also offers a Java development environment known as **JDeveloper.** JDeveloper is based on Inprise's JBuilder, but Oracle has added features to it for the database interaction.

WEBDB

Another Oracle development environment is **WebDB.** WebDB is written in PL/SQL and is a tool to develop HTML-based applications to interact with Oracle data. The WebDB environment uses standard HTML, and its components can be used from any browser, such as Internet Explorer or Netscape Navigator.

When you connect to WebDB through your browser, you interact with HTML pages to create WebDB components. You supply values for parameters, which are inserted into Oracle database tables. WebDB then creates a PL/SQL package based on these parameter values. When the PL/SQL package is called through a WebDB component, it interacts with underlying data to generate HTML pages to return to the browser.

The features of WebDB in development environment are as follows:

USER INTERFACE (UI) COMPONENTS

You can create various user interface components in WebDB, such as

- Forms, to retrieve data, insert new data, and update data.
- WebDB reports, to generate reports based on parameters and criteria passed.
- WebDB Charts, to display data graphically.
- Menus, to create menu-based applications.
- Dynamic HTML pages, to use dynamic data from Oracle database with HTML pages.
- WebDB calendars, to display data sorted by date in graphical calendar form.
- Frame drivers, to build web frames to provide lists of values to users so that they put the right data in the database and get the right data from the database.

SHARED COMPONENTS

- **Template.** A graphical style that contains buttons, colors, background images, and so on that can be applied to any user interface.
- **Link.** A connection between WebDB components, or between a WebDB component and an HTML page.

INTERACTION WITH THE DATABASE

WebDB enables you to browse a database, perform data manipulation, and create database structures.

Component Administration

You can manage your components in WebDB. You can find, export, import, copy, and monitor components in WebDB.

Create Web Sites

WebDB has a product called SiteBuilder, which enables you to create complete web sites. It can be home to your components and HTML pages. It also allows users to publish their information on the web site.

WebDB is a tool to create a front end with HTML pages that utilizes Oracle data as a back end. The data is made available to users through these dynamic pages or by creating dynamic web sites.

JDEVELOPER

JDeveloper is another Oracle tool to develop web applications. It is a visual programming environment with a library of predefined classes. The classes include buttons, labels, frames, pull-down menus, and so on. The programmer can build Java-based applications to provide users access to Oracle database over Internet or Intranet. Under JDeveloper's Integrated Development Environment (IDE), you can quickly create Java applets and applications with minimal code writing.

Java is an object-oriented programming language that is compiled but whose object code is not machine dependent. You need Java Virtual Machine (JVM) to run a Java program. Java is used to write various types of applications, such as

- **Applets.** These are small pieces of Java code that are downloaded from the web and run within a web browser. Applets have to be completely downloaded to the user's PC for verification and interpretation. If the applet code is too large and the bandwidth is low, applets can take a long time. The Just In Time (JIT) compiler included with Netscape Navigator can compile an applet while it is downloaded, to improve performance tremendously.

- **Applications.** Java applications are like programs written in other languages. They are installed on individual PCs or on the network. Java has great network connectivity and multithreading for applications running on different systems without recompilation.

- **Servlets.** Servlets are Java programs on the server side that run on Java-based web server. The executed Servlet formats results into HTML format and sends them to the user. Servlets are slower Java programs because they receive data from the client side, process it locally, take the results from the database request, and then create an HTML page.

IN A NUTSHELL . . .

- Oracle8i is a database for Internet.
- Oracle8i's core package consists of Database Engine, Enterprise Manager, SQL*Plus, precompilers, EXP/IMP, Assistants, Net8, and WebDB utilities.
- An object is a reusable component that represents a real-world thing. An object is defined with a user-defined type called the object type as its data type.
- An object contains a name, attribute(s), and methods to manipulate data. Methods are procedures and functions.
- An object-relational database provides ways to connect relational tables and objects.
- SQL statements for objects use the object's name as a qualifier for referencing its attributes.

- Oracle8i employs a three-tier architecture, with a server, clients, and a web server in the middle.
- HyperText Transmission Protocol (HTTP) is a communication protocol between an Internet server and clients.
- HyperText Markup Language (HTML) is the formatting language for web browsers.
- Java Virtual Machine (JVM) in Oracle8i is called JServer and calls PL/SQL procedures through SQLJ interface.
- WebDB is a web development environment to develop and deploy HTML-based applications to interact with Oracle data.
- WebDB is used to create user interface components, create shared components, interface with a database, administer components, and create complete web sites.
- JDeveloper is another web development tool, one that involves visual programming.
- Java is a very popular object-oriented language to create applets, applications, and servlets.

EXERCISE QUESTIONS

Answer the following questions.

1. Explain the role of Oracle8i in Internet computing.
2. What are the functions of different utilities bundled with Oracle8i?
3. State the three ways objects and relational tables are connected.
4. What is the three-tier Oracle8i architecture?
5. What are the functions of WebDB?
6. Discuss three types of Java applications.

Define the following terms.

1. Net8
2. Object Table
3. REF type
4. HTTP
5. HTML
6. Applet
7. JServer
8. Hybrid Table

Appendix A

Sample Databases:
Table Definitions

In this section, the structures of tables introduced in Chapter 3 are described. The primary key attribute is underlined. Some of the attributes, which are not used for any mathematical operations, are assigned the NUMBER data type for simplicity. They could have been assigned one of the character data types CHAR or VARCHAR2.

THE INDO–US COLLEGE STUDENT DATABASE

STUDENT

Column Name	Data Type
StudentId	CHAR (5)
Last	VARCHAR2 (15)
First	VARCHAR2 (15)
Street	VARCHAR2 (25)
City	VARCHAR2 (25)
State	CHAR (2)
Zip	CHAR (5)
StartTerm	CHAR (4)
BirthDate	DATE
FacultyId	NUMBER (3)
MajorId	NUMBER (3)
Phone	CHAR (10)

FACULTY

Column Name	Data Type
FacultyId	NUMBER (3)
Name	VARCHAR2 (15)
RoomId	NUMBER (2)
Phone	CHAR (3)
DeptId	NUMBER (1)

CRSSECTION

Column Name	Data Type
CsId	NUMBER (4)
CourseId	VARCHAR2 (6)
Section	CHAR (2)
TermId	CHAR (4)
FacultyId	NUMBER (3)
Day	VARCHAR2 (2)
StartTime	VARCHAR2 (5)
EndTime	VARCHAR2 (5)
RoomId	NUMBER (2)
MaxCount	NUMBER (2)
ActualCount	NUMBER (2)

COURSE

Column Name	Data Type
CourseId	VARCHAR2 (6)
Title	VARCHAR2 (20)
Credits	NUMBER (1)

REGISTRATION

Column Name	Data Type
StudentId	CHAR (5)
CsId	NUMBER (4)
Midterm	CHAR
Final	CHAR

ROOM

Column Name	Data Type
Room Type	CHAR
RoomDesc	VARCHAR2 (9)

TERM

Column Name	Data Type
TermId	CHAR (4)
TermDesc	VARCHAR2 (11)
StartDate	DATE
EndDate	DATE

LOCATION

Column Name	Data Type
RoomId	NUMBER (2)
Building	VARCHAR2 (7)
RoomNo	CHAR (3)
Capacity	NUMBER (2)
RoomType	CHAR

MAJOR

Column Name	Data Type
MajorId	NUMBER (3)
MajorDesc	VARCHAR2 (25)

DEPARTMENT

Column Name	Data Type
DeptId	NUMBER (1)
DeptName	VARCHAR2 (20)
FacultyId	NUMBER (3)

THE NAMANNAVAN CORPORATION EMPLOYEE DATABASE

EMPLOYEE

Column Name	Data Type
EmployeeId	NUMBER (3)
Lname	VARCHAR2 (15)
Fname	VARCHAR2 (15)
PositionId	NUMBER (1)
Supervisor	NUMBER (3)
HireDate	DATE
Salary	NUMBER (6)
Commission	NUMBER (5)
DeptId	NUMBER (2)
QualId	NUMBER (1)

DEPT

Column Name	Data Type
DeptId	NUMBER (2)
DeptName	VARCHAR2 (12)
Location	VARCHAR2 (15)
EmployeeId	NUMBER (3)

POSITION

Column Name	Data Type
PositionId	NUMBER (1)
PosDesc	VARCHAR2 (10)

SALARYLEVEL

Column Name	Data Type
LevelNo	NUMBER (1)
LowerLimit	NUMBER (6)
UpperLimit	NUMBER (6)

QUALIFICATION

Column Name	Data Type
QualId	NUMBER (1)
QualDesc	VARCHAR2 (11)

DEPENDENT

Column Name	Data Type
EmployeeId	NUMBER (3)
DependentId	NUMBER (1)
DepDOB	DATE
Relation	VARCHAR2 (8)

Appendix B

Quick Reference to SQL and PL/SQL Syntax

In the syntax for various SQL statements and PL/SQL blocks, the following convention is used:

- The keywords are in uppercase letters.
- The user-defined names are in lower or mixed case.
- The optional items are enclosed in [and].

CREATING A TABLE

```
CREATE TABLE [schema.] tablename
    (column/attribute1 datatype [ CONSTRAINT constraint_name ] constraint_type...,
    (column/attribute2 datatype [ CONSTRAINT constraint_name ] constraint_type...,
    . . .
    [ CONSTRAINT constraint_name ] constraint_type (column, ... ), ...);
```

COLUMN-LEVEL CONSTRAINT

```
    Column datatype [ CONSTRAINT constraint_name ] constraint_type,
```

TABLE-LEVEL CONSTRAINT

```
    [ CONSTRAINT constraint_name ] constraint_type ( column, ... ),
```

ADDING A COLUMN TO AN EXISTING TABLE

ALTER TABLE tablename
ADD columnname datatype;

MODIFYING AN EXISTING COLUMN

ALTER TABLE tablename
MODIFY columnname newdatatype;

ADDING A CONSTRAINT TO A TABLE

ALTER TABLE tablename
ADD [CONSTRAINT constraint_name] constraint_type (columnname/
expression) [REFERENCES tablename (columnname)]

DROPPING A COLUMN (ORACLE 8i ONWARD)

ALTER TABLE tablename DROP COLUMN columnname;

SETTING A COLUMN AS UNUSED (ORACLE 8i ONWARD)

ALTER TABLE tablename SET UNUSED (columnname);

DROPPING AN UNUSED COLUMN (ORACLE 8i ONWARD)

ALTER TABLE tablename DROP UNUSED COLUMNS;

DROPPING A TABLE

DROP TABLE tablename;

RENAMING A TABLE

RENAME oldtablename TO newtablename;

TRUNCATING A TABLE

TRUNCATE TABLE tablename;

INSERTING A NEW ROW INTO THE TABLE

INSERT INTO tablename [(column1, column2, column3, ...)]
VALUES (value1, value2, value3, ...);

CUSTOMIZED PROMPTS

ACCEPT variablename PROMPT 'prompt message'

UPDATING ROW(S)

UPDATE tablename SET column1 = newvalue
[, column2 = newvalue, ...]
[WHERE condition];

DELETING ROW(S)

DELETE [FROM] tablename
[WHERE condition];

DROPPING A CONSTRAINT

ALTER TABLE tablename
    DROP PRIMARY KEY / UNIQUE (columnname) /
    CONSTRAINT constraintname [CASCADE];

ENABLING/DISABLING A CONSTRAINT

ALTER TABLE tablename
    DISABLE CONSTRAINT constraintname [CASCADE];
ALTER TABLE tablename
    ENABLE CONSTRAINT constraintname;

RETRIEVING DATA FROM A TABLE

SELECT column, groupfunction (column)
    FROM tablename [WHERE condition(s)]
    [GROUP BY column/expression]
    [ORDER BY column/expression [ASC/DESC]];

DEFINE COMMAND

DEFINE variable [= value]

DECODE FUNCTION

DECODE (column / expr, value1, action1,
                [value2, action2, ...,]
                [, default]);

JOINING TABLES—INNER OR OUTER JOIN

SELECT tablename1.columnname, tablename2.columnname
    FROM tablename1, tablename2
    WHERE tablename1.columnname [(+)] = tablename2.columnname [(+)];

SET OPERATION

SELECT Query1
SetOperator
SELECT Query2;

SELECT SUB-QUERY

SELECT columnlist
   FROM tablename
   WHERE columnname operator
     (SELECT columnlist
       FROM tablename
       WHERE condition);

CREATING A TABLE USING A SUB-QUERY

CREATE TABLE tablename
AS
SELECT query;

INSERTING A ROW USING A SUB-QUERY

INSERT INTO tablename [(column aliases)]
SELECT columnnames FROM tablename WHERE condition;

UPDATING USING A SUB-QUERY

UPDATE tablename
SET (columnnames) operator
   (SELECT-FROM-WHERE sub-query)
WHERE condition;

DELETING USING A SUB-QUERY

DELETE FROM tablename
   WHERE columnname operator
      (SELECT-FROM-WHERE sub-query);

CREATING A VIEW

CREATE [OR REPLACE] [FORCE/NOFORCE] VIEW viewname
   [column aliases]
AS SELECT-subquery
[WITH CHECK OPTION [CONSTRAINT constraintname]]
[WITH READ ONLY];

DROPPING A VIEW

DROP VIEW viewname;

CREATING A SEQUENCE

CREATE SEQUENCE sequencename
    [INCREMENT BY n]
    [START WITH s]
    [MAXVALUE x / NOMAXVALUE]
    [MINVALUE m / NOMINVALUE]
    [CYCLE / NOCYCLE]
    [CACHE c / NOCHACHE]
    [ORDER / NOORDER];

MODIFYING A SEQUENCE

ALTER SEQUENCE sequencename
    [INCREMENT BY n]
    [MAXVALUE x / NOMAXVALUE]
    [MINVALUE m / NOMINVALUE]
    [CYCLE / NOCYCLE]
    [CACHE c / NOCHACHE]
    [ORDER / NOORDER];

CREATING A SYNONYM

CREATE [PUBLIC] SYNONYM SynonymName
FOR ObjectName;

CREATING AN INDEX

CREATE INDEX indexname
    ON tablename (columnname1 [, columnname2]...);

LOCKING ROW(S) FOR UPDATE

SELECT columnnames
FROM tablenames
WHERE condition
FOR UPDATE OF columnnames
[NOWAIT];

CREATING A USER

CREATE USER username
    IDENTIFIED BY password;

GRANTING SYSTEM PRIVILEGES

GRANT privilege1 [, privilege2...]
    TO username1 [, username2...];

GRANTING OBJECT PRIVILEGES

GRANT objectprivileges [(columnnames)] / ALL
    ON objectname
    TO user/role/PUBLIC
    [WITH GRANT OPTION];

REVOKING PRIVILEGES

REVOKE privilege1 [, privilege2...] / ALL
ON objectname
FROM users/role/PUBLIC
[CASCADE CONSTRAINTS];

PL/SQL ANONYMOUS BLOCK

DECLARE
        Declaration of constants, variables, cursors and exceptions
BEGIN
        PL/SQL and SQL statements
EXCEPTION
        Actions for error conditions
END;

PL/SQL VARIABLE/CONSTANT DECLARATION

DECLARE
        IdentifierName [CONSTANT] DataType
            [NOT NULL] [:= /DEFAULT expression];

ANCHORED DECLARATION

VariableName TypeAttribute%TYPE [value assignment];

ASSIGNMENT OPERATION

VariableName:=Literal/VariableName/Expression;

IF-THEN-END IF

IF condition THEN
        Action statements
END IF

IF-THEN-ELSE-END IF

IF condition THEN
        Action statements 1
ELSE
        Action statements 2
END IF

IF-THEN-ELSIF-END IF

> *IF condition1 THEN*
> > *Action statements 1*
>
> *ELSIF condition2 THEN*
> > *Action statements 2*
>
> *. . .*
>
> *ELSIF condition THEN*
> > *Action statement N*
>
> *[ELSE*
> > *Else Action statements]*
>
> *END IF*

BASIC LOOP

> *LOOP*
> > *Looping statement1;*
> >
> > *. . .*
> >
> > *EXIT [WHEN condition];*
>
> *END LOOP;*

WHILE LOOP

> *WHILE condition LOOP*
> > *Looping statement 1;*
> >
> > *Looping statement 2;*
> >
> > *. . .*
> >
> > *Looping statement n;*
>
> *END LOOP;*

FOR LOOP

> *FOR counter IN [REVERSE] lower..upper LOOP*
> > *Looping statement 1*
> >
> > *Looping statement 2*
> >
> > *. . .*
> >
> > *Looping statement n*
>
> *END LOOP;*

BIND/HOST VARIABLE

> *VARIABLE VariableName DataType*

SELECT-INTO IN PL/SQL

> *SELECT ColumnNames*
> *INTO VariableNames / RecordName*
> *FROM TableName*
> *WHERE condition;*

EXPLICIT CURSOR DECLARATION

CURSOR CursorName IS
SELECT statement;

OPENING AN EXPLICIT CURSOR

OPEN CursorName;

FETCHING A ROW FROM AN EXPLICIT CURSOR

FETCH CursorName INTO VariableList / RecordName;

CLOSING AN EXPLICIT CURSOR

CLOSE CursorName;

CURSOR FOR LOOP

FOR RecordName IN CursorName LOOP
Loop statements;
. . .
END LOOP;

WHERE CURRENT OF CLAUSE

UPDATE TableName
SET clause
WHERE CURRENT OF CursorName;

CURSOR WITH SELECT–FOR UPDATE

CURSOR CursorName IS
SELECT ColumnNames
FROM TableName
[WHERE condition]
FOR UPDATE [OF ColumnNames] [NOWAIT];

CURSOR WITH PARAMETERS

CURSOR CursorName
[(Parameter1 DataType, Parameter2 DataType, . . .)]
IS
SELECT query;

REF CURSOR TYPE

TYPE CursorTypeName IS REF CURSOR [RETURN ReturnType];
CursorVarName CursorTypeName;

OPENING A CURSOR VARIABLE

OPEN CursorName / CursorVarName FOR SELECT query;

FETCHING FROM A CURSOR VARIABLE

FETCH CursorVarName INTO RecordName / VariableList;

EXCEPTION SECTION

EXCEPTION
    WHEN ExceptionName1 [OR ExceptionName2, . . .] THEN
      Executable statements
    [WHEN ExceptionName3 [OR ExceptionName4, . . .] THEN
      Executable statements]
    [WHEN OTHERS THEN
      Executable statements]

PRAGMA_INIT_EXCEPTION DIRECTIVE

ExceptionName EXCEPTION;
    PRAGMA_EXCEPTION_INIT (ExceptionName, ErrorNumber);

RAISE_APPLICATION_ERROR PROCEDURE

RAISE_APPLICATION_ERROR (error_code, error_message [, TRUE/FALSE];

CREATING A PL/SQL RECORD

TYPE RecordTypeName IS RECORD
    (FieldName1 DataType / Variable%TYPE / table.column%TYPE /
      table%ROWTYPE [[NOT NULL] := / DEFAULT Expression]
    [, FieldName2. . .
    , FieldName3. . .);
RecordName RecordTypeName;

DECLARING A PL/SQL TABLE

TYPE TableTypeName IS TABLE OF
    DataType / VariableName%TYPE / TableNname.ColumnName%TYPE
    [NOT NULL] INDEX BY BINARY_INTEGER;
TableName TableTypeName;

PL/SQL PROCEDURE

```
CREATE [ OR REPLACE ] PROCEDURE ProcedureName
        [ (parameter1 [, parameter2...] ) ]
IS
      [ Constant / Variable declarations ]
BEGIN
      Executable statements
[ EXCEPTION
      exception handling statements ]
END [ ProcedureName ];
```

CALLING A PROCEDURE

```
ProcedureName [ (parameter1, ...) ];
```

RECOMPILING A PROCEDURE

```
ALTER PROCEDURE ProcedureName COMPILE;
```

PL/SQL FUNCTION

```
CREATE [ OR REPLACE ] FUNCTION FunctionName
        [ (parameter1 [, parameter2...] ) ]
        RETURN DataType
IS
      [ Constant / Variable declarations ]
BEGIN
      Executable statements
      RETURN ReturnValue
[ EXCEPTION
      exception handling statements
      RETURN ReturnValue ]
END [ FunctionName ];
```

PL/SQL PACKAGE SPECIFICATION

```
CREATE [ OR REPLACE ] PACKAGE PackageName
IS
      [ constant, variable and type declarations ]
      [ exception declarations ]
      [ cursor specifications ]
      [ function specifications ]
      [ procedure specifications ]
END [ PackageName ];
```

PL/SQL PACKAGE BODY

> *PACKAGE BODY PackageName*
> *IS*
> > *[variable and type declarations]*
> > *[cursor specifications and SELECT queries]*
> > *[specification and body of functions]*
> > *[specification and body of procedures]*
> *[BEGIN*
> > *executable statements]*
> *[EXCEPTION*
> > *exception handlers]*
> *END [PackageName];*

PL/SQL TRIGGER

> *CREATE [OR REPLACE] TRIGGER TriggerName*
> *BEFORE / AFTER TriggeringEvent ON TableName*
> *[FOR EACH ROW]*
> *[WHEN condition]*
> *DECLARE*
> > *Declaration statements*
> *BEGIN*
> > *Executable statements*
> *EXCEPTION*
> *Exception handling statements*
> *END;*

CREATING TABLESPACE

> *CREATE TABLESPACE TablespaceName*
> > *DATAFILE 'filespecs' SIZE size;*

CREATING A USER FROM THE COMMAND LINE USING ALL CLAUSES

> *CREATE USER UserName IDENTIFIED BY PasswordName*
> > *[DEFAULT TABLESPACE DefaultTableSpaceName]*
> > *[TEMPORARY TABLESPACE TemporaryTableSpaceName]*
> > *[QUOTA StorageSpace ON DefaultTableSpaceName]*
> > *[PROFILE ProfileName];*

LOGGING INTO SQL*PLUS FROM THE COMMAND LINE

> *SQLPLUS [UserName[/Password]] [@HostName] [@script] [parameter list]*

Appendix C

Additional References

In this book an attempt is made to give you in-depth understanding of relational database concepts, Oracle's nonprocedural language SQL, and the procedural language PL/SQL. Both language features apply to Oracle 8 as well as Oracle8i, although Oracle8i has some added features. The author has researched through various resources to provide an adequate amount of knowledge to the readers, by staying within the scope of this book. This appendix lists additional sources of information available for the further reference of topics covered in this book.

WEB SITES

1. **Oracle Corporation**—*http://www.oracle.com*
   Home page of Oracle Corporation.
2. **Oracle Magazine**—*http://www.oramag.com*
   For a free subscription to the bimonthly *Oracle Magazine.*
3. **Oracle Technology Network (OTN)**—*http://technet.oracle.com*
   Oracle's network to reach users—low-cost offers, free downloads, etc.
4. **Oracle Training**—*http://education.oracle.com*
   Information about Oracle training tracks, schedules, online registration, and certifications.
5. **Oracle User's Group**—*http://www.oug.com*
   The brainstorm of a number of dedicated user group officers.

6. **OracleZone**—*http://www.oraclezone.com*

A wide variety of Oracle information, real-life problems, and troubleshooting tips posted by Oracle users.

7. **Orapub**—*http://orapub.com*

A site founded by a former Oracle employee, Craig Shallahamer, devoted to all Oracle-related issues.

BOOKS AND OTHER PUBLISHED MATERIAL ON ORACLE

Part 1: Relational Database Concepts

1. Hansen, Gary W., *Database Processing with Fourth Generation Languages*, South-Western Publishing Company, Cincinnati, 1988.
2. Rob, Peter, and Treyton Williams, *Database Design and Application Development*, McGraw-Hill, Primis Custom Publishing.

Part 2: Oracle SQL

3. Abbey, Michael, and Michael J. Corey, *Oracle 8: A Beginner's Guide,* Oracle Press—Osborne, Berkeley, 1997.
4. "Introduction to Oracle: SQL," Oracle Education—Student Guide, 1998.
5. Morrison, Joline, and Mike Morrison, *A Guide to Oracle 8,* Course Technology, Cambridge, 2000.

Part 3: Oracle PL/SQL

6. Feuerstein, Steven, and Bill Pribyl, *Oracle PL/SQL Programming*, O'Reilly. Sebastopol, 1997.
7. "Introduction to Oracle: PL/SQL," Oracle Education—Student Guide, 1998.
8. Koch, George, and Kevin Loney, *Oracle 8: The Complete Reference*, Oracle Press—Osborne, Berkeley, 1997.

Part 4: Miscellaneous Topics

9. Greenwald, Rick, Robert Stackowiak, and Jonathan Stern, *Oracle Essentials—Oracle 8 and Oracle8i,* O'Reilly, Berkeley, 1999.
10. Kreines, David C., and Brian Laskey, *Oracle Database Administration—The Essential Reference,* O'Reilly, Sebastopol, 1999.
11. Scherer, Douglas, Gaynor, William, Valentinsen Arlene, Marrius, Sue, and Cursetjee, Xerxes, *Oracle8i—Tips and Techniques,* Oracle Press—Osborne, Berkeley, 1999.

Index